Confessions of the Pricing Man

Hermann Simon

Confessions
of the Pricing Man

How Price Affects Everything

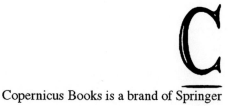

Copernicus Books is a brand of Springer

Hermann Simon
Simon-Kucher & Partners Strategy & Marketing Consultants

ISBN 978-3-319-20399-7   ISBN 978-3-319-20400-0   (eBook)
DOI 10.1007/978-3-319-20400-0

Library of Congress Control Number: 2015950470

Springer Cham Heidelberg New York Dordrecht London

Adapted from Original German Language Edition
Preisheiten: Alles, was Sie über Preise wissen müssen by Hermann Simon
Copyright © Campus Verlag GmbH 2013

Copernicus is a brand of Springer
Springer International Publishing AG Switzerland is part of Springer Science+Business Media
(www.springer.com)

Preface: Confessions

Prices are ubiquitous. We pay them and charge them many times a day, often agonizing over them, often giving them barely a second thought. Managers who understand the underlying dynamics of price can turn that knowledge into higher profits and a strong competitive advantage.

The challenge is that the game of "price" is becoming more and more complex. Intense competition, the maturing Internet, and increasing globalization are causing massive, disruptive changes in how consumers perceive values and prices, and thus how sellers need to set prices. Managers must remain vigilant and learn constantly.

When I started digging into the mysteries of prices and pricing more than 40 years ago, I could never have imagined that this fascinating area would evoke so much curiosity, intrigue, and innovation. Pricing became my vocation and my life's work. Over the span of four decades, my associates and I created a pioneering body of work which continues to guide price strategies and price setting for thousands of companies around the world. All this work has yielded an unrivaled store of accumulated experience, a treasure vault of practical pricing wisdom.

This book is your access key to that vault.

It will provide you the answers for everything you should know about the topic of price. These answers are just as relevant for executives, managers, sales professionals, and marketing experts as they are for consumers. I'll serve as your trusted guide as we look at the tricks, the tactics, and the "best" and "worst" of pricing practices. We will explore price from its rational and irrational sides, through the lens of revolutionary behavioral research. And occasionally we will do some simple math to make some points clearer.

Before we start our journey, though, I would like to introduce myself and make a few confessions.

My colleagues and I study consumer behavior in great depth in order to get to the best prices for the seller. I did that in my first life of 16 years as a business school professor and researcher. I continued to do so at the consulting firm Simon-Kucher & Partners, which I founded in 1985 together with two of my doctoral students. With 30 offices in all major countries and revenue in excess of $250 million, our firm today is the global leader in price consulting. We serve top managers and executives in all industries: health care, automotive, telecommunications, consumer goods, services, Internet, and industrial products. Simon-Kucher & Partners has provided the guidance and analysis behind many of the modern, sophisticated pricing strategies which confront the consumer or the industrial buyer. These customers are almost always unaware of who created these sophisticated price structures in the first place.

Through our recommendations, we have influenced prices of products and services with an aggregate revenue of $2.5 trillion. Only six countries in the world have a gross domestic product which is greater than this number.

Yes, I confess that there may not always be a level playing field between the seller and the consumer. This is less true for industrial buyers, the procurement specialists who are tough in negotiating prices. But generally I think that the game is fair. The reason lies in one word: value. Ultimately the customer is only willing to pay for the value he or she gets. The challenge for any seller is to find out what this perceived value is and then price the product or service accordingly. The customer stays loyal only if the exchanges with the seller cultivate a lasting sense of fairness. Customer satisfaction is the only way to maximize long-term profits.

Yes, I confess that we are occasionally confronted with ethical issues. Can you recommend to charge the highest possible price for a life-saving drug? Should a company ask the same price in poor countries as in rich countries? How far can a company go in exploiting a monopoly-like position? What is in conflict with anti-trust and cartel laws and what is still allowed? These are difficult questions without clear-cut answers. Ultimately our clients have to decide. But we, as consultants, must still consider these legal and moral aspects.

Yes, I confess that I have been helping thousands of companies to use smart pricing to maximize their profits. Some people see "profit" as the ugly side of capitalism. "Maximize profit" is an inflammatory phrase which can send shivers down these people's spines. The simple truth is that profit is the cost of survival. Making a sustainable profit is a matter of "to be or not to be" for each and every private business, for without profit the business will fail. And price, whether you like it or not, is the most effective way to generate higher profits. We try to instill a true profit orientation in managers. But I am not a fan of short-term profit maximization. My mission is to support companies in optimizing their prices to achieve sustainable long-term profitability.

Finally, I confess that this book contains a comprehensive collection of my pricing endeavors, adventures, triumphs, and failures. I am still surprised almost every day as I see new, unconventional, and creative pricing ideas popping up. The confessions will continue.

I hope you have a lot of fun exploring the vast world of price, and wish you many "a-ha" moments along the way!

In the Fall of 2015

Hermann Simon
Hermann.Simon@simon-kucher.com
Twitter:@hermannsimon

Acknowledgements

For the adaptation of the original German text into English, I would like to thank Frank Luby and Elana Duffy of Present Tense, LLC. They not only translated and edited the text, but also contributed fresh research, encouraged me to add more anecdotes and "confessions," and challenged me on how to adapt the flow to make the book more appealing to an English-language audience.

For ideas, comments, critical reviews of portions of the text, and technical support, I would like to thank the following colleagues at Simon-Kucher & Partners:

In Bonn: Dr. Philip Biermann, Dr. Klaus Hilleke, Ingo Lier, Dr. Rainer Meckes, Kornelia Reifenberg, Dr. Georg Tacke, Dr. Georg Wübker
In Boston: Juan Rivera
In Frankfurt: Dr. Dirk Schmidt-Gallas
In Cologne: Dr. Gunnar Clausen, Dr. Martin Gehring, Dr. Karl-Heinz Sebastian, Dr. Ekkehard Stadie
In London: Mark Billige
In Madrid: Philip Daús
In Munich: Dr. Clemens Oberhammer
In Milan: Dr. Enrico Trevisan, Dr. Danilo Zatta
In New York: Michael Kuehn, Andre Weber
In Paris: Kai Bandilla
In San Francisco: Joshua Bloom, Matt Johnson Madhavan Ramanujam
In Sao Paulo: Manuel Osorio
In Tokyo: Dr. Jens Müller
In Vienna: Dr. Thomas Haller

Contents

1 My First Painful Encounters with Prices 1
Pricing Student: The Journey Begins 2
Pricing Professor: Academia Was Still My Only Option 5
Pricing Consultant: We Take Theory into the Real World 6

2 Everything Revolves Around Price 9
What Does "Price" Actually Mean? 10
"Price" Goes by Many Aliases 12
Price = Value 13
Creating and Communicating Value 15
What Smart Pricing Can Achieve: The 2012 London Olympics 17
What Smart Pricing Can Achieve: The BahnCard 18
Supply and Demand 21
Scarcity and Boom-and-Bust Cycles 22
Price and Government 23
Price and Power 24
Pricing Pushes Its Boundaries 25

3 The Strange Psychology of Pricing 27
The Prestige Effect of Price 28
Price as an Indicator of Quality 29
The Placebo Effect of Price 30
Price as a Defused Weapon 31
Price Anchor Effects 31
The Magic of the Middle, or the Story of the Padlock 33
Neither the Cheapest nor the Most Expensive Wine 33
A Profit-Generating Product No One Ever Buys 34
Creating Scarcity 34
Selling More by Offering Additional Alternatives 35
Price Thresholds and Odd Prices 37
Prospect Theory 40
Prospect Theory and Price 41
Business or Economy? 41
Free or Paid: A Big Difference 42

Better to Pay in Cash... 42
The Temptation of Credit Cards 43
"Cash Back" and Other Absurdities 43
Moon Prices 44
Price Structures 45
Mental Accounting.. 46
Neuro-Pricing.. 47
In Conclusion: Be Cautious!... 48

4   Price Positioning: High or Low................................... 51
Success Strategies with Low Prices 51
Aldi 51
IKEA 52
H&M and Zara.. 53
Ryanair.. 53
Dell... 54
Less Expensive Alternatives 55
Amazon and Zalando: Revenue vs. Profit.............................. 55
Success Factors for a Low-Price Strategy.............................. 56
Ultra-low Prices: Can You Go Lower than Low? 57
Dacia Logan and Tata Nano.. 58
Honda Wave 58
Ultra-low Price Positioning in Other Consumer and Industrial
Goods 59
Ultra-low Price Products Also for Sale in Highly
Developed Countries?.. 61
Success Factors for an Ultra-low Price Strategy.................... 62
Success Strategies with High Prices 63
Premium Pricing 63
Apple vs. Samsung.. 64
Gillette.. 65
Miele 66
Porsche.. 66
Enercon 67
"Bugs" Burger Bug Killers 68
Premium Strategies Can Also Backfire.................................. 69
Success Factors for a Premium Price Strategy....................... 70
Success Strategies for Luxury Goods Pricing......................... 70
How Much Does a Luxury Watch Cost?................................. 71
Swiss Watches... 72
LVMH and Richemont.. 72
Stumbling Blocks in Luxury Goods Marketing...................... 73
Maybach.. 73
Are There Limits to Prices of Luxury Goods?........................ 75
The Challenge of Creating Enduring Value 75
Observing Volume Limits 76

Success Factors for Luxury Goods Price Strategies 77
What Is the Most Promising Price Strategy to Pursue? 78

5 Prices and Profits 81
Chasing the Wrong Goals? 83
How Does a Price Increase of 2 % Affect Profits? 86
Price Is the Most Effective Profit Driver.. 87
Now … Let's Change Your Prices and See What Happens...................... 88
Back to the Future: The General Motors Employee
Discount Program 91
Prices, Margins, and Profits 92
Price Is a Unique Marketing Instrument.. 93

6 Prices and Decisions... 97
Who, What, Where, When, Why … and How?.. 97
The Effects of a Price Decision... 99
Price and Volume 100
Using Costs to Set Prices 101
Following the Competition 102
Market-Based Price Setting 103
Sharing Value Fifty-Fifty 104
How to Determine Demand Curves and Price Elasticities 106
Expert Judgment: Making Direct Estimates of Price Elasticities 106
Asking Customers About Prices Directly 108
Asking Customers About Price Indirectly 108
Price Tests 109
The Big Data Myth: Using Market Data for Demand Curves
and Price Elasticities 109
So … What About the Competitors' Prices? 111
The Prisoner's Dilemma: Let the Game Begin 112
Price Leadership.. 113
Signaling 113
Competitive Reaction and Price Decisions... 114
Inflation: What It Is and Why It Matters for Price Decisions.................. 117
Price and Inflation: A Lesson from Brazil 119

7 Price Differentiation: The High Art.. 121
Going from the Profit Rectangle to the Profit Triangle............................ 122
What Does a Can of Coca-Cola Cost?.. 123
The Difference Two Prices Can Make 125
Why the First Beer Should Be More Expensive 126
Nonlinear Pricing for a Cinema 127
Price Bundling 129
Price Bundling for Optional Accessories.. 131
Unbundling... 132
Multi-Person Pricing... 132
The More, the Cheaper? Be Careful!.. 133

Differentiation or Discrimination? 134
Price and Location 136
Price and Time 138
Perishable Goods 140
Patents for Dynamic Pricing 140
Juggling Capacities and Prices 141
Price and Scarcity 142
Hi-Lo vs. EDLP 143
Advance Sale Prices and Advance Booking Discounts 144
Penetration Strategy: Toyota Lexus 145
Skimming Strategy: The Apple iPhone 147
Information and Profit Cliffs 149
Fencing 150
Pay Attention to Costs 151

8   Innovations in Pricing 153
Radical Improvements in Price Transparency 153
Pay Per Use 154
New Price Metrics 156
Introducing a New Price Parameter: The Case of Sanifair 157
Amazon Prime 159
Industrial Gases 159
ARM 159
Freemium 160
Flat Rates 163
Prepaid Systems 165
Customer-Driven Pricing 165
Pay What You Want 166
Profit-Oriented Incentive Systems 167
Better Price Forecasts 168
Intelligent Surcharges 169
à la Carte Pricing 172
Harvard Business Review Press 173
Auctions 174

9   Pricing in Crises and Price Wars 177
Crisis: What Does That Mean? 177
Cut Volume or Cut Price? 179
Making Intelligent Price Cuts 180
Offer Cash or Goods Instead of Lower Prices! 182
Staying Off the Customers' Radar Screen 183
The Arch-Nemesis: Overcapacity 185
Price Increases in Times of Crisis 187
Price Wars 188

10   What the CEO Needs to Do 193

Price and Shareholder Value 194
How Price Can Increase Market Capitalization 195
$120 Million More Through Pricing 196
Price and Market Capitalization 197
The Day the Marlboro Man Fell Off His Horse 197
20 % Off on Everything: The Praktiker Case 197
The Devastating Effect of Price Wars: The Potash Oligopoly Case 199
Pride Before the Fall: The Netflix Case 200
A Failed Attempt to Trade Customers Up: The J.C. Penney Case 201
Discounts and Promotions: The Abercrombie & Fitch Case 203
Price Discipline Increases a Company's Market Value:
A Telecom Case 204
Pricing and Financial Analysts 205
Price and Private Equity Investors 207
The Key Role of Top Management 208

Name Index 211

Companies and Organizations Index 213

Subject Index 217

About the Author

 **Hermann Simon** is Chairman of Simon-Kucher & Partners Strategy & Marketing Consultants, which has 30 offices in 24 countries. He is the world's leading authority on pricing.

Simon was a professor of business administration and marketing at the Universities of Mainz (1989–1995) and Bielefeld (1979–1989). He was also a visiting professor at Harvard Business School, Stanford, London Business School, INSEAD, Keio University in Tokyo, and the Massachusetts Institute of Technology. He studied economics and business administration at the Universities of Bonn and Cologne. He received his diploma (1973) and his doctorate (1976) from the University of Bonn. He has received numerous international awards and honorary doctorates, and is voted the most influential management thinker in German-speaking countries after the late Peter Drucker.

Simon founded Simon-Kucher & Partners in 1985 together with two of his doctoral students. After advising the firm for a decade, Hermann left his academic career in 1995 to assume the full-time role as CEO of Simon-Kucher & Partners, where he led the firm's international expansion. When he left that role in 2009, Simon-Kucher & Partners had become the world's largest pricing consulting practice, active in all major industries. The firm has consulted with more than 200 members of the Global Fortune 500, some in decades-long relationships.

Simon has published over 30 books in 26 languages, including the worldwide bestsellers *Power Pricing* (Free Press, 1997), *Manage for Profit, Not for Market Share* (Harvard Business School Press, 2006), *Hidden Champions* (Harvard Business School Press, 1996), and *Hidden Champions of the 21st Century* (Springer New York, 2009).

He has served on the editorial boards of numerous business journals, including the *International Journal of Research in Marketing*, *Management Science*, *Recherche et Applications en Marketing*, *Décisions Marketing*, *European Management Journal*, as well as several German journals. Since 1988 he has been a columnist for the business monthly *Manager Magazin*. He is also a board member of numerous foundations and corporations.

My First Painful Encounters with Prices

My first life lessons on the power, importance, and effects of price were emotional and left a permanent imprint. But they didn't come in the university classrooms or corporate boardrooms where I spent much of my adult life as a professor or a consultant.

No, the setting was one of the oldest forms of commerce known to mankind: a rural farmer's market.

I grew up on small livestock farm shortly after World War II. When our hogs were ready for slaughter, my father would bring them to the local wholesale market, where they would be auctioned off to butchers or traders. The sheer number of farmers who brought their hogs to market, matched by the large number of butchers and traders on the "buy" side, meant that no individual buyer or seller had a direct influence on the price of the hogs. We were at the mercy of the local cooperative, which cleared the transactions. They would tell my father the price he would receive, and thus determine how much money he could take home to our family.

The same applied to milk, which we would deliver to the local dairy. We had absolutely no influence on the price. The dairy, again part of a cooperative, told us what the price would be. The milk price would fluctuate based on supply and demand. In times of an oversupply, prices would plunge. We never had hard numbers on supply and demand, only the impressions we gained from observing the market itself. Who else delivered milk? How much did they have?

In every market my father went to, we were "price takers." We had to accept the set price, whether we liked it or not. It was an extremely uncomfortable position. As anyone with a similar experience will attest, money is tight on a farm; these sales were our only source of income.

I absorbed all these impressions as a young boy and I must admit, I didn't like them. Decades later, I would explain in interviews that these lessons taught me something which has guided me in running my own business and helping others

© Springer International Publishing Switzerland 2015
H. Simon, *Confessions of the Pricing Man*, DOI 10.1007/978-3-319-20400-0_1

improve theirs: never run a business in which you have no influence on the prices you charge.[1]

I won't claim I articulated those thoughts exactly that way in the 1950s as a young boy. But I have that same visceral feeling today whenever I think about the price of pork or buy a gallon of milk. I am rather certain that these childhood experiences shaped my opinions about how businesses operate. To this day, I don't think much of a business that doesn't make money.

Prices determine how much money you make. That much is clear. Yet how much influence can you exert on prices, so that money isn't tight and you don't need to live month to month or quarter to quarter? And if you have that influence, what is the best way to wield it? Out of my childhood experiences came a lifelong passion to get better answers to those two questions. I was hooked. Pricing would become my lifelong companion. But the journey from the small farm to global pricing expert was anything but straightforward.

Pricing Student: The Journey Begins

In college I was fascinated by lectures on pricing theories. They were mathematically elegant and often very complex. These challenging lessons gave me a solid set of ways to think about price problems, structure them, and solve them. They would become one more essential building block to my understanding of how pricing works.

But the farmer's son in me noticed something right away: the professors and their students rarely talked about how any of these theories applied to real life. At the time I had no idea that one could eventually apply these concepts to real-world problems. Only years later would I understand that the math also matters, and that it can provide companies a strong competitive edge when combined with other aspects of pricing.

Pricing became an emotional experience again when I met Professor Reinhard Selten, who would go on to win the Nobel Prize in Economics in 1994 for his work on game theory. Professor Selten conducted a pricing experiment in class with real money at stake. He offered a prize of $100. One "A" player and four "B" players could divide this money up among themselves if they could form a coalition that lasted at least 10 minutes.

Imagine now that you are the A player, which was my role. What would you do? What principles would you follow? What are your motivations? Keep those thoughts in mind as you read further. Toward the end of this chapter, I'll reveal how the experiment turned out. What I will say now, though, is that the results of this experiment cemented the word "value" in my vocabulary. They taught me first hand that pricing is about how people divide up value.

---

[1] "Hier ist meine Seele vergraben" (Here my soul is buried), interview with Hermann Simon *Welt am Sonntag*, November 9, 2008, p. 37.

Back in the 1970s, at the time I completed my master's degree in economics, no one in the business world thought of pricing as a discipline unto itself. That left me with only one practical option if I wanted to continue exploring my passion for pricing. I needed to stay in academia. The next major milestone came with my doctoral dissertation "Pricing Strategies for New Products." During my time as a teaching assistant I had the chance to work on several expert opinion papers which addressed questions about pricing policies. These papers gave me my first glimpse of how large companies priced their products. I do recall a strong feeling that their processes and policies had considerable room for improvement, but at that time I lacked specific solutions.

The next stop on my journey came in January 1979, during my time as a postdoc fellow at the Massachusetts Institute of Technology. Within a matter of a few days, I would meet three people who would not only influence my own career path, but who would also lay the groundwork for pricing to grow from an academic topic for a few passionate professors to a vital corporate function and a powerful marketing tool.

First I visited Professor Philip Kotler at Northwestern University. Kotler had become a marketing guru at a relatively young age, and I was eager to show him my research results on how a buyer's price sensitivity changes over the course of a product's life cycle. This is a topic all shoppers around the world experience nowadays, whether they are looking at high-tech gadgets in an online store or eyeing a basket of very ripe fruit at a local market: the value we perceive changes as the product ages. I wanted to know how that translated into opportunities for smart pricing.

In 1978 I had published a paper in *Management Science*, the leading journal at that time, which showed that one of Kotler's models on the dynamics of prices during a product's life cycle had implications which were nonsensical. My own empirical research on the dynamics of price elasticity over the product life cycle also contradicted the prevailing conventional wisdom.

Full of self-confidence, I told Professor Kotler that I wanted to conduct unconventional research into pricing. I wanted to go outside the realm of sophisticated functions and elegant theories and actually produce something that a manager or salesperson could understand and apply to his or her own business decisions.

He quickly burst my bubble.

"Most scientific marketing researchers want to uncover something that is relevant for day-to-day business," Kotler told me. "Few succeed."

I knew that Kotler was correct. Most of the science around pricing came from microeconomics. If pricing remained limited to the boundaries and shifts in microeconomics, its real-world relevance would be marginal at best.

Kotler did offer me one bit of encouragement, though. He knew someone who called himself a "price consultant," someone who apparently made a decent living by helping companies with pricing problems. The term "price consultant" sounds intuitive now, but it struck me as unimaginable when I first heard it. How did he do that? What did he recommend to his clients? I filed the term away and vowed to track down this "price consultant" after my trip and learn more about his work.

The same trip to Northwestern took me several miles south along Lake Michigan to the South Side campus of the University of Chicago, where I had appointments with assistant professors Robert J. Dolan and Thomas T. Nagle the next day.

I arrived in the evening and walked about four blocks through the biting cold and wind from the Illinois Central train station to the University guesthouse. When I met my hosts at the business school the next morning and told them that I walked in the night from the train station to the guesthouse, they were horrified.

"How could you be so careless!" they said. "This is a high crime area. You were really lucky you didn't get mugged."

Weather and crime risks aside, the University of Chicago was the place for me, as a quantitatively educated economist. It was something like visiting the Vatican. The business school had young professors who focused on the same research areas I did, namely Dolan and Nagle, at a time when so many new, exciting ideas started to percolate: empirical measurements of price elasticity and demand curves, nonlinear pricing, price bundling, dynamic modeling, the effect of price on the diffusion of new products, and many others. I stood out as a controversial figure, the unknown from Germany who had dared to attack the great Philip Kotler. Though Kotler himself took the criticisms in stride (the two of us remain friends to this day), many others viewed my comments as an insult. These feelings faded into the background though. As young professors focused on pricing research, we had plenty to discuss. Nagle left UChicago several years later and founded the Strategic Pricing Group, which concentrated on pricing training. He would also write *Strategies and Tactics of Pricing*, which would become one of the best-selling books on the topic. Nagle and I would usually meet when I visited Boston over the years.

Dolan and I, however, forged a lifelong friendship among ourselves and our families. He would later switch to Harvard Business School, where I was a Marvin-Bower-Fellow[2] for the 1988/1989 academic year. Dolan and I began an intensive cooperation and started publishing jointly, culminating in the book *Power Pricing* in 1996.[3]

A little later in 1979, I did indeed follow up on the referral Kotler gave me. I contacted Dan Nimer, the man who called himself a price consultant. He sent me some of his articles, and the differences between his publications and the theoretical papers I'd read and written in my academic career could not be more striking. The scientific papers on price in the academic world were long on theory but devoid of practical advice. Nimer's papers were the exact opposite, chock full of simple but useful insights. He had a very good intuitive feel for pricing tricks and tactics, without exploring or perhaps even knowing their theoretical underpinnings. For instance, he had recommended price bundling a couple of years before a Stanford professor presented the theory and showed why price bundling can be optimal.

---

[2] Marvin Bower (1903–2003) is the co-founder of McKinsey & Company. He also was very interested in my pricing work.

[3] Dolan RJ, Simon H (1996) *Power pricing – how managing price transforms the bottom line.* Free Press, New York.

Nimer was the practice-oriented consultant who had a toolbox, before this toolbox was proven by academia. His enthusiasm for price consulting was contagious; it certainly infected me. And he was interested in what we young guys were doing. When people who are older, more experienced, and more famous than you are taking an interest in your work, it provides a tremendous motivation.

I would see Nimer on occasion in the ensuing years. Into his 90s, his enthusiasm did not wane. He still lectured on pricing and advised clients. In 2012, members of the pricing community honored this visionary of pricing with a voluminous book of almost 400 pages for his 90th birthday.[4] I had the honor to contribute a chapter titled "How Price Consulting is Coming of Age" to Nimer's anniversary publication.

All of these encounters and relationships made 1979 a watershed year in my understanding of pricing and its future. It would still take me six years, though, before I would find a way to weave all of these strands together—emotion, incentives, theory, math, value, and research—to offer companies the support I knew deep down inside that they needed. Between 1979 and 1985, I continued within academia to raise awareness about the importance of pricing and the fascinating areas of study within it.

Pricing Professor: Academia Was Still My Only Option

In the fall of 1979, I started teaching business administration at various universities and business schools. My research focused primarily on pricing. This culminated in the publication of my first book, *Preismanagement* in 1982. The English title *Price Management* under which I published a book in 1989[5] may seem very simple, but I thought long and hard about what to call the book. The idea of managing prices was not in the mainstream back then. If any terms had common usage, they were "price theory" or "price policy." The former dealt with the highly quantitative concepts I first encountered in my studies of economics. Prices must ultimately be quantitative. We express them in numbers. The latter term, "price policy," described what businesspeople actually did. It was highly qualitative, a sort of oral or written history passed on from one generation to the next at a company.

With the term "price management" I wanted to integrate these seemingly incompatible worlds in a way that would serve the managers, salespeople, and the finance teams that make price decisions every day. In other words, I tried to take the quantitative, theoretical concepts and make them accessible and useful so that these businesspeople could make better pricing decisions at their own companies.

During my tenure as a university professor, I regularly gave speeches and seminars on price management to businesspeople. I also sponsored numerous master's theses and dissertations on the topic. Many of these papers raised as many new questions as they answered. They combined with other research to expand and

---

[4] Smith GE (ed) Visionary pricing: reflections and advances in honor of Dan Nimer. Emerald Publishing Group, Bingley.

[5] Simon H (1989) Price management. Elsevier, New York.

deepen the body of knowledge on price management. That helps explain why the second edition of the book *Price Management*, published in 1992, swelled to 740 pages. This growth in knowledge met a demand for more insights into pricing.

Pricing Consultant: We Take Theory into the Real World

Since 1975 I had been teaching in a 3-week management seminar for "high potentials" for Hoechst, a large chemical company and the world's largest pharmaceutical firm at the time. I extended my teaching activities to business schools around the world, through guest professorships at INSEAD, London Business School, Keio University (Tokyo), Stanford, and Harvard. And I started to advise companies. In the beginning it was a small side business and a nice change of pace from the academic grind. The time had now come to take the next step and take on the job title that Dan Nimer had coined in the 1970s. I dared to call myself a "price consultant."

My very first consulting project was for the chemical giant BASF. The BASF management told me that they needed to reconsider their market segmentation in the industrial paint business, and asked for our support. We also received projects from Hoechst, which became our biggest client in those early years. By 1985, I was well known in German and European industry and earned an appointment as director of the German Management Institute, which almost all large German companies belong to. Within a very short time, I got to know the top brass of German industry.

We soon realized that the only way to do all this work professionally was to form a consulting firm. So in 1985 I founded a firm together with my first two doctoral students, Eckhard Kucher and Karl-Heinz Sebastian. Similar to the motivation behind the book *Price Management*, we wanted to apply the methods and theories of academic research to actual business problems. Eckhard and Karl-Heinz ran the fledgling company, taking advantage of my industry connections before developing their own. With three additional employees, we achieved $400,000 in revenue in the first year. In 1989 the firm had 13 employees and $2.2 million in sales. The growth continued slowly but steadily, as we gained more and more confidence that we had tapped an unmet need for businesses.

As I said about Dan Nimer: when people who are older, more experienced, and more famous than you are taking an interest in your work, it provides a tremendous motivation. Around this time we received further support and inspiration from the world-renowned management thinker Peter Drucker. He and I had many interesting discussions about pricing, and he always encouraged me to pursue the goal of finding practical applications for pricing theory and research.

"I am impressed by your emphasis on pricing," he told me during a visit to his home in Claremont, California, adding that it is the "most neglected area of marketing." Drucker saw a clear link between pricing and profit and also sensed the same improvement potential I first noticed in my doctoral research.

Pricing intrigued Drucker from an economics and also from an ethical perspective. He understood profit to be the "cost of survival" and sufficiently high prices to be a "means for survival," two points which resonated deeply with me. In the 21st century, the word "profit" has become a magnet for protests and negative headlines. Drucker always tried to strike a clear ethical balance. He warned against the abuses of market power. He commented on price transparency, and advocated fair behavior. At the same time, he understood the importance of making money, and described it very eloquently in an opinion piece in *The Wall Street Journal* in 1975:

> It is not the business that earns a profit adequate to its genuine costs of capital, to the risks of tomorrow and to the needs of tomorrow's worker and pensioner, that 'rips off' society. It is the business that fails to do so.

"Pricing policy today is basically guess work," he told me in the early 2000s. "What you are doing is pioneering work. And I think that it will be quite some time before any of the competitors catch on."[6] Shortly before his death in 2005, he provided a testimonial for *Manage for Profit, not for Market Share*, a book which I co-wrote with two colleagues: "Market share and profitability have to be balanced and profitability has often been neglected. This book is therefore a greatly needed correction."[7]

By 1995, our little consulting firm had 35 employees and revenues of $7.9 million. At that point, I decided to stop serving two masters. I ended my academic career and devoted myself full time to the firm and its emphasis on price management. In 1995, I became the full-time CEO of Simon-Kucher & Partners and fulfilled that role until 2009. Since then I have served as the firm's chairman.

In 2015, Simon-Kucher & Partners achieves revenue of $235 million. At the end of 2015, the firm had more than 850 employees working out of 30 offices in 24 countries around the world. Simon-Kucher & Partners is now widely considered to be the global market leader in the specialized area of price consulting.

From that first visit to a farmer's market to my latest trip to give a speech in China, I have encountered prices in thousands of forms. This challenging lifelong journey to understand prices — where they come from, why they work, and how they work — has been immense fun at times, especially during those "Eureka" moments when my colleagues and I unlocked another secret with the real-world relevance which Professor Philip Kotler said was so elusive. You will read about many of those moments in this book. But I have also experienced frustration, confusion, and occasional helplessness. You will read about some of those moments as well.

---

[6] Personal letter from Peter Drucker, July 7, 2003.

[7] Personal letter from Doris Drucker, the wife of Peter Drucker, on November 2, 2005. She wrote: "I am sorry to tell you that Peter is very ill. Before his collapse he dictated a letter to you. The secretary just brought it here for his signature." This note was followed by his testimonial for the book. He and I were scheduled to meet on November 12, 2005, at his house in Claremont, CA. The evening before the meeting, I called from Mexico City to confirm. Mrs. Drucker answered the phone and said, "Peter died this morning." I was shocked.

The biggest pricing triumphs came when we helped companies create and launch new pricing approaches that resulted in a big win for consumers and the company. In 1992, we introduced a discount card with an upfront fee for the huge German Railroad Corporation. Consumers loved it, because it made travel planning much simpler and provided unprecedented price transparency. The company loved it, because they would have a steady income stream from the card fees and earned higher revenue as more people saw the train as a practical, affordable option.

I was also proud that we helped Daimler implement a relatively high price when it launched the revolutionary Mercedes A-Class. Our teams have helped Porsche launch new models and have helped most major Internet companies use better pricing to turn their breakthrough ideas into sustainable, successful businesses.

A critical part of these triumphs is the ability to anticipate future trends and estimate their impact. In some industries, such as petroleum exploration, events may take years to unfold. A few times, though, the world changed in a matter of minutes. We developed new pricing for TUI, the world's largest tour operator, and we were on target to launch the system with them on October 1, 2001. The terrorist attacks on September 11 rendered every assumption, every analysis, and every recommendation behind that system obsolete. Nonetheless, it was comforting to receive an e-mail from TUI's top management a year later which explained that the work on the new pricing system was not for naught. They said that the company would have been much worse off if they had kept the previous system in place.

You might call Professor Selten's game the first pricing triumph I ever had, because it taught me about the importance of value, incentives, and communication. Unlike the experiences at the farmer's market, I had an opportunity to influence the amount of money I would take away from a negotiation. What were your thoughts about being Player A? When I had that role that afternoon long ago, the B players and I had a lot of back-and-forth negotiations before a coalition finally stood for the required 10 minutes. Two of the B players took home $20, and I left with $60, a lot of money for a student at that time, 20 % above the expected value.[8] Pricing is always a reflection of how people divide up value. This experiment was one of the highlights of my studies.

Naturally, I have experienced some flops as a pricing consultant, either because the client couldn't implement our price recommendation or because the price change did not yield the anticipated effects in the market. Fortunately these flops were few and far between. I have also had many intense discussions with clients who resisted our recommendations. In hindsight it is still hard to tell sometimes which party was right. A business team may have many viable options, but can choose only one. These decisions involve so many factors and face so many market dynamics that black-and-white certainty is rare.

Everyone creates and consumes value. We are constantly making decisions about whether something is worth our money, or trying to convince others to part with their money. That is the essence of pricing. Please join me in this book on a journey through that amazing world. Enjoy the confessions of the pricing man!

---

[8] Since the A player has double the weight of the B players the expected distribution is $50 for the A player and $25 for two B players. But any other outcome is possible. It depends all on the negotiations.

Everything Revolves Around Price

2

Prices are the central hinges of a market economy. Think about it: every dollar of revenue and profit that a company generates is the direct or indirect result of a price decision. Each expenditure in your personal budget gets you something in return, which means you paid a price each time. Everything revolves around prices. Yet despite this pervasiveness—and the thousands of books and millions of articles dedicated to pricing—so many people still know precious little about prices, where they come from, and what effects they have. In 2014, former Microsoft CEO Steve Ballmer stressed this point in a talk with entrepreneurs:

> [T]his thing called 'price' is really, really important. I still think that a lot of people under-think it through. You have a lot of companies that start and the only difference between the ones that succeed and fail is that one figured out how to make money, because they were deep-in thinking through the revenue, price, and business model. I think that's under-attended to generally.[1]

What comes to mind when you think about the word "price"? Of course, you can type "price" into Wikipedia and get a summary of theory not too far removed from what many of us saw in our college days. Flip open any economics textbook and you see that prices help balance supply and demand. In highly competitive markets, price is a manager's weapon of choice, the most frequently used form of aggression. The common notion among managers is that no other marketing instrument is better suited to increase sales volumes quickly and effectively than price cuts. That's why price wars are the rule rather than the exception in many markets, often with devastating effects on profits.

Managers tend to have fear of prices, especially when they need to increase them. The fear has one legitimate source: one can never know with absolute certainty how customers will react to a price change. If we raise prices, will customers remain loyal or will they run in droves to the competition? Will they really buy more, if we cut prices?

---

[1] Be all-in, or all-out: Steve Ballmer's advice for start-ups. The Next Web, March 4, 2014.

© Springer International Publishing Switzerland 2015
H. Simon, *Confessions of the Pricing Man*, DOI 10.1007/978-3-319-20400-0_2

Special discounts and price promotions—two standard forms of price cuts—are an everyday occurrence in retail, but they seem to occur with increasing frequency and depth. In recent years, promotions accounted for 50 % of beer sales in one of the world's largest beer markets.[2] Just two years later, some 70 % of all beer sales at the retail level came on special offer, with discounts as high as 50 %.[3] Whether driven by opportunity or perceived necessity, this is clear evidence that managers think that aggressive prices help their business. But is this really true?

To appreciate this uncertainty, you need only to listen to the simple explanation offered by Best Buy CEO Hubert Joly after his company suffered disappointing sales during the 2013 holiday season in the USA: "The highly promotional environment has not led to higher industry demand." In fact, *The Wall Street Journal* reported that Best Buy's aggressive discounting "appeared to do nothing to persuade shoppers to buy more electronics. Instead, they just reduced the price of what was sold."

Price changes are high-stakes decisions with dramatic consequences when they go wrong. Shares in Best Buy fell by almost 30 % the day after the news about the holiday sales broke. This catastrophic, nationwide effect on customer and shareholder opinion is why managers will keep their hands off the pricing lever if they have doubt, turning their attention to something more tangible and more certain: cost management. Cost management involves internal matters and supplier relationships, which managers generally feel are less sensitive and easier to handle than their customer relations.

Yes, uncertainty and mystery surround pricing. As with any branch of science, the deeper we dig and the more we learn, the more questions we get. But over the last 30 years, we have made enormous progress in understanding and applying pricing actions, strategies, tactics, and tricks. Classical economics has developed new price structures such as nonlinear pricing, bundling, and multi-person pricing. The beginning of the 21st century saw a surge in interest and research into behavioral economics, revealing many phenomena that classic economics cannot explain. We will touch on more of these fascinating behavioral findings in Chap. 3. But first, let's take a closer look into prices, where they come from, and the effects they have.

What Does "Price" Actually Mean?

Most people probably think of "price" in its simplest form: it is the number of monetary units you need to pay for a good or service. Keeping things rough and round, a gallon of gas costs around $4, a large regular coffee costs around $2, and a ticket to a movie can run you $10. Most products and services we encounter day to day have that characteristic. Or do they?

---

[2] Kapalschinski C (2013) Bierbrauer kämpfen um höhere Preise. Handelsblatt, January 23, 2013, p. 18. The beer market in this case is Germany.
[3] Brauereien beklagen Rabattschlachten im Handel. Frankfurter Allgemeine Zeitung, April 20, 2013, p. 12.

❑ Base price
❑ Discounts, bonuses, rebates, conditions, special offers
❑ Differentiated prices by package size or product variant
❑ Differentiated prices based on customer segment (e.g. child, senior), time of day, location, or phase of the product cycle
❑ Prices for complementary products (razors and blades; smartphones and data plans)
❑ Prices for special or additional services
❑ Prices with two or more dimensions (e.g. upfront charge and a usage fee)
❑ Bundles
❑ Prices based on personal negotiations
❑ Wholesale, retail, and manufacturers' suggested retail prices (MSRP)

Fig. 2.1 The many dimensions of prices

If you fill up your tank, you may get a discount on a car wash. Combine your coffee with a donut or bagel, and you may get a discount. Stop at the concession stand at the movies, and you will probably notice the bundles (large drink, large popcorn) before you ever see their individual prices.

It gets even more complicated. Try to answer these questions quickly: How much does one minute cost on your mobile phone plan? How much do you pay for 1 kWh of electricity? How much does your daily commute cost you? It is hard to answer these questions spontaneously, because for many goods and services, prices have many dimensions. That makes it hard for you to tease out the real, relevant number.

Even when prices have just one dimension, the "how much?" question can depend on many different variables, as Fig. 2.1 shows.

Prices, in terms of what you actually pay, are the by-product of this complexity. Few can make sense of the pricing structures of telecom companies, banks, airlines, or utilities. The Internet has increased price transparency, but the sheer volume of available information plus the overwhelming number of products and sellers often neutralize that advantage. Prices often change from minute to minute or hour to hour, which can also make any advantage fleeting. You remain confused, just to a greater extent.

The price list of a bank typically has hundreds of line items. Wholesalers carry tens of thousands of products, each with its own pricing quirks. Carmakers and heavy machinery makers need hundreds of thousands of spare parts, meaning they need hundreds of thousands of prices. And if there is a grand prize in this escalation, it probably goes to major airlines, who make millions of price changes every year.

How do customers cope with this jumble of prices, price variables, and price changes? At a workshop in Dubai, I asked a manager from Emirates, one of the world's largest airlines, to explain how the pricing works for their New York-Dubai stretch.

"That is a difficult question," he responded with a resigned smile.

"Yes it is," I agreed. "But millions of travelers need to figure out questions like that every day."

Doing that task manually would be almost impossible. Price comparison sites like kayak.com make the task somewhat easier for customers, who still need to trust the level of price transparency and the quality of the comparisons. But how does this work within the company itself, if managers have a hard time explaining their pricing? How well do they understand the effects of their decisions on volume, revenue, and profit?

I am not trying to single out Emirates or the airline industry. Many industries share this same challenge. The complexity and the many dimensions of pricing create opportunities which can be very lucrative if you make the right decision, but that same complexity also increases the downside risk if you make a mistake. There is always one "right" price or price structure and a multitude of "wrong" ones. The Russians have a saying which sums this up: "In every market there are two kinds of fools. One charges too much, the other charges too little." Consumers face a similar challenge. Everyone can recall that euphoric feeling when your research and efforts yielded a deal which saved you a lot of money. But at one time or another, all of us have also been burned. Whether you are a manager or a consumer, a seller or a buyer, you need to strike the right balance between value and money.

You will never make perfect decisions all the time, as a buyer or seller. But my decades of experience have taught me that an adequate level of "pricing wisdom" goes a long way. The more we understand about prices and become aware of how they work, the greater our chances of using pricing to build a more successful business or sort through the tsunami of price information to find better deals.

"Price" Goes by Many Aliases

Normal goods and services have a "price" or a "price tag." But that term is too crude for other industries. Insurance companies do not talk about prices; they talk about their "premiums," a more genteel and harmless term. Lawyers, consultants, and architects have fees or receive an honorarium. Private schools charge tuitions. Governments and public authorities have fees and taxes and sometimes surcharges and surtaxes, to cover everything from trash removal to schools to driver's licenses and inspections. Highways, bridges, and tunnels frequently require tolls. Apartment dwellers pay rent. Brokers charge commissions. An English private bank didn't send me a price list for its services, but they happily made their "schedule of charges" available.

The price you see on the list or the sign, however, isn't always the final price. In business-to-business transactions, where most prices are negotiated, suppliers and middlemen see "price" as a battle on many fronts. Using the list price at best as guidance or starting point, they negotiate intensely over terms and conditions, such as discounts, payment terms, order minimums, and on-invoice and off-invoice rebates. Some cultures still use barter for business or personal transactions.

"Compensation" is another term that clouds the nature of a transaction and the prices within it. At your last performance review, it probably never crossed your mind to talk about the price you charge for your contribution to your company. Instead you used terms like salary, wage, bonus, or stipend.

No matter what you call it, though, price is price. We are constantly making decisions about whether something is worth our money, or trying to convince others to part with their money. That is the essence of pricing, regardless of what we call the money or the means by which the parties close the transaction. Everything has a price.

Price = Value

People have asked me thousands of times to name the most important aspect of pricing. I answer with one word: "value."

When asked to elaborate, I will use the term "value to customer." The price a customer is willing to pay, and therefore the price a company can achieve, is always a reflection of the perceived value of the product or service in the customer's eyes. If the customer perceives a higher value, his or her willingness to pay rises. The converse is equally true: if the customer perceives a lower value relative to competitive products, willingness to pay drops.

"Perceive" is the operative word. When a company tries to figure out the price it can achieve, only the *subjective* (perceived) value of the customer matters. The *objective* value of the product or other measures of value, such as the Marxian theory that value is defined by the human labor time invested, do not matter intrinsically. They matter only to the degree that the customer thinks they matter *and* is willing to a pay a price in return.

The Romans understood this connection so well that they incorporated it into their language. In Latin the word "pretium" means both price and value. Literally speaking, price and value are one and the same. This is a good guideline for businesses to follow when they make their price decisions. It leaves managers with three tasks:

- *Create value*: The quality of materials, performance, and design all drive the perceived value of customers. This is also where innovation comes into play.
- *Communicate value*: This is how you influence customers' perception. It includes how you describe the product, your selling proposition, and last but not least the brand. Value communication also covers packaging, product performance, and shelf or online placement.
- *Retain value:* What happens post-purchase is decisive in shaping a lasting, positive perception. Expectations about how the value lasts will have a decisive influence on a customer's willingness to pay for luxury goods, consumer durables, and cars.

The process of price setting begins at the conception of the product idea. A company must think about prices as early and often as possible in the development process, not just after a product is ready to launch. Customers and consumers also have homework to do. The age-old maxims of "buyer beware" and "you get what you pay for" are appropriate warnings. As a customer you have to make sure that you understand the value the product or service offers you, and then decide how much you are willing to pay for it. This knowledge of value is your best protection prior to purchase, in order to avoid regretting the decision.

I have to confess that I learned this lesson the hard way. The farms in my home village were so small that two or three farmers needed to share a reaping-and-binding machine. That also meant that we all needed to help each other with our harvests. When I was 16, I had had enough of this time-consuming routine and decided to do something about it. My family would become independent. Without asking my father, I spent $600 on a second-hand reaping-and-binding machine. The price seemed very reasonable, and I was proud to have found such a bargain! Then we used it for the next harvest and quickly made a frustrating discovery. The machine used a new and unfamiliar system, which proved unreliable in practice. The damn thing kept breaking down. So much for my bargain! The frustration dogged us for two years, before we scrapped the machine for good. I had learned my lesson. As the French say, *"le prix s'oublie, la qualité reste."* Loosely translated, that means that the quality you bought endures long after you have forgotten the price.

The famous Spanish philosopher Baltasar Gracian (1601–1658), whose wise words I would not encounter until many years after that episode with the harvesting machine, summed up the same sentiment this way: "That is the worst and yet easiest error. Better be cheated in the price than in the quality of goods."[4] I wonder sometimes whether public authorities or corporations take that into account when they insist on choosing the lowest bidder for a job.

Yes, it is very frustrating to pay more than you should have. But the anger over this form of "rip-off" fades if the product still gets the job done. Worse is the situation when the product is flawed. The frustration stays with you until you finally use up the product or get rid of it. The moral here is that one should not lose sight of quality in pursuit of a better deal. Admittedly, that is easier said than done.

This reminds me of my first encounter with an international tax advisor. The first time I had a complex tax issue, he took about 30 minutes to answer it. Then he sent me a bill for $1,500. This amount was so outrageously high that it had to be an honest mistake. So I called him up.

"Don't you think that amount is a bit too high for a half hour of work?" I asked.

"Look at this way, Mr. Simon," he explained. "You could have asked a normal tax consultant. They would have probably taken three days to answer your question, and their answer may still have been sub-optimal. I understood your problem within 15 minutes, and then needed 15 more to come up with the optimal solution for you."

He was right. When I look back now, his answer was indeed the optimal one for me. I learned that good advice is not expensive. It is quite affordable, if you can recognize its value. The challenge, of course, is that we tend to appreciate the value of advice only with the benefit of hindsight. Paying that kind of money requires trust and sometimes a leap of faith. The time spent on the solution often has little correlation with its quality.

---

[4] Gracian B (1991) The art of worldly wisdom. Doubleday, New York, p. 68.

Price is often ephemeral and quickly forgotten. Consumer research and behavioral studies show time and again that we struggle to remember prices, even for products we just purchased. But quality, good or bad, stays with us. Every one of us has quickly seen a deal, bought a product, and then realized that the product didn't live up to even our most modest expectations. Many of us have also paid a price that seemed too high, but ended up surprised by the exceptional quality of the product. When my mother bought her first washing machine in 1964 she chose a Miele. The price was outrageously high for a poor farming family, but she never regretted this purchase. The machine lasted until she passed away in 2003.

Creating and Communicating Value

Offering true value is a necessary but by no means sufficient condition for success. Far too often I have heard managers claim that if you make a good product, it will sell itself. This is especially common among managers with a background in engineering or sciences. A board member of a major carmaker believed this wholeheartedly. "If we build good cars, we won't have to worry about our sales figures," he told me in the mid-1980s. Today this company is in big trouble.

What a mistake!

Fortunately, managers nowadays strike a much different tone. Martin Winterkorn, the CEO of Volkswagen Group, the largest car company in the world in 2014, said at a recent workshop that "we need to build excellent cars, but the brand is just as important as the product."[5] That is an impressive statement for someone trained as an engineer, and the kind of statement one would not have heard a couple of decades ago.

What has changed in the meantime? Managers have become keenly aware that value alone does you little good unless you can communicate it successfully. That means that customers understand and appreciate what they are buying. Remember, the only fundamental driver of willingness to pay is the *perceived* value in the eyes of the customer.

Nonetheless, the struggles continue. What makes the understanding of value to customer so complicated is that this value is often inextricably linked to outcomes which managers fail to truly understand and quantify: second-order effects and intangible benefits.

To understand the power of second-order effects, imagine that you work in the air-conditioner business. Your company designs special air conditioners for heavy trucks, the kind that logistics companies use for long-haul traffic. If I asked you about the quality of your product—what makes it *good*—you could pull out a spec sheet and tell me how fast it cools, how intuitive it is to use, and how quiet it is. But

---

[5] Workshop on the implementation of multibrand strategies within pricing, Wolfsburg, Germany, March 5, 2009.

if I asked you to tell what really determines the value of your product to your customer, the trucking company, and how much that value is, what would you say?

Don't worry if you just shook your head or shrugged your shoulders. I got the exact same response when I posed that question to a company that really does make those products. To find out the answer, they commissioned an occupational health and safety study which documented two things that determined the value of the air-conditioning devices: they reduced the number of accidents and the number of sick days. This is a common example of a second-order effect. By keeping the drivers cool and comfortable (first order) the product showed its true value by keeping them safer and keeping them healthy and on the job (second-order effect). Noticing the subjective improvement in driver comfort was easy, but this soft factor is hard to quantify. What a logistics company can measure, though, is its savings from fewer accidents and sick days. These hard benefits far outweighed the costs of equipping their trucks with the air-conditioning units. The manufacturer used the study to support its value communication in its negotiations with customers.

The card for the rail service in Chap. 1 shows the power of intangible benefits. As you might recall, my team helped the German Railroad Corporation launch a discount card with an upfront fee. The promise of a 50 % discount on each ticket convinced millions of people to sign up and take the train more often. But the company noticed that many cardholders, even those who renewed from year to year, did not fully amortize their cards. In other words, their savings were less than the fee for the card.

That makes no economic sense unless you take the intangible benefits into account. Two of the most powerful intangible benefits we willingly pay for every day are convenience and peace of mind. Rail passengers saved a lot of time and frustration because they could purchase a ticket on any stretch at any time at a discount of 50 %, knowing that they have likely chosen the least expensive way to get to their destination. By adding this intangible value, the rail service justified the price of the card in the mind of the customer, even when consumers didn't ride enough to cover the card's fee.

Modern methods allow market researchers to put a monetary value on intangible factors such as brand, design, and service friendliness. Armed with this knowledge, companies can design quality products without over-engineering them, and offer those products at prices which have a better chance of resonating with customers.

For many products, especially industrial goods, the most effective way to communicate value is to express it in terms of money. Witness the table below which General Electric, often a pioneer in better pricing, included in its 2012 annual report. Figure 2.2 shows in dollar terms the dramatic impact of energy savings. The time frame is 15 years, because the products GE sells require a significant investment and are expected to last at least that long.

Whenever possible, you should try to communicate value using hard data, especially in a business-to-business situation. This is of course a bigger challenge for consumer products. As advertising guru David Ogilvy once wrote, Coke doesn't try

The Power of 1%		
A 1% change can deliver tremendous value to customers		15-year savings
Aviation	1% Fuel Savings	$30B
Power	1% Fuel Savings	$66B
Rail	1% Reduction in System Inefficiency	$27B
Healthcare	1% Reduction in System Inefficiency	$63B
Oil and Gas	1% Reduction in Capital Expenditures	$90B

Fig. 2.2 Value communication by General Electric

to beat Pepsi by saying how many more cola berries it uses in its mix.[6] Prestige, quality, and design are harder to put numbers on. The appliance maker Miele has found a way around this, though, by regularly communicating that its machines last for 20 years. The washing machine my mother bought actually lasted almost 40 years. Consumers are free to do their own extrapolations on what that means in terms of reliability, peace of mind, and convenience. But the bottom line is that the claim is true and Miele customers know it. That explains why the company has a repeat purchase rate of almost 100 % in spite of its high prices. Only perceived value creates willingness to pay.

What Smart Pricing Can Achieve: The 2012 London Olympics

Pricing played a decisive role in the spectacular success of the 2012 Olympic Games in London. Paul Williamson, who was responsible for managing the ticket program, used prices not only as an effective revenue and profit driver but in addition as a powerful communications tool.[7] The digits of the prices themselves were designed to send a message without any additional commentary. The lowest standard price was £20.12, and the most expensive was £2,012. The number "2012" appeared over and over again in the price points, and everyone knew immediately that such price points referred to the Olympic Games.

For children under 18, the motto was "Pay Your Age"; a 6-year-old would pay £6, and a 16-year-old £16. This price structure generated an extremely positive resonance; the media reported on it thousands of times. Even the Queen and the Prime Minister publicly praised the "Pay Your Age" tactic. These prices were not only an effective means of communication, but also perceived as very fair. Seniors could also purchase lower price tickets.

---

[6] Ogilvy D (1985) Ogilvy on advertising. Vintage Books, New York.

[7] Vgl. Williamson P (2012) Pricing for the London Olympics 2012. Speech at World Meeting of Simon-Kucher & Partners, Bonn, 14 Dezember 2012.

Another important feature of the price structure: there were absolutely no discounts. The management of the London Olympics remained firm about this policy, even when certain events did not sell out. This sent the clear signal about value: the tickets and the events were worth their price. The team also decided not to offer any bundles, a common practice in sports under which a team combines attractive and less attractive games or events into a single package. Local public transportation, however, was bundled together with the tickets.

The organization relied very heavily on the Internet both for communications and sales. Approximately 99 % of tickets were sold online. The goal prior to the Olympic Games was ticket revenues of £376 million ($625 million). With his ingenious price structure and communication campaign, Williamson and his organization blew that target away, generating ticket revenues of £660 million ($1.1 billion). That was 75 % more than anticipated, and more ticket revenue than from the preceding three Olympic Games (Beijing, Athens, and Sydney) combined. The London ticket team's work demonstrated that the powerful combination of high perceived value and excellent communication can drive higher willingness to pay. The following case is even more spectacular.

What Smart Pricing Can Achieve: The BahnCard

A new price system can have revolutionary impact. In the early 1990s, the German Railroad Corporation Deutsche Bahn (DB for short) was in deep trouble. More and more people switched to driving and shunned the train. The price of a train ticket was one big cause of that: it was almost twice the price of gasoline for a car trip of the same distance.

In the fall of 1991, Hemjö Klein, DB's CEO for passenger traffic at the time, issued us a challenge: find a way to make travel by rail more price competitive with travel by car. Our research revealed that when drivers compare the costs for rail and car travel, they tend to consider only the cost of gasoline, their so-called out-of-pocket costs. At that time, the price for a second-class ticket on DB was the equivalent of about 16 US cents per kilometer, while the cost for gas for a typical mass-market car such as a Volkswagen Golf was only about 10 US cents per kilometer. That meant that a trip of 500 km would cost about $80 on the rails, while the cost of gas for a drive of identical distance would be only about $50. With this kind of price disadvantage, the chances for DB looked dismal. An outright cut in the price of a train ticket to below 10 cents per kilometer, in order to compete better against car travel, was out of the question.

If an outright price cut wouldn't work, what would? The breakthrough came when we realized that the true cost of a car trip has two components: the variable costs we notice every day (gas) and the fixed costs that go largely unnoticed on a daily basis (e.g., insurance, depreciation, excise taxes). Was it possible to split the costs of a train trip into fixed costs and variable costs as well?

Yes, it was. The BahnCard was born.

Instead of one single price for a train trip, the price now had two components: the price of the ticket (variable) and the price of the BahnCard (fixed). The first BahnCard was launched on October 1, 1992, for second-class tickets at an annual price of roughly $140 per year, and the first-class version followed a few weeks later at an annual price of $280 per year. Seniors and students paid half-price for their cards. Whoever had a BahnCard could purchase tickets at a discount of 50 % off the regular price. This reduced the variable cost for a train trip to 8 cents per kilometer, noticeably below the 10 cents per kilometer for the typical car trip.

The BahnCard 50 (so named because of its discount) became an immediate hit. Within four months, DB had sold over one million cards. And the number grew year by year to four million around the year 2000, when Hartmut Mehdorn took over as CEO of DB. He had a strong affinity to the airline business and is known as one of the toughest managers in Germany. He called in airline consultants, who killed the BahnCard 50 in 2002 and introduced a new system which required passengers to reserve in advance, similar to air travel. But Mehdorn's calculations took neither the individual consumer nor the general public into account. In the spring of 2003, Germany stood on the verge of a consumer revolt, because the DB had killed off the beloved BahnCard 50. At the beginning of May, I met Mehdorn at a conference in Frankfurt and asked him why he scrapped the BahnCard.

"It didn't fit into the system anymore," he replied. "And I'm not about to let people ride at half-price on Friday afternoon or Sunday evening, which are our peak times!"

"You're missing the point," I replied. "These people have already paid several hundred Euros before they even got their first discount. Their real discount for a trip is actually much less than 50 percent." I must confess that I didn't know the true average discount BahnCard holders got at that time. The amount is hard to calculate.

A few days later Mehdorn called me. On Sunday, May 18, 2003, I met him in Berlin's most famous hotel, the Adlon. I was accompanied by Georg Tacke, who had written his doctoral dissertation on two-dimensional price schemes and had also played a key role in the development of the initial BahnCard 50 ten years earlier. Just two days later, we started on a fresh revision to the railroad's price system. We worked day and night. We turned over each stone of the "airline" system. Every Tuesday at 6 p.m. we presented to the DB Board. I still remember the heated discussions, especially with the super-tough Hartmut Mehdorn (*nomen est omen*: Hartmut literally means "hard courage" in German). Eventually we convinced him and his colleagues. On July 2, 2003, only six weeks after we had started the project, DB announced at a major press conference that it would reintroduce the BahnCard 50 on August 1. In the meantime, another version of the card, the BahnCard 25 (giving a discount of 25 %) had been introduced. And we added a new card, the BahnCard 100, which allows its holder to ride free of charge for an entire year after paying the (high) upfront fee (100 stands for 100 % discount). DB later fired the "airline" managers who had been responsible for the disaster.

Today about five million people have a BahnCard. The annual fees range from 61 Euros (roughly $80) for the BahnCard 25 in second class up to $8,900 for the BahnCard 100 in first class. The BahnCard 50 costs 249 Euros (roughly $325) in

Revenue at normal prices	BahnCard variant	Revenue with the BahnCard	Savings	
			in €	in %
500 €	BC 25	436 €	64 €	12.8%
750 €	BC 25	624 €	126 €	16.9%
1,000 €	BC 50	749 €	251 €	25.1%
2,500 €	BC 50	1,499 €	1,001 €	40.0%
5,000 €	BC 50	2,749 €	2,251 €	45.0%
10,000 €	BC 100	4,090 €	5,910 €	60.1%
20,000 €	BC 100	4,090 €	15,910 €	79.6%

Fig. 2.3 Savings with the BahnCard (second class)

second class and 498 Euros (around $650) in first class. There are also business versions of the card with additional services. As Fig. 2.3 shows, the variants of the BahnCard offer very different levels of savings against the regular ticket prices. The data are for the second-class versions on the card. The percentage savings for the first-class BahnCards are roughly similar.

For every BahnCard variant, the effective discount off the regular prices increases, the more the cardholder uses the card. This gives cardholders a strong incentive to "earn back" their investment in the card. In this way, the BahnCard becomes a very effective customer retention instrument.

The project in 2003 revealed an intriguing insight. The BahnCard 50 customers saved on average just under 30 % off regular prices. But in the customers' perception the savings is 50 % on every ticket. In other words, DB's customers feel that they have gained an advantage of 50 %, but it only cost the company a little less than 30 % to create that impression. Not a bad deal!

The BahnCard opens up opportunities for DB, but it is not without risks. One critical aspect is how many BahnCard cardholders travel by train instead of by car after they have made their investment in a BahnCard. One well-known economist told me that he purchased the BahnCard 100 to force himself to travel by train and give up his car entirely. DB would sacrifice a tremendous amount of revenue, if the only ones who bought BahnCards were already heavy users. Such customers pay considerably less with the BahnCard than they would have without it. In contrast, the company earns more than before from BahnCard customers who before didn't travel by train frequently. Only a small number of customers know the exact break-even points between the different BahnCard variants. Quite a few of the BahnCard 50 holders are unlikely to reach their break-even point, but they still enjoy getting a discount of 50 % each time they buy a ticket.

The BahnCard 100 deserves special mention. DB had offered a personalized annual "network pass" for ages, but in an awkward form. One had to fill out a kind of "application." DB did not actively promote the network pass; few people knew of its existence. It sold less than 1,000 passes per year. The inclusion of the BahnCard

100 into the BahnCard system caused sales to multiply, despite a slight price increase. Today 42,000 people have a BahnCard 100. This card has an unbeatable convenience advantage. Its holders never need to buy a ticket. They can simply board any train they want and go as far as they want.

Today the revenues from the BahnCard and the associated ticket sales run into the billions. BahnCard customers account for the lion's share of DB's revenues from long-distance passenger traffic. The BahnCard is by far the most popular product of DB. And it is also DB's most effective loyalty instrument.

Two-dimensional price systems of the BahnCard type are still quite rare. We once developed a similar system for a major airline under the working title "Fly & Save." The card, which gave a discount on all tickets for the continent (not the world), would have had a price of around $7,000. The risk was higher here, because there was a substantial number of heavy travelers who would have saved a lot of money with the "Fly & Save" card. But the ultimate reason the airline did not launch the card was antitrust. It would have created such a strong preference for this airline on the part of the cardholders, because each customer who bought such a card would use only this airline if at all possible. The lawyers concluded, probably rightly so, that the antitrust authorities would prohibit the scheme. The "Fly & Save Card" project was shelved. I wonder whether it will return some day. The dilemma here is that an airline with a high market share runs into antitrust problems. For an airline with a weak market position and a smaller network, such a card would not be as effective, and people's willingness to pay for it is most likely substantially lower.

Yes, I confess that I am still proud today to have contributed to the BahnCard, both in its initial launch in 1992 and its resurrection in 2003. I am convinced that we will see more of these two-dimensional price schemes. The success of the BahnCard and also Amazon's Prime, another popular two-dimensional pricing scheme, make me believe that this concept can be fruitful in many other industries. But their introduction requires a deep understanding of the economic, psychological, and in some cases legal factors involved. They are not without risk.

Supply and Demand

In economic terms, the most important role price plays is in creating a balance between supply and demand. Higher prices mean that supply increases. The supply curve has an upward (positive) slope. Higher prices also mean that demand goes down. The demand curve, therefore, has a downward (negative) slope. The point where the two curves intersect is known as the market-clearing price, the only price at which supply and demand are in equilibrium.

Equilibrium means that every supplier willing to sell at that price can sell his or her desired volume, and likewise every buyer can find his or her desired volume at that same price. In a market with free supply and free demand, a market-clearing price always emerges. If the government intervenes through regulation, taxation, or other barriers, the result is almost always an imbalance between supply and demand.

Scarcity and Boom-and-Bust Cycles

Price is the most powerful indicator of a good's scarcity. A rising price is an indicator that the supply for the good will soon grow. Higher prices tend to yield higher profits for producers, leading them to expand their production volumes. This expansion diverts resources away from less scarce goods, allowing the company to produce more of the scarce good faster. The opposite happens when prices decline. Lower prices indicate an oversupply, if not a glut, and suppliers cut back on production. The lower prices eventually encourage more consumers to buy, thus creating an equilibrium.

In one of the first economics lectures I attended in college, I asked the professor why it always seemed to work out, more or less, that the right volume of product ended up in a marketplace. He simply stared me down, aghast that someone would ask such a stupid question which had nothing to do with the formulas and theories up on the board. Yet the question is central to any functioning market economy. In a controlled and short-term manner, we see it in action every time we see the word "clearance" in an advertisement or on a sign in a store window. Sometimes it takes many years for these cycles to run their course, and as they do they exert an extremely strong influence on national economies and their policy making.

Changes in prices often have a delayed effect, which is sometimes referred to as a "boom-and-bust cycle" or "hog cycle." When hogs are in short supply, prices for hogs rise. This encourages farmers to raise more hogs for the next season. When this increased supply hits the market after a few months it causes prices to drop. This encourages farmers to raise fewer hogs the next time … and the cycle continues on and on.

In some markets, such as petroleum exploration and production, these price cycles may take 10–15 years to unfold. In 1997 my team conducted a global survey for Deminex, a large oil and gas exploration company. We interviewed all major oil companies in the world. We wanted to gather long-term forecasts for the crude oil price, which stood at around $20 per barrel at that time. Most of the forecasts clustered around $15 per barrel, and by the beginning of 1999 the price had actually plunged to $12 per barrel.

The expectations of a downward price trend had already manifested themselves in investment decisions. They would later become the underlying cause for the high crude oil prices in recent years, peaking at more than ten times the prices of 1999. That may sound like a paradox until you look more closely at how this "hog cycle" unfolded. Overall investment in new exploration projects fell sharply during the period of low oil prices. Only the most promising projects received funding. Fewer projects meant less oil as those new fields came online and older fields matured. That factor, combined with rising demand for oil in China and emerging markets, led to a wide and enduring gulf between demand and supply.

Price changes reflected this differential. In July 2008, the oil price reached $147.90 per barrel, an all-time high. That 10-year period, not coincidentally, coincides with the amount of time it can take for a development project to go from initial exploration to full production. This decade-long run-up in price encouraged companies to invest more in exploration and also to scale up new sources and methods of production, which were impossible to fund at $12 per barrel but could turn a nice profit with oil over $100 per barrel. Demand from emerging markets, heightened sensitivity to environmental impacts, and more efficient uses for fuel are wild cards in the equation and make an exact forecast impossible. An increase in supply is inevitable, even if it takes a few more years to come online. The lesson—whether from oil or hogs—is that price cycles are natural occurrences, much more likely than sustained upward or downward trends in prices. One part of the world experiencing the "boom" part of the cycle right now is the state of North Dakota, where new discoveries and extraction technology have boosted oil production so rapidly that the state now trails only Texas in terms of output in the USA.[8] The side effect is a boom in other parts of the North Dakota economy. The most expensive rents (again, prices!) in the USA in early 2014 were not in Manhattan or Silicon Valley. They were in the town of Williston, North Dakota.[9] But this didn't last. In 2015 the oil price dropped below $50 per barrel.

Price and Government

Imbalances occur whenever price mechanisms get disrupted. And the biggest disrupter of all, across the globe and throughout history, is government, which intervenes in pricing in many ways. This intervention can cause oversupply, whether it is mountains of butter or oceans of milk. It can also cause undersupply, which some of you might know of from rent control or from conditions in former socialist or communist countries.

You can get a better sense for my viewpoint when you look at how the government sets prices. Under names such as tolls, fees, and taxes instead of prices, the government actually does a lot of price setting. Your utilities, the cost of a passport, the price to register a business, and the cost of a subway ride can come directly from government entities or government oversight. The problem is that governments rarely rely on market signals to set these prices. These "prices" are political decisions, not economic ones.

American readers are familiar with the current financial performance of Amtrak and the postal service, but older readers will recall the monopoly that AT&T had in phone services through 1984 and the effects of airline and rail regulation which lasted until the 1970s. The situation was even more extreme in Europe in the decades after World War II, as large parts of Western European economies came under the control of government-sponsored monopolies or market-dominating companies. The sectors ranged from telephony, television, utilities, and postal services to trains and airlines. Many of these monopolies endure until today.

The lesson here is that to the greatest extent possible, one should leave price setting to markets themselves and let events run their course. I understand that this

---

[8] Data from the US Energy Information Administration for January 2014.
[9] North Dakota wants you: Seeks to fill 20,000 jobs. CNN Money, March 14, 2014.

stance is controversial, especially to those who feel that the government should intervene to prevent price gouging, or, in broader context, feel that greater regulation may have prevented events which helped trigger the Great Recession in 2008.

Nonetheless, some types of government involvement do ensure that competition and price mechanisms operate smoothly and fairly. In the USA, the Department of Justice and the Federal Trade Commission have this watchdog role. In Europe, the responsibility falls to national antitrust authorities and the European Commission. All these authorities and agencies have become far stricter and vigilant over the last decade. One of these authorities' mandates is to break up cartels, which occur when companies explicitly or tacitly agree to divide up markets in terms of prices, conditions, or volumes. When they do bust a cartel, they levy fines which often total in the billions of dollars. In December 2012, the European Commission fined seven manufacturers of tubes for televisions and computers a total of $1.9 billion. In December 2013, the European Commission struck again. It fined six financial institutions a total of $2.3 billion for an alleged interest rate cartel in the derivatives industry.

The largest punishment against an individual European company came in 2008, when the EU fined St. Gobain roughly $1.2 billion for its role in a cartel for automotive glass. In the USA the "largest price fixing investigation ever" has targeted automotive suppliers and has resulted in prison time for 12 managers so far and fines of over $1 billion.[10]

Tighter antitrust regulation contributes to better price competition. It is one of the rare examples of government intervention which actually allows pricing mechanisms in markets to function more freely.

Price and Power

"The single most important business decision in evaluating a business is pricing power," investor Warren Buffett said. "And if you need a prayer session before raising price, then you've got a terrible business."[11] Here is a case of true pricing power: In a *Fortune* interview media mogul Rupert Murdoch talks about the business of Michael Bloomberg. Murdoch said that Bloomberg created a great company, and then "he kept pushing it. And now those who use it buy it at a huge price—can't live without it. When their costs go up a bit, they put the prices up, and no one cancels."[12] Wouldn't each company love to have such pricing power?

Pricing power is indeed critical. Pricing power determines whether a supplier can achieve his or her desired prices. It also determines the degree to which a brand can earn a premium price. The flipside of pricing power is buying power: to what extent can a buyer get the desired prices from his or her suppliers? In some

---

[10] Probe Pops Car-Part Keiretsu. The Wall Street Journal Europe, February 18, 2013, p. 22.

[11] Interview with Warren Buffett before the Financial Crisis Inquiry Commission (FCIC) on May 26, 2010.

[12] Sellers P (2014) Rupert Murdoch - The Fortune Interview. Fortune, April 28, 2014, pp. 52–58.

industries, such as car manufacturing, purchasing power is high and buyers wield significant buying power over suppliers. Likewise, retailers can exert their buying power over suppliers when market concentration is high.

One unusual interpretation of pricing and power goes back to the French sociologist Gabriel Tarde (1843–1904), who considered every agreement on a price, wage, and interest rate to be equivalent to military truce.[13] Price negotiations are similar to war, eventually ending in a truce. You have this sense often after wage negotiations between unions and employers. The peace lasts only until the next round of fighting begins. In a business-to-business negotiation, the agreement on a price reflects a power struggle between supplier and customer. Fortunately it is not a zero-sum game. But price plays a pivotal role in how a pool of money gets divided up between a supplier and a customer.

In reality, the pricing power of most companies is relatively modest. Simon-Kucher & Partners interviewed over 2,700 managers in 50 countries for its "Global Pricing Study"[14] and found that only 33 % of respondents felt that their companies had a high level of pricing power. The remaining two-thirds admitted that their companies are not able to implement their desired prices in the market, which puts their profitability at risk.

The study's insights into the sources of pricing power offer guidance for those firms looking for an edge. Pricing power was 35 % higher in companies if top management was involved in setting the framework for pricing decisions instead of delegating that authority. Companies with dedicated pricing departments had 24 % more pricing power than companies without such departments. The key lesson is that it pays for top managers to make a strong and serious commitment to better pricing and to invest time and energy into this endeavor. This sparks a positive spiral, as higher pricing power leads to sustainably higher prices and higher profits.

Pricing Pushes Its Boundaries

For centuries, certain goods and services had no prices. The use of streets was free, going to school cost nothing, and many services came with an all-inclusive price. Governments, churches, or charities delivered goods and services at no charge, because it would help others or because charging a price would be considered immoral or taboo. But that is changing quickly.

In his book *What Money Can't Buy: The Moral Limits of Markets*, Harvard philosopher Michael J. Sandel reports that prices are creeping into all realms of our lives.[15] The airline Easy Jet charges passengers $16 to be among the first to board the aircraft. It costs a foreigner $14 to enter the USA. That is the cost of an entry into

---

[13] Tarde G (1902) Psychologie économique, 2 volumes. Alcan, Paris.

[14] The study was conducted in 2012.

[15] Sandel MJ (2012) What money can't buy: the moral limits of markets. Farrar, Straus and Giroux, New York.

ESTA (Electronic System for Travel Authorization). In some countries you can pay extra during rush hour to travel in exclusive lanes, with the prices dependent on the current traffic. For a fee of $1,500 per year, some doctors in the USA offer a dedicated cell phone access number and 24/7 availability. In Afghanistan and other war zones, private companies paid mercenaries between $250 and $1,000 per day, with the price based on qualifications, experience, and the mercenary's country of origin. In Iraq and Afghanistan, these private security and military companies had more people on the ground than the US armed forces did.[16]

Moving further along the moral spectrum, one can pay a surrogate mother in India $6,250 to carry a baby to full term. If you want to immigrate to the USA, you can purchase that right for $500,000.

Someday many more things will have a price tag attached to it, as more and more of our lives and routines come under market and pricing mechanisms. This creep across moral and ethical boundaries is one of the most significant economic trends of our time.

Sandel commented on this development. "When we decide that certain goods may be bought and sold, then we decide—at least implicitly—that it is appropriate to treat them as commodities, as instruments of profit and use. But not all goods are properly valued in this way. The most obvious example is human beings."[17]

In my childhood on the farm I experienced an entirely different world. Despite my remarks about prices for our hogs and our milk, money played a secondary role in our lives. Self-sufficiency was the priority; neighbors helped neighbors without any formal "price" mechanism in effect. The money-based part of our economy was small. Nowadays, prices are pervasive. They are inescapable. You see them everywhere, sometimes in unexpected or troubling roles. An important question we all wrestle with is how much more these market forces—and with them, prices—will take over our lives. This makes it all the more important for us to understand how prices and pricing mechanisms work.

---

[16] Christian Miller T (2007) Contractors Outnumber Troops in Iraq. Los Angeles Times, July 4, 2007 and Glanz J (2009) Contractors Outnumber U.S. Troops in Afghanistan. New York Times, 2.

[17] Sandel MJ (2012) What money can't buy: the moral limits of markets. Farrar, Straus and Giroux, New York; see also Kay J (2013) Low-cost flights and the limits of what money can buy. Financial Times, January 23, 2013, p. 9.

The Strange Psychology of Pricing

The principles of classical economics assume that buyers and sellers act rationally. Suppliers try to maximize their profits, while buyers try to maximize their value, or their "utility" in the vernacular of the economist. Under these principles, all parties have complete information. The sellers know how the buyer will respond to different prices, which means that they know their demand curves. The buyers know all available alternatives and their prices, and can make qualified judgments on the utility that each alternative provides, independent of its price.

Nobel Prize winners Paul Samuelson (1970) and Milton Friedman (1976) are prominent advocates of this view. Friedman said that buyers behave rationally, even though they don't explicitly make their decisions using clever mathematics or elegant economic theories. Gary Becker (Nobel Prize, 1992) extended the idea of utility optimization or maximization to other aspects of life, such as crime, drug dealing, and family relationships. In his models, all parties likewise act rationally by seeking to maximize their gains and their utilities.

These assumptions about rationality and information first came into doubt through the work of Herbert A. Simon[1] (Nobel Prize, 1978). In his view, people have only limited capacity to absorb and process information. For that reason, they do not strive to maximize their profit and their utility. Instead, they content themselves with a "satisfactory" outcome. He coined the term "satisficing" to describe this behavior.

Akin to this initial doubt, psychologists Daniel Kahneman and Amos Tversky published their groundbreaking paper on "prospect theory" in 1979 and gave rise to a new school of thought called behavioral economics.[2] Kahneman won the 2002 Nobel Prize.[3] The number of authors and publications devoted to behavioral economics has exploded since then. Research in this direction—noteworthy that it was

---

[1] Herbert Simon and I are not related.

[2] Kahneman D, Tversky A (1979) Prospect theory: an analysis of decision under risk. Econometrica: pp. 263–291.

[3] Tversky (1937–1996) had passed away by that time.

© Springer International Publishing Switzerland 2015
H. Simon, *Confessions of the Pricing Man*, DOI 10.1007/978-3-319-20400-0_3

initiated largely by noneconomists — may permanently alter economic theory. Price plays a central role in behavioral economics, with surprising and often counterintuitive outcomes and, thus, consequences for price management. The entire field of behavioral economics is too complex and comprehensive to cover here. For now, we focus on the basic elements of behavioral pricing. If you would like a deeper treatment of behavioral economics, I would recommended Daniel Kahneman's best-selling book *Thinking Fast and Slow*.

The Prestige Effect of Price

In classical economics, price plays a role in a purchase decision only because of its impact on the customer's budget. The demand curve has a negative slope, which means the higher the price, the less the customer buys. There are exceptions to this situation, however, which give rise to apparently irrational consequences.

In his classic *The Theory of the Leisure Class*, the American economist and sociologist Thorstein Veblen revealed way back in 1898 that prices signal status and social prestige and therefore offer the buyer an additional level of psychosocial utility. This is known as the Veblen or "snob" effect. The price itself becomes an indicator for the quality and exclusivity of luxury products. A Ferrari wouldn't be a Ferrari if it costs only $100,000. The demand curve for such products — at least within a certain range — has an upward (positive) slope, not a downward (negative) one. That means that a price increase leads to *higher* sales. This increases profits not only because of the higher unit margins, but also because of higher unit sales. This powerful combination results in a veritable profit explosion if the price is raised.

Such cases do indeed exist in real life. Delvaux, a Belgian manufacturer of exclusive handbags, raised prices massively in conjunction with a repositioning of the brand. Unit sales rose sharply, as consumers now viewed the product as a viable alternative to Louis Vuitton handbags. Sales of the famous whiskey brand Chivas Regal were in the doldrums in the 1970s. In order to reposition the brand, the company developed a label with a more high-end look and raised the price by 20 %. The whiskey itself remained exactly the same. In spite of the price increase, sales rose significantly.[4]

MediaShop Group, one of the leading direct-response TV networks in Europe, introduced a new cosmetic accessory at a price of 29.90 Euros. Sales were sluggish, and management pulled the product, in order to free up valuable airtime for better-selling products. A few weeks later, they relaunched it with a new sales offensive and a new price: 39.90 Euros, a hefty increase of 33 %. This time, management apparently found the sweet spot for the price. Sales skyrocketed in a matter of days, leading to temporary supply shortages. The product became one of MediaShop's top sellers, not in spite of its higher price, but *because* of it!

---

[4] Müller K-M (2012) NeuroPricing. Haufe-Lexware, Freiburg.

For premium and luxury goods, one needs to know whether such prestige effects exist and whether the demand curve has a part which slopes upward. If it does, the optimal price never lies in that portion of the demand curve. It always lies higher, in the part where the curve slopes downward again. This reinforces a key lesson in this book: you need to know what your demand curve looks like, the more precisely, the better. When companies do not know their demand curves—especially in the case of premium and luxury goods—they will be poking around in the dark searching for the optimal price to charge.

If some uncertainty remains, I recommend feeling your way along by gradually raising prices toward that higher range. It is also often wise—as the cases of Delvaux and Chivas Regal show—to combine the higher price positioning with an enhanced design or a packaging upgrade.

Price as an Indicator of Quality

An effect similar to the prestige phenomenon occurs when consumers use the price as an indicator of the product's quality. A lower price can prompt a consumer to forgo a purchase, because the price raises concerns about the quality. Many customers act according to the motto "you get what you pay for" and steer clear of low-priced products. But the flipside of that statement is also valid for many customers. For them, the simple equation "higher price = higher quality" becomes a handy rule of thumb. In such cases, a price increase can lead to higher unit sales. How does price end up serving as an indicator of quality? I have several plausible explanations:

- *Experience*: A high price is seen as more likely to guarantee better quality than a low price, if a consumer has had a positive experience with a high-priced product before.
- *Ease of comparison*: Consumers can use price to compare products immediately and objectively. This is especially true in situations—such as most consumer products—when the price is fixed and nonnegotiable. In situations where prices are negotiated, such as industrial goods or at a bazaar, prices rarely serve as quality indicators.
- A *"cost-plus"* mentality: In the minds of many customers, the price is closely related to the seller's costs. In other words, consumers have a "cost-plus" mindset. They think that sellers base their prices on costs such as raw materials, manufacturing, and shipping.

When do consumers assess a product primarily or solely based on its price? Price is likely to serve as an indicator of quality when buyers are uncertain about a product's underlying quality. This happens when they are confronted with a product that is entirely new to them or one which they rarely buy. Consumers are also prone to make such price-based judgments when the absolute price of the product is not very high, when they have little transparency on prices for alternatives, or when they are under time pressure.

There are countless empirical observations of the role of price as a quality indicator and the related upward slope on a portion of the demand curve. It has occurred for products as diverse as furniture, carpet, shampoo, toothpaste, coffee, jams and jellies, and radios. Researchers have reported that unit sales rose after a price increase for nasal spray, panty hose, ink, and electrical goods. For one electric razor, sales increased by a factor of four after the company raised prices sharply in order to come closer to the prices of Braun, the market leader. The price difference was still sufficient to offer a purchase incentive, but no longer so large that consumers would start to doubt the razor's quality.

I have observed similar effects in the service sector, particularly in restaurants and hotels. It also occurs in the business-to-business world. A software firm offered cloud software for businesses at an extremely low monthly fee of $19.90 per workstation. The price for the comparable competitive product stood at more than $100. Several months after the launch, the company's CEO told me that "small businesses are really excited about our prices. For the first time, they can afford this kind of software. But larger companies think our price point is so low that they have no faith in our product. Our extremely low price becomes a barrier to sales rather than an advantage."

The solution lay in product and price differentiation. The company loaded up its product with additional features, and then offered the new package to larger companies at a significantly higher fee per month. The package was still rather inexpensive, but it now fit better into a more conventional price-value framework. Through this adaptation, the firm succeeded in getting rid of the negative image the previously low price had created.

The Placebo Effect of Price

The effect of price as a quality indicator sometimes goes beyond the mere level of perception and creates a true placebo effect. A placebo effect is therapeutic improvement in a patient who has received a treatment of no real medicinal value. In one test, study participants received a pain reliever at different prices. One group saw a tag with a high price, and the other group saw a low price. Without exception, the participants in the high-price group claimed that the pain reliever was very effective. In the low-price group, only half of the participants made that claim.[5] In both cases, however, the pain reliever was actually a vitamin C placebo, which has no objective ability to relieve pain. The only difference between the two groups was the price the participants in each group saw.

Another finding: after consuming a power drink priced at $2.89, a group of athletes reported significantly better training results than a group which drank the exact same power drink priced at 89 cents. The most surprising result, though, came in a study on intellectual skills among two groups: "Participants who consumed an

[5] Ariely D (2010) Predictably irrational. Harper Perennial Edition, New York.

energy drink they purchased at a discount price performed worse on a puzzle-solving task than did equivalent participants who purchased the same drink at its regular price."[6] Price differences really can create significant placebo effects.

Price as a Defused Weapon

If prestige, quality, or placebo effects are present in a market, this has a major impact on both price positioning and price communication. These effects defuse price as a competitive weapon. If a supplier wants to increase its market share through aggressive pricing, the attempt will fail. One cannot rule out that both unit sales and market share will actually drop rather than increase. These effects make it very difficult for an unknown supplier or an unknown brand to break into a market where these phenomena exist. Attempts to win over customers through lower prices don't work. These effects also explain why discounts on no-name products or weaker brands also fail to work: customers associate the reduced price with lower quality or with low prestige. According to automotive experts, Volkswagen's Phaeton is a good luxury car, objectively in the same category as BMW, Mercedes, and Audi. Yet the Phaeton doesn't sell well in Germany, because it lacks sufficient prestige. The VW brand—which is very strong in the company's mass market segment—does not have the power to carry a product in the premium/luxury segment. As a result, even the offer of very low prices and leasing rates had little effect on sales of the Phaeton. If you offer those kinds of low prices on a strong brand, though, sales will explode, because high prices have already established the quality judgments about strong brands.

What should a company do when it can't use price as a competitive weapon? The best method may be to position the product in a price range which corresponds to its true quality and accept lower sales initially. This may require considerable patience until customers actually learn and appreciate the product's quality and its price-value relationship. Audi had this problem in the 1980s, and it took 20 years to get the brand to the price and prestige position it deserved.

Price Anchor Effects

What does a buyer do when he or she has neither the knowledge or means to make a qualified assessment of a product's quality, nor the information about the price range for this product category? One method is to do thorough research to reduce the information gaps by looking online, reading test reports, or asking friends. This time-consuming approach may make sense for a major purchase, such as a new car. But what does a buyer do when it is something of much lesser value, and this intensive research is not worth the investment? Buyers look for reference points or "anchors."

---

[6] Shiv B, Carrnon Z, Ariely D (2005) Placebo effects of marketing actions: consumer may get what they pay for. Journal of Marketing Research, pp. 383–393, November 2005, here p. 391.

Here is an old story about such a price anchor effect.[7] The brothers Sid and Harry ran a clothing store in New York in the 1930s. Sid was the salesman, and Harry the tailor. If Sid noticed that a customer liked a suit, he would play dumb. If the customer asked about the price, Sid would call out to Harry back in the tailor shop.

"Harry, how much does this suit cost?"

"That nice suit? $42," Harry would yell back.

Sid would act as if he didn't understand.

"How much?"

"$42!" Harry would say again.

Sid would then turn to the customer and say that the suit's price is $22. The customer didn't hesitate, immediately putting $22 on the counter and leaving with the suit. The brothers' price anchor had worked as planned.

This approach can also work for bigger ticket purchases, especially when combined with a premium or prestige effect. Two young construction workers became frustrated in their attempts to join a local union in California, so they decided to form their own company. Instead of describing themselves as masons, they claimed to be "European bricklayers. Experts in marble and stone." To underscore this positioning, one of them would make the measurements at a prospective job site in meters and centimeters, and then show them to his colleague. The two of them would argue in German until the customer came over and asked what was going on.

"I don't get why he thinks this patio will cost $8,000," the one who took the measurements explained, pulling the customer aside. "Between you and me, I think we can build it for $7,000." After some discussion with the customer and a little more arguing in German, the customer accepted the $7,000 bid.

The two immigrants built a solid business in this manner, before one of them left to pursue another career path. The one who took the measurements at the job site was a young Austrian bodybuilder named Arnold Schwarzenegger. [8]

The most diverse information sources can end up serving as price anchors. This process of anchoring doesn't even have to be a conscious one. As consumers and buyers we often use price anchors subconsciously. Price anchors also work effectively on professionals, not just on consumers. In one study, car experts were asked to assess the value of a used car. Someone stood next to the car, apparently just by chance, and remarked unprompted that the car is worth "x." In one study with 60 automotive experts, the participants assessed the value of the car at $3,563 after the neutral observer gave $3,800 as the price anchor. But when the neutral person gave $2,800 as the anchor price, the experts' average estimate came to $2,520.[9] The casual remark by a random person had created a price anchor which altered the price perception of the experts by $1,043 for the identical car. Based on the average anchor

[7] Cialdini RB (1993) Influence: science and practice. Harper Collins, New York.

[8] Schwarzenegger A (2013) Total recall: my unbelievably true life story. Simon & Schuster, New York, p. 119.

[9] Mussweiler T, Strack F, Pfeiffer T (2000) Overcoming the inevitable anchoring effect: considering the opposite compensates for selective accessibility. Personality and Social Psychology Bulletin, pp. 1142–1150.

price of \$3,300 across the two studies, this is a shift of 32 %. Similar anchor effects have occurred in many other studies. The researchers concluded that "anchoring is an exceptionally robust phenomenon that is difficult to avoid."[10]

The Magic of the Middle, or the Story of the Padlock

Another interesting effect of price anchors is the "magic of the middle." How a price looks in relation to other prices can have a strong influence on a consumer's behavior. An identical price of \$10 can trigger widely different reactions, depending on whether it is the highest, lowest, or middle price in an assortment. Likewise, the number of alternatives in an assortment can exert a strong influence on customers' choices.

I once needed a padlock for a barn door on my farm (the one where we raised hogs in the 1950s). When was the last time I had purchased a padlock? I had no idea. Nor did I have any clue about how much a padlock costs. So I went to the home improvement store and found a large assortment of locks, priced in a range of \$4–\$12. What did I do? On the one hand, I didn't require a high level of security which would warrant the purchase of one of the expensive locks. On the other hand, I didn't trust the quality of the cheaper locks. So I chose one from the middle of the range, priced at \$8.

What does this teach us? When buyers know neither the price range of a product category nor have any special requirements (e.g., high quality, low price), they gravitate toward a price in the middle of the range. What does this mean for sellers? Quite simply, it means that a seller can use the price range in his assortment to steer customers toward certain price levels and away from others. If the price range for the locks at the home improvement store was \$4–\$16, I would have probably spent \$10 on a new padlock. That would have generated 25 % more revenue for the store, and higher profit margins as well.

Neither the Cheapest nor the Most Expensive Wine

We observe the same behavior at restaurants when guests select a wine. After looking at the wine list, most guests order a wine with a price in the middle of the list. Only a few guests opt for the most expensive or least expensive wine. The middle has a magical allure. The same effect occurs with the food menu. Let's assume that a restaurant offers its entrées in a price range from \$10 to \$20, and 20 % of the demand goes to the dish priced at \$18. If the restaurant then adds an entrée at \$25, the share of the \$18 entrée is very likely to increase. Analogously, if the restaurant adds an entrée which is less expensive than the previously least expensive entrée, sales for the latter option will likely increase, even though few customers ever

---

[10] ibidem, p. 1143.

bought it in the past. The explanation is simple. The price of the formerly least expensive entrée has now moved closer to the middle of the price range.[11]

The less a buyer knows objectively about the quality of the products and prices in an assortment, the stronger the pull of the "magic of the middle" will be. One could even argue that this purchase behavior is rational, as the buyer tries to make the best possible decision with very limited information. By selecting a product from the middle of the price range, buyers simultaneously reduce the risk that they buy something of poor quality and the risk that they overspend. Sellers should not go to extremes to take advantage of this, however. They should be cautious setting price anchors at extremely high or extremely low levels. An extremely high price may scare off buyers who don't want to spend that much, whereas an extremely low price may scare off buyers who become suspicious of the quality.

A Profit-Generating Product No One Ever Buys

Price anchor effects can make it worthwhile to carry a product in an assortment even though no customer ever buys it. The next case illustrates this. A customer enters a luggage store to purchase a new suitcase. The saleswomen asks how much he is willing to spend.

"I was thinking about $200," the customer said.

"You can get a good suitcase for that amount," the saleswoman responded.

"But before we take a closer look at the suitcases in that range, may I show you one of our finer pieces?" she asked. "I'm not trying to upsell you to a more expensive suitcase. I just want to inform you about our whole product range."

The saleswoman then brings out a suitcase for $900. She emphasizes that in terms of quality, design, and brand name, it is truly a top-of-the-line model. Then she returns to the products in the customer's desired price range, but also calls his attention to some models with slightly higher prices, between $250 and $300. How will the customer react? It is highly likely that he buys a model in the $250–$300 price range and not something near his original target price of $200. The anchor effect created by the $900 model drew the buyer's willingness to pay upward. Even if the store never sells even one $900 suitcase, it makes sense to keep it in the assortment, purely because of the anchor effect it creates.

Creating Scarcity

One of the cleverest tricks to boost sales is to create the perception of scarcity. The impression of consumers that a product is available only in limited supply can create a stronger urge to buy. In an in-store test in the USA, one group of shoppers was shown a sign for Campbell's Soup which said "Limit of 12 per person." The other

---

[11] Huber J, Puto C (1983) Market boundaries and product choice: illustrating attraction and substitution effects. Journal of Consumer Research 10: pp. 31–44.

group was confronted with a display sign which read "No Limit per Person." Shoppers in the first group bought seven cans on average, and the shoppers in the latter group only half as many. At play here is not only an anchor effect—the sign suggests that buying 12 cans is normal—but also a hoarding effect. Buyers interpret such a sign as a signal that some kind of scarcity is looming. Similar reactions result when long lines form at the gas pump or at the cinema. In former socialist economies, scarcity was an everyday occurrence. Lines were everywhere. People bought whatever they could get their hands on. One never knew what might happen.

Selling More by Offering Additional Alternatives

At Simon-Kucher & Partners we have observed time and again that the introduction of additional alternatives can significantly increase sales and shift demand toward higher priced products. This finding is one of the most astounding in behavioral pricing research.[12] Figure 3.1 shows the results of a study with two sets of alternatives. In Test A, respondents saw a checking account for $1 per month and a checking account plus credit card for $2.50 per month.[13] In test group A, 59 % selected the combination, while 41 % chose the checking-only alternative.

In test group B the credit card was included as a stand-alone option at the same price as the combination (checking account and credit card). Only 2 % of respondents chose the stand-alone option for the credit card; the share of respondents selecting the combination jumped from 59 to 81 %. The average monthly revenue per customer rose from $1.89 to $2.42, an increase of 28 % … without implementing a price increase! The only thing that changed was the structure of the offering itself. Banks serve a large number of customers. If the bank in Fig. 3.1 has one million customers, the additional revenue works out to $530,000 per month, or $6.36 million per year, revenue essentially created out of nowhere.

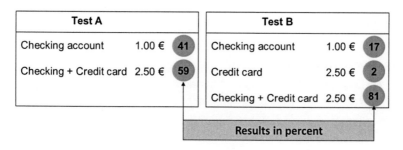

Fig. 3.1 Banking products with two and three alternatives

---

[12] Trevisan E (2013) The irrational consumer: applying behavioural economics to your business strategy. Gower Publishing, Farnham Surrey (UK).

[13] Trevisan E (2012) The impact of behavioral pricing. Presentation at the Simon-Kucher University, August 14, 2012, Bonn.

In terms of rational, classical economics, this result makes no sense. The addition of one alternative—which hardly anyone wanted—caused the share of respondents' choosing the combination to rise sharply. What explains such a shift in purchase behavior? One possible explanation is the "magic of zero." Setting the credit-card-only option and the combination at the same price means that the customer receives added value with the combination at no extra charge. This temptation is too much for many customers to resist, so they choose the combination. The anchoring argument can also play a role here. Test B has two of its three alternatives set at $2.50, which pulls the overall price anchor upwards, and, thus, creates higher willingness to pay.

The following case comes from telecommunications.[14] In the first test, respondents could choose between two plans, one with a basic monthly price of $25 and one with a fee of $60. Some 78 % of the respondents chose the less expensive plan, while the remainder selected the more expensive one. The average revenue per user (ARPU) from this test came to $32.80. In the second test, the respondents could choose among three plans priced at $25, $50, and $60. The highest and lowest prices remained the same; the only difference is the $50 plan inserted in between them. As you might now expect, the shift similar to the bank case occurred here as well. In the second test, only 44 % of respondents chose the cheapest plan, compared with 78 % in the first test. Almost as many (42 %) went for the new $50 plan, and the remaining 14 % chose the most expensive plan. The ARPU increased to $40.50, or 23 % more than in the first test, an enormous amount of additional revenue. What are the possible explanations for selecting the middle option in this case? Here are four hypotheses:

- *Uncertainty*: Customers don't have a good estimate of their monthly usage, so they fall back on the "magic of the middle."
- *Quality expectations*: The customer thinks: "If the basic fee is so low, the service probably isn't all that good."
- *Peace of mind/risk avoidance*: "If I end up making a lot of calls, it can get really expensive with the low base fee and high variable charges."
- *Status*: "I can afford it."

In reality, these motivations don't manifest themselves in their pure forms, but rather work in concert. These two cases demonstrate clearly that psychological effects are extremely important and relevant for price setting and assortment planning. Small changes in the assortment or price structure can have a dramatic impact on revenue and profit, without any increases in costs.

---

[14] Simon-Kucher & Partners project from 2011, led by Dr. Philip Biermann.

Price Thresholds and Odd Prices

A section on pricing psychology would not be complete without some mention of price thresholds and pricing on the 9s. A price threshold is a price point which triggers a pronounced change in sales whenever it is crossed. You might think of a price threshold as a kink in the demand curve. This price-threshold effect normally happens at round price points, such as $1, $5, $10, or $100. That is why many prices lie just under those thresholds, very often ending in a 9.

Eckhard Kucher, one of the co-founders of Simon-Kucher & Partners, examined 18,096 prices of fast-moving consumer goods and found that 43.5 % of them ended in a 9.[15] No prices in his sample ended in a zero. Another study found that 25.9 % of the prices ended in 9.[16] At the gas pump, almost all prices end in 9, but go one step further: they are posted in tenths of a cent rather than in full cents, i.e., 0.1 cent under a full cent. If you fill a 20-gallon tank at a price of $3.599 per gallon, you pay $71.98. If the price were $3.60, you would pay $72.00, an absurdly small difference of just two cents.

The most important argument for the existence of odd prices is that customers perceive the digits in a price with decreasing intensity as they read from left to right. The first digit in a price has the strongest influence on perception; that is, a price of $9.99 comes across as $9 plus something rather than $10. Neuropsychologists have confirmed that the further to the right a digit is, the less influence it has on price perception. According to this hypothesis, customers underestimate prices which lie just under round numbers.

Another hypothesis claims that customers tend to associate prices ending in 9 with promotions or special offers. Reducing a price from $1.00 to 99 cents sometimes results in a sharp jump in sales. Should one attribute this sales increase to its appearance as a special offer, rather than to the price reduction of a mere 1 %? The question of cause and effect remains open.

The fact—or rather the belief—that price thresholds exist has led to the widespread practice of using odd prices, which are prices not ending in zero. When consumers grow accustomed to these odd prices, they can show heightened sensitivity to prices and price increases which breach nearby thresholds. The comparison of price increases in three brands of sparkling wine—Mumm, Kupferberg, and Fürst von Metternich—indicates the presence of a price-threshold effect, as Fig. 3.2 shows.[17]

---

[15] Kucher E (1985) Scannerdaten und Preissensitivität bei Konsumgütern. Gabler-Verlag, Wiesbaden.

[16] Diller H, Brambach G Die Entwicklung der Preise und Preisfiguren nach der Euro-Einführung im Konsumgüter-Einzelhandel. In Handel im Fokus: Mitteilungen des Instituts für Handelsforschung an der Universität zu Köln 54(2): pp. 228–238.

[17] Rotkäppchen-Mumm steigert Absatz. LZnet, April 26, 2005; Rotkäppchen will nach Rekordjahr Preise erhöhen; Jeder dritte Sekt stammt aus dem ostdeutschen Konzern; Neuer Rosé; Mumm verliert weiter. Frankfurter Allgemeine Zeitung, April 26, 2006, p. 23; and Sekt löst Turbulenzen aus. LZnet, November 29, 2007.

	Mumm		Kupferberg		Fürst von Metternich	
	before	after	before	after	before	after
Price (€)	4.99	5.49	3.45	3.90	7.75	8.50
Volume (index)	100	63.7	100	64	100	94
Price elasticity	3.64		2.77		0.62	

Fig. 3.2 Price increases and their effects for three brands of sparkling wine

The only price which crossed a price threshold was Mumm's, which went above 5 Euros. The volume decline for Mumm was much greater than what Kupferberg and Fürst von Metternich experienced, when we look at it from the perspective of price elasticity. The price elasticity—which we will explore in greater detail in Chaps. 5 and 6—is defined as the percentage change in volume, divided by the percentage change in price.[18] Mumm's price elasticity of 3.64 is significantly higher than Kupferberg's. It means that for Mumm, a price increase of 1 % would cause volume to drop by 3.64 %. It is hard to say precisely how much of the volume decline resulted from the price-threshold effect and how much from the normal effects of a price increase. If we make a rough approximation of 50:50, the price-threshold elasticity would be 1.82.

Despite the frequency of reported cases such as these, convincing scientific evidence for a general price-threshold effect is still lacking. Columbia University professor Eli Ginzberg investigated the price-threshold effect as far back as 1936.[19] In 1951, business economist Joel Dean reported on a mail-order company's experiment, in which the company systematically varied prices around various thresholds. "The results are shockingly variable [...] sometimes moving a price from $2.98 to $3.00 dollars greatly increased sales, and sometimes it lowered them. There was no clear evidence of concentration of sales response at any figure."[20] Eckhard Kucher was also unable to isolate systematic effects when prices crossed thresholds.[21] In another study on women's clothing, a store tested three prices for the same item: $34, $39, and $44. The results were surprising. The highest sales came at the price of $39. Sales at $34 and $44 were each 20 % lower.[22] That indicates, as already mentioned above, that a price ending in 9 can signal a particularly favorable price.

---

[18] Price elasticity is usually a negative number, because normally volume rises when prices falls and vice versa. But for simplicity's sake, we generally leave off the negative sign and just write the absolute value.

[19] Ginzberg E (1936) Customary prices. American Economic Review (2): pp. 296.

[20] Dean J (1951) Managerial economics. Prentice Hall, Englewood Cliffs, NJ, p. 490 f.

[21] Kucher E (1985) Scannerdaten und Preissensitivität bei Konsumgütern. Gabler, Wiesbaden, p. 40.

[22] Anderson ET, Simester DI (2003) Effects of $9 price endings on retail sales, evidence from field experiments. Quantitative Marketing and Economics (1): pp. 93–110.

These overall unclear findings speak in favor of the hypothesis that economist Clive Granger (Nobel Prize, 2003) and Professor Andre Gabor put forward in 1964, namely, that the belief in the price-threshold effect is a consequence of predominant marketing practices[23]; that is, it must be effective because so many people do it.

Price thresholds—real or theoretical—can prove problematic when inflation hits. At some point, a company needs to exceed a price threshold, which can lead to a sharp decline in sales. Another—sometimes admittedly problematic—way to get around a price increase is to change the package size in order to stay on the favorable side of a price threshold. The idea is that the average consumer will not notice if the new package they buy has slightly fewer units or fewer ounces than the package they used to buy, as long as the price is the same. This tactic caused an uproar after the financial crisis hit in 2008. Skippy peanut butter gained nationwide attention when its manufacturer introduced a new jar with an indentation in the bottom. Outwardly a consumer noticed no difference at the shelf, but the jar contained less peanut butter.[24] In 2009, Häagen-Dazs reduced the size of its standard ice cream container to 14 from 16 ounces, yet still called the container a "pint." This prompted its archrival, Ben and Jerry's, to issue this statement:

> One of our competitors (think funny-sounding European name) recently announced they will be downsizing their pints from 16 to 14 ounces to cover increased ingredient and manufacturing costs and help improve their bottom line. We understand that in today's hard economic times businesses are feeling the pinch. We also understand that many of you are also feeling the same, and think now more than ever you deserve your full pint of ice cream.[25]

Believing in the price-threshold effect can also result in missed opportunities, as the papers from several contemporary economics and psychology researchers show. One study demonstrated that clinging to prices that end in 9 can lead to considerable profit sacrifices if there is no proof that the price threshold exists.[26] Other authors argued that misconceptions about price thresholds can have negative consequences.[27] Resellers (retailers, distributors, wholesalers) often have a return on sales of just 1 %. An across-the-board price increase from 99 cents to $1.00 would double their profits, assuming no change in volume.[28] Even if volume dropped significantly—say by 10 %—the price increase would still have a positive effect on profit.

---

[23] Gabor A, Granger CWJ (1964) Price sensitivity of the consumer. Journal of Advertising Research (4): pp. 40–44.

[24] Hirsch J (2009) Objects in store are smaller than they appear. Los Angeles Times, November 9, 2008.

[25] Ben and Jerry's Calls Out Haagen-Dazs on Shrinkage. Advertising Age, March 9, 2009.

[26] Diller H, Brielmaier A (1996) Die Wirkung gebrochener und runder Preise: Ergebnisse eines Feldexperiments im Drogeriewarensektor. Schmalenbachs Zeitschrift für betriebswirtschaftliche Forschung, July/August, pp. 695–710.

[27] Gedenk K, Sattler H (1999) Preisschwellen und Deckungsbeitrag – Verschenkt der Handel große Potentiale? Schmalenbachs Zeitschrift für betriebswirtschaftliche Forschung, January, pp. 33–59.

[28] Müller-Hagedorn L, Wierich R (2005) Preisschwellen bei auf 9-endenden Preisen? Eine Analyse des Preisgünstigkeitsurteils. Arbeitspapier Nr. 15, Universität zu Köln, Seminar für Allgemeine Betriebswirtschaftslehre, Handel und Distribution, Köln, p. 5.

My own findings show that it makes no sense to set prices at \$9.90 or \$9.95. If you want to remain below a price threshold, then you should set your price as close to the threshold as possible, which means \$9.99 in this case.

Prospect Theory

The law of declining marginal utility was first formulated in 1854. It has become one of the most widely known economic principles. It says that the marginal utility of a product declines with each additional unit that one consumes. This law makes no distinction, however, between positive and negative marginal utility. Kahneman and Tversky suggested that positive and negative marginal utility may be asymmetrical. Figure 3.3 shows the basic concept which they called "prospect theory." In the upper right quadrant, we see the positive portion of the utility curve, which corresponds to the traditional law from 1854. The perceived utility of a gain increases steadily, but at a diminishing rate. In other words, the utility of the first \$100 you win or earn is greater than your utility from the next incremental \$100.

Prospect theory differentiates between positive marginal utility (from gains) and a negative marginal utility (from losses). Perhaps a more fitting term for the negative utility would be "marginal harm." The curve for marginal harm is shown in the lower left quadrant. Similar to the pattern for gains, the marginal harm gets smaller as the size of the overall loss increases. That is not surprising. The real breakthrough message from prospect theory is this: for any absolute gain or loss of identical size, the negative utility from the loss is greater than the corresponding positive utility

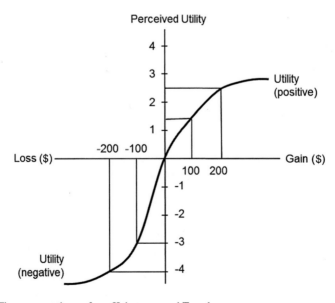

Fig. 3.3 The prospect theory from Kahneman and Tversky

from the gain. In other words, the pain we feel from a loss is greater than the happiness we feel from a gain, even if the magnitude of the loss and gain themselves is equal. This leads to some surprising consequences with real-life relevance. One such consequence: prospect theory shows that it is not only the net utility that matters to an individual, but how that net utility comes about.

What is the simplest way to explain this? Imagine someone who has entered a lottery. The sponsor calls him to say that he has just won $1 million. Then one hour later, the sponsor calls back to say: "Sorry. Tonight's drawing was not valid. You didn't win." Suddenly the "winner" has experienced an extreme loss. His presumptive gain has been taken away. On a net basis, nothing changed. He wasn't a millionaire before the first call, nor was he a millionaire after the second one. But we can safely assume that his net utility from the entire experience was very negative, requiring days if not weeks to overcome the disappointment.

Prospect Theory and Price

What does prospect theory have to do with price? The theory is vitally important to pricing, even though the term "pricing" appears just twice in Kahneman's seminal book. Paying a price generates negative utility. The amount that an individual parts with is a sacrifice, a loss. The purchase and use of a product or service, in contrast, represents a gain and generates positive utility. The asymmetry between the utility from gains and losses can cause some unusual effects. One is known as the endowment effect, which you can see in an experiment that Kahneman conducted with his students. The students in one group received mugs bearing the university's logo. They were worth about $6 each. The students in the other group received nothing, but they could buy the mugs from the students in the other group. How would you expect the potential buyers and sellers to behave?

The average asking price for the mugs was $7.12. The students who could buy the mugs offered on average only $2.87, a big difference. Because the students were split randomly into two groups, we should assume that each group would have the same price expectations. Classical economics cannot explain the large discrepancy between the two prices. But prospect theory can. The negative utility of giving up something we already own is significantly greater than the positive utility we get from a good that we first need to buy. We are all reluctant to part with what we have.

Business or Economy?

Prospect theory can also explain my own occasionally peculiar behavior. On October 27, 2011, I was scheduled to fly back to Frankfurt from the Chinese city of Guangzhou. When I went to Lufthansa's business-class counter to check in, the agent informed me that business class was overbooked. He wanted to know if I would be willing to "downgrade" to economy and offered me 500 Euros. I said no. Then he immediately increased his offer to 1,500 Euros. That made me think.

As reluctant as I am to wedge my 6-ft-5 frame into an economy seat for a long-haul flight, and to give up the opportunity to get a lot of work done, I had to admit that 1,500 Euros for 12 hours works out to a decent hourly wage.

Something similar happened to me a few years earlier in Boston. The offer to switch from business class to economy was $1,000.

"For a six-and-a-half hour flight, that isn't bad," I remarked to my wife, who accompanied me on that trip. But she had a more rational view of the situation, and also the appropriate response.

"That is the exact same amount that you were willing to pay extra to fly business class when you bought the tickets," she said. "So why didn't you just book economy to begin with and save the $1,000 then?" Of course, she was right. When I originally booked our flights, I never imagined making this red-eye flight in economy class. Why was I suddenly willing to accept the offer and the downgrade to economy? Prospect theory offers a plausible explanation. The negative utility from the original booking—which I paid for via credit card—was less than the positive utility from the cash amount that the Lufthansa agent offered.

Free or Paid: A Big Difference

Prospect theory also explains another phenomenon. Let's assume you have received a ticket for an open-air concert. On the day of the show, it rains. The odds that you go to the concert despite the weather are much greater if you paid for the ticket with your own money than if you had received the ticket as a gift. Both situations have to do with "sunk costs." The money is gone, regardless of whether you attend the concert. But the urge to "earn back" the price of the ticket is much higher if you paid with your own money. In the spirit of prospect theory, the negative utility is greater when the ticket cost you something.

Better to Pay in Cash

Nowadays you can pay with credit cards almost anywhere. It is convenient and fast and you also don't need to carry cash around with you. Nonetheless, some people still prefer to pay with cash. Why do people do that? Economists previously thought that differences in transaction costs determined which form of payment someone would use. But paying in cash has other characteristics which can prove advantageous to consumers. Prospect theory tells us that it is harder for us to part with cash than to pay via credit card, because the negative utility from a cash payment is greater. If you want to rein in your spending and resist the temptation to buy things, trying to pay in cash as much as possible will better help you achieve that goal.

Two economists discovered another effect. In their analysis of 25,500 individual transactions, they found that consumers who want to have an overview of their expenditures tend to avoid paying with credit cards. They described this as the "reminder effect" of cash.[29] When you look into your purse or wallet, you immediately see how much you have spent and how much money is left. It is particularly advisable for people with limited financial means to use cash payments as a control mechanism. According to the researchers, people actually do this; they make two-thirds of their purchases in cash. The clear advice of the researchers for anyone who is deep in debt or who wants to live within a tight budget: always pay in cash!

The Temptation of Credit Cards

There are many reasons why paying by credit card is so tempting. Doing so lets us consume something several weeks before the bill comes due. In other words, credit card payments are a way of postponing the actual separation from our money. We also don't "feel" the payment as much, because we don't have to reach into our pockets, give physical money to a cashier, and watch them put it away. We simply sign our names or type in our PIN codes. As a result the negative utility is smaller when we pay with plastic.

When we receive our monthly statement and see that long list of transactions, the effect of any individual transaction gets watered down. This also hurts less. Some cards offset the negative utility even more by conferring positive utility, such as prestige. This matters, for example, when someone checks into a hotel or pays in a place where the type of card is visible to other people. American Express has its Centurion Card—informally known as the "black card"—which is accessible only to select wealthy individuals for a substantial annual fee. To serve these cardholders even better, American Express opened its own exclusive "Centurion" airport lounges whose "free amenities set them apart." The lounge at the Dallas-Fort-Worth airport includes a spa, a complimentary buffet featuring food from the chef at Dallas's Ritz-Carlton Hotel, and full-size, first-class showers.[30]

Consumers can also use the credit card as a weapon to achieve slight discounts. At some retailers, you can get some flexibility when you "threaten" to pay with credit card, and then offer to pay cash if you can get a discount. Retailers often prefer cash payments, because they receive their money right away and also avoid having to pay a transaction fee.

"Cash Back" and Other Absurdities

Prospect theory also helps to explain some price structures that would seem absurd if you only took the perspective of classical economics. "Cash back" is a common sales tactic at car dealerships. You purchase a car for $30,000 and receive $2,000 in cash

---

[29] von Kalckreuth U, Schmidt T, Stix H (2011) Using cash to monitor liquidity-implications for payments, currency demand and withdrawal behavior. Discussion Paper Nr. 22/2011. Deutsche Bundesbank, October 2011.

[30] McCartney S (2014) The airport lounge arms race. The Wall Street Journal, March 5, 2014.

back. How does that make any sense? Prospect theory provides the answer. The payment of $30,000 generates a significant negative utility, balanced out by the positive utility of acquiring the new car. Then on top of that comes an additional positive utility in the form of $2,000 in cash. This constellation apparently leaves many car buyers with a perceived net utility that is higher than if they had just paid $28,000 for the car straight up. If the dealership accepts payment via check, transfer, or credit card, the positive utility may even be greater. The payment is made in an intangible form. The "cash back," in contrast, comes in the form of physical money. In addition, this cash may represent a rare opportunity for heavily indebted consumers to get their hands on real money once in a while. Within the context of prospect theory, this access can add to make "cash back" an effective tactic.

Many discount tactics work along similar lines. Older readers may remember collecting S&H Green Stamps. The concept was popular in many countries; I experienced something similar in my childhood. We collected stamps and pasted them into an album. For every dollar, we received three stamps, each with a value of one penny. This is a discount of 3 %. When we filled the album with 150 stamps, we could redeem it for $1.50. Why would a retailer or a store owner go through the hassle of handing out and redeeming stamps, when they could simply offer the direct discount of 3 %? Redeeming the stamp album created a high positive utility, especially for children. We perceived it as a much bigger gain than if the store owner had offered a 3 % discount, which would have generated only a tiny positive utility to offset the negative utility of parting with cash at checkout. The joy of collecting also provided a positive reward, especially for us children, while the store owner profited from the loyalty effect as we and our parents bought more in an effort to get more stamps.

Moon Prices

In our daily lives we constantly encounter list prices which no one ever pays, so-called moon prices. Is it better for a seller to offer a product at $100 with a discount of 25 %, or simply ask for $75? Classical economics cannot answer the question because it only looks at the end result: the customer ends up paying $75.

Prospect theory has an answer, however. The rebate provides the customer with additional positive utility. This means that the net utility is greater when one sees a price of $100 and receives a 25 % discount than when one pays $75. This trick is typical for car dealers. They have list prices, but they hardly ever sell cars at those prices. So why do such moon prices make sense? There are two answers. First, the high prices create an opportunity for price differentiation. Not all buyers receive the same discount. One role of the seller is to offer the smallest possible discount without losing the customer. The second answer stems from prospect theory. I experienced it myself the last time I bought a car. At first I was pleased with the new car (positive utility). But I had also negotiated a large discount, which contributed in no small way to my net utility from the transaction. Hardly anyone can deny that a successful price negotiation which results in a discount—even a slight one in absolute terms—will trigger such positive feelings. Most of us have experienced that at one time or another.

The situation with magazine subscriptions is similar. Subscriptions will continue only if we renew them, and as the expiration date approaches, the hard sell begins. One opens the mailbox or clicks on an e-mail and gets a message similar to this one, which I have personally received: "I have authorized our business office to extend your subscription for as little as $0.81 per issue. That's a savings of up to 82 % off our cover price." Who can resist a discount of 82 % off the cover price? And in addition to the extremely large discount, many publishers also throw in a "mystery gift" or "an invaluable business tool" or "full unrestricted access" to the magazine's online version. The problem with such offers is that over time, the exaggerated list prices lose their credibility. When that happens, they cease to function as proper price anchors.

Price Structures

Prospect theory provides concrete guidance on how to set up price structures. One question is the price metric, which is the unit a seller will use to express the price. Let's look at car insurance. The standard way to express the price is an annual premium. So let's use $600 in this example. Wouldn't it be wiser to express the price on a quarterly or even a monthly basis? The numbers a customer sees would then be much smaller—$150 for the quarter or $50 for the month—and may therefore create a more favorable price perception.[31]

When a customer actually pays the premium, however, it can make sense to have him or her pay in one lump sum of $600 rather than pay $50 in 12 monthly installments. When you pay monthly, you "hurt yourself" 12 times in a year, and the sum of this negative utility is greater than what you experience with the one-off payment. On the flipside, incentives or reimbursements may work much better when paid out in installments, because they trigger positive feelings in the recipient each time. Prospect theory would imply that paying someone a bonus of $100 per month for a year would enhance the positive utility of payment versus making a one-off payment of $1,200. I suspect, however, that we should be wary of small amounts in such situations, because the effects indicated by prospect theory diminish. It's probably better to pay someone back $10 at once rather than pay them $1 over 10 periods. It can also make more sense for a newspaper to receive a subscription payment as a lump sum (say $360) than receive its money in 12 equal payments of $30, each of which it needs to process.

Likewise, one should avoid making generalizations here. Nor should we rush to judgment on whether an approach that works in one context can be transferred to another. One study looked at the question of whether a fitness studio is better off

---

[31] Schmidt-Gallas D, Orlovska L (2012) Pricing psychology: findings from the insurance industry. Journal of Professional Pricing (4): pp. 10–14.

charging an annual fee or 12 monthly installments.[32] Prospect theory would presuppose that the one-time payment is better because the customer "feels the pain" only once. The fitness studio also has two advantages from the one-off payment: immediate access to the money, and lower transaction costs. But fitness studios are a special case, and the study found another effect. After making a payment, the customers want to "earn it back" and visit the studio on a regular basis. The frequency of visits starts to decline, though, the further the most recent payment recedes into the past. By encouraging monthly payments, the studio restores the customers' incentive to get their money's worth back. With monthly payments, the usage intensity remains strong over time and—most importantly for the studio— the renewal rates are significantly higher. The clear recommendation is to ask for monthly payments, a contradiction to prospect theory.

Mental Accounting

University of Chicago professor Richard Thaler developed the theory of mental accounting, which claims that consumers allocate their transactions into different mental accounts. How easily or carefully they spend their money depends on which account the money is in.[33] These accounts may be based on different criteria or needs such as food, vacation, hobby, car, or gift-giving. This kind of categorization helps consumers to budget their money, plan expenditures, and monitor their spending. Each account is subject to different spending behaviors and price sensitivities. Each account will have its own negative utility curve, according to prospect theory.

I also apparently have my spending for cars and other products in separate accounts, each with its own price sensitivities and limits. When I was looking for a new office chair, I shopped around and compared prices before settling on a model I liked. Around the same time, as I was buying a new car, I invested almost three times as much on a special comfort seat without batting an eye. With the possible exception of an airline seat, I probably spend more time sitting in my office chair and car seat than any others. Yet my behavior in purchasing them, my mental accounting, was much different.

One famous experiment by Kahneman and Tversky showed the absurd effects of false mental accounting. The participants did not distinguish between costs which are relevant for their decision making and those which aren't (such as sunk costs). Assume that a ticket to a play costs $10. Participants were divided into two groups. The participants in the first group were informed that they were standing in front of

[32] Gourville JT, Soman D (1998) Payment depreciation: the behavioral effects of temporally separating payments from consumption. Journal of Consumer Research (2): pp. 160-174.

[33] Thaler RH (1999) Mental accounting matters. Journal of Behavioral Decision Making (3): p. 119, and Thaler RH (1994) Quasi-rational economics. Russell Sage, New York; see also Thaler RH, Sunstein CR (2009) Nudge: improving decisions about health, wealth and happiness. Penguin, London.

the theater and had lost their ticket. The participants in the second group were told that they would need to buy a ticket at the window, and that they had just lost $10 moments earlier.

Among those in the group who lost their ticket, 54 % decided to buy a new one. Among those in the group who had lost the $10 bill, some 88 % decided to buy a ticket. Mental accounting helps explain this discrepancy. The ones who lost the ticket booked both the price for their lost one and their new one to the "going to a play" account, whose mental price now rose to $20. That price was too expensive for 46 % of the participants. The ones who lost the $10 bill, however, booked that loss to their "cash" account. Since their mental price for the theater ticket remained unaffected at $10, the vast majority of them decided to buy the ticket for $10. In other words, the participants allocated their gains and losses to different mental accounts. Loss aversion, the desire to avoid or postpone losses, is a strong human trait. It helps explain why many people wait too long before getting out of stocks when their prices have gone down.[34]

Neuro-Pricing

New research into the field of neuro-pricing builds on behavioral pricing and broadens it by measuring physical responses to price stimuli, using modern technologies such as magnetic resonance imaging (MRI).

"The perception of prices is no different than the perception of other stimuli," says one researcher.[35] This simple revelation means that price perception triggers responses in the brain which scientists can now measure with ever-increasing precision. Important emotions in the context of pricing are trust, value, and longing. Researchers track these emotions in order to assess the success of a marketing campaign. The most interesting finding thus far in neuro-pricing research is that price information activates the brain's pain center. That is not surprising. Associating prices with pleasure is probably the rare exception rather than the rule.

Neuro-pricing is a form of behavioral research which can yield useful information to supplement the existing knowledge. MRIs and other scans allow researchers to objectively measure processes that subconsciously influence consumers' decisions, without needing to coax a verbal or written answer from their study participants. The goal is to understand these subconscious processes better and offer sellers new ways to influence them. I know what you are now thinking, and you are correct: this kind of research gets into ethically sensitive territory. But that is just one problem with neuro-pricing. The validity of the results is also an issue, and that starts with the sampling process. Selecting a sample for this kind of research follows the same principles as classical market research. Many potential participants, however, are unwilling to

---

[34] Tversky A, Kahneman D. The framing of decisions and the psychology of choice. Science 211(4481): pp. 453–458.

[35] Müller K-M (2012) NeuroPricing. Haufe-Lexware, Freiburg.

subject their brains to physiological research for marketing purposes. Personally, I would also refuse. Neuro-marketing studies require participants to go to special labs, which puts even more limitations on how representative the results are. In light of all these factors, how well do the study results project to real-life situations? How well can they be extrapolated to larger populations? Those questions remain open.

Thus far, the research has yielded relatively few findings and insights from which someone could derive practical price recommendations. Kai-Markus Müller, a neuro-pricing researcher, reported on a brain study he conducted on Starbucks coffee. His conclusion: "… the willingness to pay for a cup of coffee at Starbucks is significantly higher than the company assumes … Starbucks is letting millions of dollars in profits slip through its fingers, because it is not taking its customers' willingness to pay into account."[36] Even people with only a passing familiarity with Starbucks knows that its prices are already very high. With all due respect to Dr. Müller, I must admit I do not think that this finding is valid.

Brain research has, however, provided some useful insights into how prices are displayed and communicated. The standard way of expressing a price—for example $16.70—causes a pronounced response in the brain's pain center. The response is weaker, however, when the respondent only sees 16.70 and the dollar sign is omitted. Apparently the brain does not immediately perceive that number to be a price. The activation of the pain center is even weaker for a round number, such as 17.

This form of price communication has become more common recently in restaurants. The form which results in the least pain, and therefore the least amount of negative utility, is actually the word itself, in this case "seventeen." It remains to be seen whether menus and price lists start to appear with prices displayed in that manner.

The research has also yielded insights into the influence of colors; for example red price tags indicate special offers. Paying by cash, as I implied earlier, activates the brain's pain center to a higher degree than paying by credit card. Marketers should also avoid using currency symbols in advertisements, unless the product in question can boost the self-image or prestige of the customer.

Using brain research for marketing and pricing is still in its infancy. Many of the claims from this field should be challenged. But the researchers are learning, and we can expect progress and new discoveries in due time. Right now, though, I feel that it is premature to speculate on how the findings from brain research will have a practical and lasting impact on pricing.

In Conclusion: Be Cautious!

Behavioral and neural economics are exciting new areas which have yielded surprising and fascinating results. The research in these areas has already changed our understanding of economics and will continue to do so. These new approaches can explain many phenomena which classical economics cannot.

---

[36] Ibidem.

Having said that, I would still warn you to be cautious with how freely you interpret and try to apply the findings and insights I've highlighted in this chapter. I am convinced that most transactions still follow the fundamental laws of economics. Yes, a higher price may lead to higher unit sales under certain circumstances. But that remains an exception, not the rule. It applies in perhaps 5 % of cases. A bigger concern, however, is the attempt to generalize these findings. When is it better to pay once a year, and when is it better to pay in 4 or 12 installments? There is neither a general answer to those questions, nor a set of unequivocal guidance on how to answer them. Philip Mirowski, an economic historian and philosopher at the University of Notre Dame, is correct when he says that behavioral economics may be "undermining the foundation of rational activity, but it's putting nothing up in its place."[37] Behavioral economics does not yet offer a complete, unified theory.

The test results which support behavioral economics have begun to face increasingly critical challenges. Most of the findings come from laboratory settings, which casts doubt on how well the findings transfer to real life. Some of the stimuli were presented in a way that could lead participants toward a particular answer. A business writer drew this conclusion: "the theoretical and empirical body of evidence against behavioral economics should serve as a warning against throwing the idea of the 'rational human' completely overboard."[38] Human beings are not as rational as classical economics claims, nor are they as irrational as some behavioral economists claim. What does this mean for pricing? It means that you should take both of these research traditions into account, but proceed with caution.

---

[37] Die Ökonomen haben ihre Erzählung widerrufen. Frankfurter Allgemeine Zeitung. February 16, 2013, p 40.

[38] Beck H (2013) Der Mensch ist kein kognitiver Versager. Frankfurter Allgemeine Zeitung. February 11, 2013, p. 18.

Price Positioning: High or Low

Are high prices or low prices better for the profit and the survival of a company? You should avoid becoming one of the fools in the Russian proverb: neither the one whose prices are too high nor the one whose prices are too low. Both fools sacrifice profit unnecessarily. The question remains, though: Where is a company's optimal price position? A company must make a conscious decision about price positioning. In fact, whether a company selects a high-price or low-price positioning is one of its most fundamental strategic decisions. Often the founders of the company make that call. For many reasons—as we will see throughout this chapter—a company's chances of changing course later on are limited.

The choice of the price position affects the overall business model, the product quality, branding, and the company's innovation activities. It also determines which market segments the company will serve and what channels it will use to reach them.

Success Strategies with Low Prices

One can run a successful business with either low prices or high prices; the success factors in each case, however, are very different. Let's begin with the more surprising of the two options: spectacular success stories with low prices.

Aldi

This deep discounter, which also owns Trader Joe's, is one of the world's most successful retailers and has expanded internationally for years. At the end of 2014, Aldi operated more than 10,500 stores worldwide, including 1,300 in 32 US states, and planned to increase that US footprint by 50 % by 2018.[1]

---

[1] ALDI press release, December 20, 2013.

© Springer International Publishing Switzerland 2015
H. Simon, *Confessions of the Pricing Man*, DOI 10.1007/978-3-319-20400-0_4

While Trader Joe's competes against higher end food and grocery retailers such as Whole Foods, and enjoys a cult following, Aldi's core strategy is simple: offer an acceptable level of quality at very competitive prices. Its assortment consists almost entirely of private-label products whose prices undercut popular brand-name products by 20–40 %. Nonetheless, Aldi achieves significantly higher returns than food and grocery chains who command higher price positions. How can that be? Three reasons explain why Aldi's return on sales is more than double the returns of a traditional supermarket: higher efficiency, lower costs, and capital management.[2] The gross return per square meter of floor space is 30.3 % higher in Aldi than in a supermarket. Personnel costs alone save Aldi the equivalent of 8.2 % of sales. Aldi puts bar codes on all sides of its packages, so that the cashiers do not need to search for the code to scan. Aldi also saves costs in procurement, where its enormous volume—combined with its negotiation skills—enables it to win favorable prices from its suppliers.

Aldi turns its inventory over almost three times as fast as a traditional supermarket. In other words, goods in their system spend far less time at a warehouse or on a store shelf. Aldi gets its money quickly, but pays its suppliers much later, and invests this so-called float to earn short-term interest.

Taking all these factors into account, Aldi uses a very aggressive low-price strategy to earn consistently higher returns than the rest of the sector. Recent data show that Aldi Süd (one of the two Aldi operating units) had a pretax return on sales of 5.0 % and an after-tax return of 3.7 %. The comparable numbers for its counterpart Aldi Nord were 3.5 and 3.0 %.[3] The profits from Aldi have made its founders extremely wealthy. For years, Karl Albrecht and his late brother Theo ranked among the world's wealthiest people. They and their descendants had a combined fortune estimated at over $44 billion.

IKEA

This Swedish company is one of the world's most successful retailers. In 2011 IKEA cut its already low prices by another 2.6 %. In 2013 it "continued to lower prices on some of its best-selling items"[4] and it cut prices overall by 0.2 %.[5] Despite this ongoing price-cut strategy, IKEA's revenue grew by 3.1 % to $36.2 billion in 2013 and its net profit likewise by 3.1 % to $4.2 billion. This corresponds to a return on sales of 11.6 %, a very high number for a retailer. One analyst commented: "A key contributor were aggressive price investments (new lower pricing strategy) on top selling products." IKEA focuses all of its activities on achieving the maximum cost efficiencies. The company can offer such low prices because of its

---

[2] The profit metric here is Earnings before Interest and Taxes (EBIT); one also uses operating profit. Because Aldi Nord has no debt, the after-tax yield may be even higher.

[3] Manager-Magazin. April 16, 2012.

[4] IKEA annual financial report. January 28, 2014.

[5] IKEA's Focus Remains on Its Superstores. The Wall Street Journal, January 28, 2014.

extremely high procurement volumes, its use of lower cost materials, and its "do-it-yourself" model under which customers pick up and assemble the furniture themselves.

H&M and Zara

The fashion retailers H&M and Zara have a similar cost strategy to IKEA's. H&M has around 3,000 stores and Zara has 5,500. H&M has revenues of roughly $19.3 billion and an after-tax profit of $3.6 billion, which works out to a return on sales of about 13.3 %.[6] Zara's profit margin is practically the same. Like IKEA, Aldi, and Walmart, the name of the game at H&M and Zara is "efficiency." These companies do nothing unless it is absolutely required by the consumer. All of their activities are trimmed and slimmed to achieve the highest efficiency. This is particularly true for their logistics processes, which ensure that the companies can time their new product lines to reflect prevailing customer tastes, and can order the right amount of goods to avoid unsold inventory when tastes shift again. This extreme precision, speed, and efficiency make them very profitable despite low prices.

Ryanair

The revenue of the Irish no-frills airline Ryanair rose by 21 % to $5.85 billion in its fiscal year 2011/2012, but profit jumped by 50 % to $750 million. That represents a return on sales of 12.8 %, an unusually high number for an airline. In contrast, Lufthansa, Europe's biggest airline, earned just under $600 million in profits in 2011 on revenue of $38.3 billion, for a return of sales of 1.6 %. Ryanair is much more profitable than the American icon of low-cost airlines, Southwest Airlines, which generated $17.1 billion in revenue in 2012 and earned a pretax profit of $685 million. That is a return on sales of 4.0 %, far below Ryanair's.

How can Ryanair be so profitable despite its famously low prices? The story begins with its capacity utilization. Ryanair boasts a load factor of around 80 %. The story continues with Ryanair's passion for focusing on costs in minute detail. Ryanair is the epitome of the "no-frills" airline business model. The flight attendants go to great lengths to make sure that passengers leave nothing behind, not even a newspaper or magazine. This frees up time once the plane arrives at the gate. While a conventional airline would need 15–20 minutes after a flight to clean the cabin, Ryanair uses that time to board passengers for the next flight. Southwest, in service since 1973 and one of the role models for airlines like Ryanair, takes a similar approach and is the record-holder in minimizing an aircraft's time on the ground. It can turn a plane around completely—deplaning and then boarding new passengers—in as little as 22 minutes. That gets the plane back in the air faster, and planes generate revenue only when they are flying. The difference is substantial: a conventional airline might

---

[6] H&M Full-Year Report, 2013.

have a plane in the air for eight hours a day on average, while the no-frills carriers average 11–12 hours per day in flight. Their capital productivity is almost 50 % higher. Another way in which Ryanair focuses on costs is to serve airports which usually lie outside of major city centers and thus have lower landing fees.

Ryanair is also a master at inventing and implementing surcharges, a topic we will explore in more detail in Chap. 8. The price that Ryanair communicates is often extremely low, with a basic ticket sometimes free of charge or for as low as 99 Euro cents (roughly $1.30). This kind of price communication plays a major role in the airline's ability to attract passengers, who often end up paying much more than the advertised price of the base ticket, because their total fare usually includes a number of surcharges.

Ryanair apparently achieves very low prices on the procurement side, too. The airline supposedly received a discount of 50 % off the list price when it placed a major order with Boeing some years ago. According to market rumors, it received a similar discount in March 2013 when it ordered another 175 Boeing 737 aircraft.[7]

Dell

In November 1988 I heard a 23-year-old entrepreneur named Michael Dell give a speech at Harvard Business School. Just four years earlier, he had founded his eponymous computer company in his dorm room at the University of Texas at Austin.

"As a student, I worked at a computer store," Dell said, describing how he came up with the idea for his company.

"We sold computers, but we ourselves didn't deliver much value to the customers," he said. "Yet we still kept 30 % of the purchase price. I thought to myself: I could save this margin through a direct-sales model and pass on those savings to customers in the form of lower prices. So I started my own firm."

From this idea grew what would become the world's largest seller of personal computers. Dell now employs over 100,000 people. In 2012 the company had $57 billion in revenue and posted an after-tax profit of $2.37 billion. That is a return on sales of just over 4.2 %, an exemplary return in such an intensely competitive sector. The margins of Dell's three biggest competitors were much lower. Hewlett Packard has a margin of −10.5 %, Lenovo's profit margin is 1.8 %, and Acer's −0.7 %.

The entire Dell system is centered on the highest cost efficiency. Dell became famous for its "configure to order" concept, which meant it built nothing in advance to store in a warehouse. It would build a computer only after a customer ordered it. That doesn't just save on warehouse costs; it also reduces the cost of returns and increases customer satisfaction. Each customer receives exactly the configuration he or she wants. Eliminating the retailer margin enabled Dell to offer lower prices and still make a good profit.

---

[7] Ryanair Orders 175 Jets from Boeing. Financial Times. March 20, 2013, p. 15 and "Ryanair will von Boeing 175 Flugzeuge," Handelsblatt, March 22, 2013, p.17.

Less Expensive Alternatives

Many firms face the question of whether to respond to competitors by offering a cheaper alternative, a so-called less expensive alternative (LEA). Such a low-price product is often marketed under a second brand, in order to differentiate it clearly from the primary brand and reduce the risk of cannibalization. A world market leader in specialty chemicals observed that its unique silicon-based products were losing their competitive edge. Low-price imitators had entered the market, posing a major threat to the 7,000 products in the market leader's portfolio. Instead of meeting these threats head on by cutting the prices for its primary brand, the market leader introduced an LEA, with a price position around 20 % below the lead brand. The LEA offered only minimal service and no customization, and was shipped only by the full tank carload. Customers would need to wait between seven and 20 days for delivery.

After introducing the LEA, the company started to achieve strong double-digit growth. Its revenue rose to $6.4 billion from $2.3 billion within four years, and the company swung from an annual loss of $27 million to a profit of $475 million. The LEA became a new growth engine for the company, in part because it complemented rather than cannibalized the primary brand.

Amazon and Zalando: Revenue vs. Profit

The previous cases prove that one can achieve high profits with low prices. I could continue with more cases, but not forever. The list of companies who have experienced enduring success with the "low price–high profit" combination is not very long. Far more low-price companies have failed with that strategy than have achieved consistently high profits. That list includes retailers such as Woolworth's, the home improvement chain Praktiker (famous for its "20 % off everything!" sales), and many no-frills airlines.

The widely praised online retailer Amazon has still not joined the "low price–high profit" club, at least not yet. Amazon reported revenue of $61.1 billion in 2012 and a net loss of $39 million. In 2013 revenue grew by 22 % to $74 billion and net income improved to $274 million. This is much better than the loss in 2012 but still only a profit margin of 0.4 %. The German online retailer Zalando, founded in 2008 with the same business model as Amazon, also seems stuck consistently in the red despite its growth. The company grew by 50 % and topped $2.4 billion in sales in 2013, but had a negative profit margin of −6.7 %.[8] Zalando's management say that they are in no hurry to become profitable. Are Amazon and Zalando betting on low-margin sales, in order to earn high profits later? Or are these firms forced to offer low prices in order to remain competitive and grow, without any prospects for attractive margins down the road? In Amazon's case, equity markets seem to believe the former scenario. Its share price has climbed more or less steadily from $55 in

---

[8] Der milliardenchwere Online-Händler. Frankfurter Allgemeine Zeitung, February 16, 2013, p. 17.

early 2009 to around \$400 by the end of 2013. The view is not unanimous. Said one critical analyst: "Investors could get tired of this and it could end up imploding Amazon's market capitalization."[9] In the course of 2015 Amazon's share price climbed further up to over \$500.

One obstacle to profitability for Amazon and Zalando is the massive investments in infrastructure and logistics required by their business models. Other popular e-commerce destinations for consumers—such as eBay or China's Alibaba—don't have that problem, and it helps explain their profitability. In 2013, eBay earned \$2.86 billion on revenues of \$16.05 billion, for a return on sales of 17.8 %. Alibaba, which executed its initial public offering in 2014, earned \$3.52 billion on just \$7.95 billion in revenue, for return on sales of 44.2 %.[10]

Success Factors for a Low-Price Strategy

The list of companies who have succeeded with a low-price strategy tends to be short, but their strategies share a set of factors which help create and sustain that success.

1. *They began with that strategy from day one:* All successful low-price companies focused on low prices and high volumes from the very beginning. In many cases, they created radically new business models. I am not aware of any company having made a successful transformation from a high-price or mid-price position to a low-price one.
2. *They are extremely efficient:* All successful low-price companies operate with extreme cost and process efficiency, which enables them to enjoy good margins and profits even while charging low prices.
3. *They guarantee adequate and consistent quality:* With poor and inconsistent quality, success is unlikely, even if you offer low prices. Sustainable success requires adequate and consistent quality.
4. *They have a strong focus on their core products:* The term no-frills is often applied to airlines, but it could apply to companies such as Aldi or Dell as well. They do nothing that isn't absolutely required by the customer. That saves costs, without putting the essential value to customer in jeopardy.
5. *They have a high-growth, high-revenue focus:* This creates economies of scale which they exploit to the greatest extent possible.
6. *They are procurement champions:* That means they are tough and forceful in their purchasing, but not unfair.
7. *They have little debt:* Only very rarely do they turn to banks or debt markets for financing. Instead they rely on self-financing or supplier credit.

---

[9] Woo S (2012) Amazon Increases bet on its loyalty program. The Wall Street Journal Europe, November 15, 2012, p. 25.

[10] Alibaba flexes its muscles ahead of U.S. Stock Filing. The Wall Street Journal Europe, April 17, 2014, pp. 10–11.

8. *They control as much as they possibly can:* This means they carry only their own brands (Dell, Ryanair, IKEA); even Aldi's assortment is over 90 % private label. They also exercise strong control over the entire value chain.
9. *Their ads focus on price:* To the extent they even advertise at all, they focus almost exclusively on price (Aldi, Lidl, Ryanair).
10. *They never mix their messages:* Almost all of the successful "low price–high profit" companies stick to an "everyday low price" strategy rather than a "hi-lo" which relies on frequent temporary promotions.
11. *They understand their role:* Most markets have room for only a small number of "low price–high profit" competitors, often just one or two.

Yes, it is absolutely possible for a company to achieve consistently high profits with low prices. But only a few who try are ever blessed with that kind of success. It only happens when a company has a clear, significant, and sustainable cost advantage over its competitors. The skills to pull that off must be anchored in the company and its culture from its very beginning. I doubt that a company with another operating style and tradition could make the switch and meet the "low price–high profit" requirements. The key challenge is to establish an acceptable (not a minimal) level of value to customer, delivered with the highest cost efficiency. This category of companies also places special demands on executives, entrepreneurs, and managers. Only those with the will and the nerves to be Spartan, thrifty, and stingy day in and day out should venture into the realm of low-price positioning.

Ultra-low Prices: Can You Go Lower than Low?

So far this chapter has focused on prices at the low end of ranges in highly developed, industrialized countries. In recent years, an entirely new "ultra-low price" segment has coalesced in emerging markets, where prices are as much as 50–70 % lower. Two Indian-American professors have anticipated the evolution of this segment for many years. Vijay Mahajan of the University of Texas in Austin referred to this segment as the "biggest market opportunity of the 21st century" in his book *The 86 % Solution.*[11] The 86 % in the book's title refers to the fact that the annual family income of 86 % of mankind is below $10,000. People with this income level are unable to afford the typical products (everything from personal hygiene products to cars) which we take for granted in highly developed countries.

In his book *The Fortune at the Bottom of the Pyramid*, the late C. K. Prahalad, formerly a professor at the University of Michigan, took a deeper look at the opportunities in the ultra-low price segment.[12] The ongoing growth in China, India, and other emerging economies means that every year millions of consumers acquire enough purchasing power to afford mass-produced products for the first time, albeit

---

[11] Mahajan V (2006) The 86 % Solution—how to succeed in the biggest market opportunity of the 21st century. Wharton School Publishing, New Jersey.
[12] Prahalad CK (2010) The fortune at the bottom of the pyramid. Pearson, Upper Saddle River, NJ.

at "ultra-low" prices. The ultra-low price position opens up a new, rapidly growing, and very large segment of the world's population to a wide range of consumables and durables. Every company needs to decide whether and how it wants to serve this segment. However, this requires a radically different approach, if one wants to make money.

Dacia Logan and Tata Nano

The emergence of an "ultra-low price segment" is not limited to Asia; one has already emerged in Eastern Europe. Nor is it limited to consumer categories such as personal hygiene, cleaning, or infant care. Taking all makes and models together, consumers around the world currently buy 10 million ultra-low price vehicles per year. That number is expected to increase to 27 million vehicles over the next decade, which means that it is growing more than twice as fast as the overall car market.

The French car company Renault has enjoyed success with its model Dacia Logan, which it assembles in Romania. The car costs around $9,600 and Renault has already sold over 1 million units. The price is less than half the price of a typical VW Golf. In France, people already speak of a "Loganization" process, similar to how the Germans occasionally talk of an "Aldization." These developments show that ultra-low-price products can enter the mainstream of Western markets, and are not doomed to be niche or fringe products.

Yet the price of cars in the ultra-lowprice segment in developing countries is far below the price of a Dacia Logan. The Nano, a car from the Indian manufacturer Tata, garnered considerable attention worldwide. The car has a price of around $3,300, and yet it contains a surprising amount of technology from leading Western suppliers. Some German suppliers saw the Nano not only as an opportunity but also as a necessity for them, and took on a key role in its launch in 2009. Bosch developed a radically simplified and much less expensive fuel injection system for use in the Nano. Bosch components account for more than 10 % of the value of the car. But Bosch is not alone. Nine German automotive suppliers have their parts or their technologies in the Nano. This demonstrates that companies from a high-priced, highly developed country (such as Germany) can hold their own in the ultra-low price segment. But the whole value chain, including R&D, procurement, and manufacturing, must reside in the emerging market. It remains to be seen whether this segment can also become a significant source of profit, not just revenue.

Honda Wave

Does a huge, global company such as Honda have the capability to outmaneuver ultra-low price competitors? Honda is the world market leader in motorcycles. It is also the number one global manufacturer of small gas-powered engines, producing over 20 million units per year.

Honda used to dominate the motorbike market in Vietnam, with a share of 90 %. Its best-selling model, the Honda Dream, sold for the equivalent of around $2,100. Chinese competitors then entered the market with ultra-low-price products. Their bikes sold for between $550 and $700 each, or between a quarter and a third of the price of the Honda Dream. These extremely aggressive prices turned market shares upside down. The Chinese manufacturers moved over one million bikes per year, while Honda's volume dwindled from about one million to just 170,000.

Most companies would have thrown in the towel at this point, or withdrawn into the premium segment of the market. But not Honda. Its initial short-term response was to cut the price of the Dream to $1,300 from $2,100. But Honda knew that it could not sustain this low price over the long term. And this price was still roughly twice the price for a Chinese motorbike. Honda developed a much simpler and extremely inexpensive new model which it called the Honda Wave. The new bike combined acceptable quality with the lowest possible manufacturing costs.

"The Honda Wave has achieved low price, yet high quality and dependability, through using cost-reduced locally made parts as well as parts obtained through Honda's global purchasing network," the company said. The new product entered the market with an ultra-low price of $732, which is 65 % less than the former price of a Honda Dream. Honda reconquered the Vietnamese motorcycle market so successfully that most of the Chinese manufacturers eventually withdrew.

This case proves that premium manufacturers such as Honda can indeed compete against ultra-low price suppliers in emerging markets, but not by selling their existing products. Success in the ultra-low price position requires a radical reorientation and redesign, massive simplification, local production, and extreme cost consciousness.

Ultra-low price Positioning in Other Consumer and Industrial Goods

Ultra-low price positionings have begun to permeate many different markets. With his "One Laptop per Child" initiative, MIT Professor Nicholas Negroponte proposed a personal computer with a price of $100. Nowadays one can find a laptop with acceptable performance for less than $200; slimmed-down devices cost even less. So Negroponte's $100 price position is almost within reach. In 2013 one could purchase a very rudimentary PC for $35.[13] If you are wondering what kinds of volumes companies can achieve in markets with ultra-low prices, look no further than the market for smartphones. The total number of mobile handsets was expected to exceed the world's population sometime in 2014, and an increasingly larger share of them are smartphones.[14] Right now there are more than two billion of them in circulation[15] and shipments of smartphones reached 1.2 billion in 2014. What we now

---

[13] The Future is Now: The $35 PC. Fortune, March 18, 2013, p. 15.

[14] Number of mobile phones to exceed world population by 2014. Digital Trends, February 28, 2013.

[15] One billion smartphones shipped worldwide in 2013. PCWorld, January 28, 2014.

consider to be an ultra-low price position may become normal in a few years. "Dirt-cheap smartphones," rumored to be available for as low as $35, "will have astonishing implications for the global economy," according to one report.[16]

More and more companies are trying to pursue an ultra-low price strategy. The manufacturers of athletic shoes are considering offering products in emerging markets for under $1.50 per shoe. Consumer product giants such as Nestlé or Procter & Gamble sell tiny package sizes for just pennies apiece, so that even consumers with the smallest incomes can occasionally afford to buy such a product, such as a single-use pack of shampoo. Companies used that same approach successfully after World War II, as the rebuilding began in Europe. I remember single-use shampoo packets, as well as boxes of four cigarettes, sold for the equivalent of 20 cents. Gillette, which is part of Procter & Gamble, now sells a razor blade in India for the equivalent of 11 cents, or 75 % below the price for the Mach3, the razor with three blades.

Ultra-low prices are by no means limited to consumer products or even durable goods such as cars and motorbikes. This price positioning is becoming increasingly common for industrial products, too. In the Chinese market for injection molding machines, the premium segment comprises roughly 1,000 machines per year, supplied primarily by European manufacturers. The midrange price segment has an annual volume of around 5,000 units and is the domain of Japanese manufacturers. The Chinese firms do battle in the ultra-low price segment, which includes 20,000 machines per year. In other words, that segment is 20 times larger than the premium segment and four times the size of the midrange segment.

With that kind of market structure, even a premium supplier cannot restrict itself to the premium segment and neglect the ultra-low price segment. This is not a viable, long-term alternative. The premium segment represents just 4 % of the market. Even in a market as vast as China's, that is still too small to warrant a singular focus at the expense of other segments. Another risk of an exclusively premium strategy is that competitors with acceptable quality at significantly lower prices will attack the premium segment from below.

"Machinery manufacturers need to radically simplify their product concepts if they want to take a large share of growth markets such as China and India," said a study conducted by a European trade association.[17] The manufacturers of high-tech and industrial products need to give serious consideration to entering the low-price segment. This means building not only a manufacturing base in emerging markets, but a research and development department as well. It is an illusion that a company can develop ultra-low price products within an advanced economy such as Germany or the USA.[18] The only way is for companies to relocate their value chain to the emerging markets themselves. Many years ago, the late Nicolas Hayek, who invented the Swatch watch and served for many years as CEO of Swatch, warned

[16] Kessler A (2014) The cheap smartphone revolution. The Wall Street Journal Europe, May 14, 2014, p. 18.

[17] VDI-Nachrichten March 30, 2007, p. 19.

[18] Ernst H (2009) Industrielle Forschung und Entwicklung in Emerging Markets – Motive, Erfolgsfaktoren, Best Practice-Beispiele. Gabler, Wiesbaden.

against conceding the lower price segments to competitors from low-wage countries. Personally, I would go one step further and raise a provocative question—a serious challenge if you will—for companies in developed countries: Why don't you try to beat the Chinese on costs?[19] The Honda story with the Dream and the Wave shows that the question is worth considering. In India, Bangladesh, or Vietnam, hundreds of millions of people work for wages which lie well under Chinese levels.

Vijay Govindarajan and Chris Trimble, both on the faculty of Dartmouth's Tuck School of Business, analyzed this process in their book *Reverse Innovation: Create Far From Home, Win Everywhere.*[20] An effective defense strategy for the premium and midrange segments is to become competitive in the price segments further downmarket. The Swiss company Bühler, the world market leader in milling technology, acquired a Chinese company in order to compete in the lower price range in China, with an eye toward simplification. Bühler CEO Calvin Grieder said that this move enabled the company to achieve a better match between its products and customer expectations, something it could never have done successfully with the high-priced, complex products produced in Switzerland. The company Karl Mayer, the world market leader for warp knitting machines with a global market share of 75 %, pursues an interesting dual strategy. Its goal is to secure a solid, sustainable market position in both the high and the low ends of the market. From a base level of performance and cost, it challenged its developers to create products for the lower priced segments which offer constant performance at 25 % lower costs, and at the same time create products for the top segment which offers 25 % better performance without cost increases. The company met both of these extremely ambitious goals, according to CEO Fritz Mayer. By extending its price and performance range both upward and downward, Karl Mayer won back the market share it had previously lost in China.

Ultra-low Price Products Also for Sale in Highly Developed Countries?

Can the ultra-low price products from emerging markets can penetrate high-income countries? That has already started to happen. Renault's Dacia Logan, originally meant for the Eastern European markets, has proven successful in Western Europe. In India, Tata is working on variants of the Nano which meet European and American regulatory requirements.[21] Siemens, Philips, and General Electric have developed radically simplified medical devices in Asia, conceived for those markets. Yet they are now selling those same ultra-low price devices in the USA and Europe.

[19] Podium discussion on "Ultra-Niedrigpreisstrategien" at the 1st Campus for Marketing, WHU Koblenz, Vallendar, September 23, 2010.

[20] Vgl. Govindarajan V, Trimble C (2012) Reverse Innovation: Create Far From Home, Win Everywhere. Harvard Business Press, Boston.

[21] Talk with Tata Auto CEO Carl-Peter Forster in Bombay on May 11, 2010.

These devices do not necessarily cannibalize the much more expensive devices, which get used in hospitals or specialty practices. In some cases, the ultra-low price products have opened up entirely new segments, such as general practitioners, who can now afford these kinds of diagnostic devices and can make some of the simpler diagnoses themselves.[22]

Grohe, one of the global leaders in bathroom fittings, instantly became one of the leading suppliers in China after it acquired the domestic market leader Jouyou. Now Grohe is trying to position Jouyou outside of China as a less expensive second brand. Simplified products which still deliver a desirable level of functionality at extremely low costs and prices definitely have an opportunity to sell well in advanced economies. When deciding whether to pursue an ultra-low price position, managers should look not only at how attractive that segment is in emerging markets. They should also think through the consequences—good and bad—that such a strategy could have on the higher price positions in developed countries.

Success Factors for an Ultra-low Price Strategy

It is still unclear whether companies can sustainably generate adequate profits with ultra-low price strategies. Nonetheless, the success factors for such a strategy are quite clear:

1. *Think "simple yet robust":* A company must strip down a product to the bare essentials, but without making it too primitive or rendering it dysfunctional.
2. *Develop locally:* The company must develop the product in emerging markets; that is the only way to guarantee that it meets the customer requirements in the ultra-low price segment.
3. *Lock in lowest cost production:* This requires the right design and the ability to manufacture in the lowest wage locations which still ensure adequate productivity.
4. *Apply new marketing and sales approaches:* These will also require keeping costs as low as possible, even if that means forgoing traditional channels and approaches.
5. *"Easy to use, easy to fix":* These two aspects are of paramount importance, because customers may lack the background to understand complicated functionality and service providers may lack the resources to make anything but the most basic repairs or adjustments.
6. *Provide consistent quality:* Sustained success is only possible if the quality of ultra-low price products is not only adequate, but above all consistent.

The key challenge in the ultra-low price segment is to find an acceptable level of value to customer which will attract enough buyers and still keep costs at extremely low levels.

---

[22] Talk with Siemens CEO Peter Löscher at the Asia-Pacific Conference in Singapore, May 14, 2010.

Success Strategies with High Prices

High prices. High margins. High profits. Intuitively that trio seems to fit together well, at least at first glance. But the relationship is not quite that simple. If a high-price positioning always guaranteed success, every single company would adopt one.

At least two other conditions must come into play in order to make this equation work. Namely, you need to make sure that the two other drivers of profit—costs and volume—are managed well. If you have high costs, a high price does not guarantee a high profit margin. A high margin results only in high profit if you achieve a sufficient gap between price and costs. That is not a trivial observation. Customers will only pay high prices for a product or service when they receive high value in return. High value, in turn, often requires high costs to produce and in real life, that is often the case: it costs too much to achieve and sustain the level of value needed to support a high price. But even when a company does achieve high margins, it still needs to sell enough units to make a high profit. If the price is so high that volume remains very low, the company will struggle on the profit front. We will now take a look at two categories of high-price strategies: premium and luxury.

Premium Pricing

How much higher are premium prices than "normal" or "average" prices? Of course it's impossible to give a general answer. A 16-ounce package of pistachio ice cream from Ben & Jerry's costs $3.49; this amounts to 22 cents per ounce. A 32-ounce package of pistachio ice cream from the regional New England brand Brigham's has a price of $2.99 or 9.3 cents per ounce. That is a price difference per ounce of 133 %. A box of 24 Crayola crayons costs $1.37, but a box of 24 crayons from Cra-Z-Art costs just 57 cents, a price difference of 140 %. All-natural peanut butter, a product consisting of just two or three ingredients, also shows a wide spread. A jar of Skippy has a price of $2.68, while Smucker's costs $2.98 and a local New England brand Teddy's costs $3.00. But specialty suppliers selling peanut butter online charge between $5.59 and $7.79 for a jar. All of these jars are the same size (16 ounces), except for Skippy, which is still 15 ounces due to the indentation in the bottom, as we explained in the previous chapter.

To get a Miele washing machine, you may need to pay roughly twice as much as you would for a Maytag or GE model, which means that you pay several hundred dollars more. Huge price differences exist even for industrial goods. The wind turbine company Enercon's prices are more than 20 % above the competition, but Enercon still holds a market share of over 50 % in its home market. 3M has many market-leading industrial products which command premium prices.

We aren't talking about small price differences here; in both percentage terms and absolute terms, we are talking about massive price differences. Nonetheless, it is not unusual for a premium product to have a higher market share than cheaper alternatives. Often the premium product is the market leader. How is that possible?

And what does it mean for profit? The answer lies in the higher perceived value or utility. This higher level of value to customer is no accident. It derives from excellent product or service performance. Premium pricing means offering higher value and demanding a premium price in return.

Apple vs. Samsung

On September 3, 2001, on a trip to Seoul, I met with Dr. Chang-Gyu Hwang, then the CEO of the memory division of Samsung Electronics. Dr. Hwang, who is now CEO of KT Korean Telecom, gave me a small device for storing and playing music. The quality of the music already stored on the device was superb, the design less so. I found the device so cumbersome to use that I wasn't able to store any additional music on it.

A few years later I bought an iPod nano. In contrast to Samsung at that time, Apple was already a very strong global brand. The iPod featured a very elegant design; I could use it right away without consulting a manual. And more importantly Apple's iTunes system allowed me to load more music onto my iPod. Over the last several years I have seen Dr. Hwang often. Every time we meet, the "iPod story" inevitably comes up. Together with the late Steve Jobs, Dr. Hwang developed the iPod, which at its core is the device he gave me back in September 2001.

What did Apple do differently? Its iPod combines four important things: a strong brand, a cool design, user-friendliness, and system integration. That combination resulted in much higher customer-perceived value, higher prices, higher volume, and astronomical profits. Apple has sold more than 350 million iPods. I have already described some of the price differences between premium products and their no-name products or competitors with weaker brands. In Apple's case, the price for an iPod is easily double or triple the price of other MP3 players. Apple followed a similar strategy with the iPhone and iPad: innovation, design, strong brand, user-friendliness, and system integration … in other words, higher value to customer which supports higher prices. Once again, Apple was extremely successful with that strategy. In 2012 Apple earned $41.7 billion as its revenue grew by 45 % to $156.5 billion. This corresponds to a return on sales of 26.6 %. In light of these numbers, Apple moved ahead of Microsoft to become the world's most valuable company in August 2012, when its market capitalization reached $622 billion. Realistically, one couldn't expect Apple to sustain this extraordinary run of success. Only time will tell if someone can fill the shoes of a genius like Steve Jobs. In August 2015, the market capitalization of Apple stood at around $642 billion, a very high number. Regardless of what happens, though, Apple has proven that a company can use innovation, a strong brand, attractive products, and system integration to generate higher value to customer, achieve high prices, and earn astronomical profits, all founded upon the customers' higher perceived value. Samsung has learned this lesson, and has tried to catch up in recent years with its own smartphones.

Gillette

The global shaving and personal hygiene giant Gillette offers a classic example of premium pricing. The company invested $750 million to develop its Mach3 system, the first razor with three blades. As Fig. 4.1 shows, Gillette priced the Mach3 razor 41 % higher than its previously most expensive product, the Sensor Excel. Gillette followed up the Mach3 with a series of innovations, including the Fusion, which has five blades. With each new innovation, the company continued to charge higher prices.[23] Gillette practices premium pricing of the best kind: creating value through innovation, communicating that value, and then extracting it with premium prices. Fusion's price is almost three times the price of the original Sensor. Is Gillette going too far?

Today Gillette has a global market share of almost 70 %, its highest market share in 50 years.[24] Its competitors Wilkinson Sword (12.5 %) and BIC (5.2 %) trail by a wide margin. Resistance to Gillette's high prices has, however, been growing in recent years. Online competitors have sensed an attractive opportunity.[25]

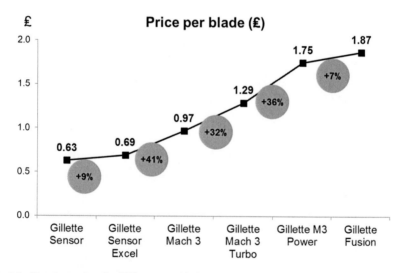

Fig. 4.1 Premium prices for Gillette razor blades

---

[23] Data collected by the London office of Simon-Kucher & Partners. The price per blade is based in the largest available pack size.

[24] Annual Report Procter & Gamble 2012.

[25] Newcomer Raises Stakes in Razor War. The Wall Street Journal, April 13, 2012, p. 21.

Miele

I have mentioned the home appliance manufacturer Miele a few times. The value is unmistakable: you might recall that my mother's Miele washing machine lasted for 40 years. Miele charges at least 20 % more than its competitors. Co-managing director Markus Miele explained how they do that: "We are at home in the premium segment. Our products are engineered to last for 20 years. In terms of technology and ecology, they are among the best you can buy. People are willing to pay higher prices for this promise of quality."[26]

Markus Miele's words capture the essence of premium pricing. But even the manufacturers of premium products need to keep their eye on the competition. In Miele's words: "Of course Miele needs to make sure that our price gap to the relevant competitors does not become too big. For that reason, we continuously work on our cost structure. We never neglect our company's motto 'forever better'. We cannot win a battle based on having the lowest price, but we will win when the battle is about having the best product."[27]

In some parts of the world, Miele is viewed as a true luxury good. Said Reinhard Zinkann, grandson of one of Miele's founders and co-managing director: "In Asia and Russia, wealthy people want to surround themselves with the best and the most expensive products on the market. That is why we positioned Miele as a pure luxury brand in those markets."[28] In 2012/2013, Miele's revenue reached a record \$4.25 billion. The company does not publish profit data. But Miele has a very high equity ratio (45.7 %) and no debt on its balance sheet, which proves that it must earn solid profits year after year. Its motto "Forever Better" hasn't changed for 100 years; it is the core and heart of Miele's strategy, the cornerstone of its lasting success as a premium brand.

Porsche

Should a company follow established industry practices when it chooses the price position of a new product? Not necessarily. More relevant than traditional industry practices or rules is the true understanding of a product's perceived value. The following case of the Porsche Cayman underlines the key role of the value to customer for the price positioning. The Cayman S is a coupé based on the Porsche Boxster convertible.[29] At what price should Porsche launch the Cayman? The automotive industry had its own clear, experience-based answer: the price of the coupé must be roughly 10 % below the price of the convertible. At that time, market data showed

---

[26] "Erfolg ist ein guter Leim, Im Gespräch: Markus Miele und Reinhard Zinkann, die geschäftsführenden Gesellschafter des Hausgeräteherstellers Miele & Cie.", Frankfurter Allgemeine Zeitung, November 13, 2012, p. 15.

[27] Ibidem.

[28] Ididem.

[29] A coupé is a hard-top.

that coupés were indeed 7–11 % less expensive than convertibles. Because the Boxster's price was €52,265, standard industry practice would call for the price of the Cayman to be around €47,000.

The CEO of Porsche at that time, Wendelin Wiedeking, decided to buck that industry trend. A big fan of value pricing, Wiedeking wanted to get a deeper understanding of the Cayman's value to customer. He asked us to do a very thorough global study which revealed that Porsche should do the exact opposite of what conventional wisdom said. The higher than expected value of the Cayman was driven by a mixture of factors, including the design, a stronger engine, and, of course, the Porsche brand. The Cayman's price should not be 10 % less than the Boxster's price, but rather 10 % higher. Porsche followed our recommendation and launched the Cayman at a price of 58,529 Euros.[30] The new model became a big success, despite the higher price. Once again, a deep understanding of value to customer proved to be the foundation for an appropriate premium pricing strategy.

Enercon

When introducing many of the concepts in this book, I have repeatedly said that their application is by no means limited to consumer products. They apply just as well to industrial products. Premium pricing is no exception. In fact, it may be even a better fit for industrial products, because industrial buyers investigate value more thoroughly and make economically more rational assessments than consumers tend to.

Founded in 1984, Enercon is the third largest manufacturer of wind turbines in the world. This company holds more than 40 % of all wind power technology patents in the world. The prices for its wind turbines are around 20 % higher than the competition's. If you consider that the average price for wind energy generation equipment is around $1.3 million per megawatt, that 20 % works out to a bit more than $250,000 per megawatt. For the 3,500 megawatts of capacity which Enercon installs each year, the additional revenue amounts to more than $600 million. Despite the higher prices, Enercon enjoyed a market share of 55 % in Germany in 2014; its global market share is around 10 %.[31] Enercon's premium price position is based on hard facts about value to customer. Its wind turbines have no gears, which means that they break down less often than competitors' products. It is, thus, rational for customers to accept a higher price for an Enercon product and the results show up in Enercon's financials. In 2012 Enercon had revenue of $6.6 billion and an after-tax profit of $783 million, for a return on sales of 11.9 %. Enercon was the only profitable supplier of wind power technology over the last few years.

Enercon also practices a very successful pricing model which involves a new form of risk sharing. Under its Enercon Partner Concept (EPC), a customer can sign up for maintenance, security services, and repairs at a price which depends on the yield of

---

[30] A slight modification boosted the Cayman's engine performance by 10 horsepower.

[31] Enercon doesn't do business in the USA and in China and it is not in offshore. In spite of these confinements it is the third largest wind technology manufacturer in the world.

the Enercon turbine. In other words, Enercon reduces its customers' entrepreneurial risks by sharing those risks with the operator of the wind park. Customers have found the offer very attractive, and more than 90 % of them sign an EPC contract.

As with all risk assumptions and guarantees, the provider needs to consider the potential costs. In Enercon's case, the costs are manageable because of its superior product quality. The absence of a gear (the number one cause of a breakdown) means that Enercon can guarantee its customer uptime of 97 %; competitors typically do not guarantee more than 90 %. In reality, Enercon products achieve 99 % uptime. It costs Enercon nothing to guarantee uptime of 97 %. This is an ideal example of optimal risk sharing between a supplier and a customer, which can noticeably lower a customer's resistance to buy. Enercon also assumes half of all service fees for the first half of the 12-year contract period. This provides substantial and much appreciated financial relief for the wind park investor, who is liable to be financially strapped in the few years it takes to ramp up a wind park.

"Bugs" Burger Bug Killers

What does high value mean for a pest control company? The highest possible value is quite simple: the pests are not only temporarily eliminated, but also gone for good. "Bugs" Burger Bug Killers (BBBK) offers an absolute unconditional

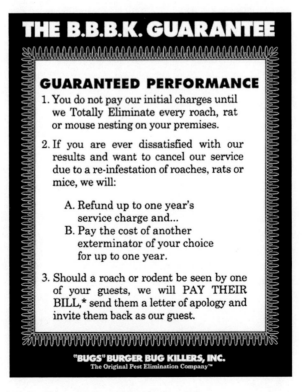

Fig. 4.2 The highest possible value through an absolute guarantee

guarantee for that kind of service. There are no exceptions or excuses. It is worth reading how BBBK expresses it (Fig. 4.2).

It is impossible to top this level of customer value. These kinds of promises make the guarantee credible. And what does the flipside of that customer value look like? BBBK's price is ten times as high as its competitors' prices.[32]

Premium Strategies Can Also Backfire

Not all attempts to extract higher value succeed. Energy-efficient light bulbs are an example. They were introduced in the early 1990s and offered big savings compared to traditional incandescent bulbs. They required only a fraction of the energy and lasted ten times longer. Over the entire lifetime of a bulb, these cost advantages could total as much as $65. Yet the manufacturers did not even come close to extracting this added value through correspondingly higher prices. The bulbs were priced at around $20 at launch, and the price trended downward year after year as cheap Chinese imports entered the market. These imports didn't have the same quality, nor did they last as long, but those facts were hard for customers to recognize at the time of purchase. The lower prices for the imported bulbs also served as strong anchors. In addition, light bulbs are a low-interest product. Consumers did not accept premium prices.

Electric motor scooters face a similar problem. They tend to be more expensive than gas-powered scooters, because of the additional costs of the battery. The energy costs for a traditional scooter are around $8 per 100 km versus just $1 for the battery-powered model, for a savings of $7 for per 100 km. If the price difference between the two scooters is $1,300, the buyer of an electric scooter reaches the break-even point within a few years, depending on actual usage. As attractive as savings of $7 per 100 km might sound, most consumers are not going to make the effort to do a break-even analysis. They tend to decide whether the claim seems reasonable at face value. This applies generally to most claims about "life cycle costs" or "total cost of ownership." In this case, the actual break-even point for the scooter described above is at about 18,000 km.

Capitalizing on the added value of innovations is often more successful when a company introduces a new price metric. Instead of selling light bulbs, the light bulb manufacturer could have offered light per hour and charged a price for that service. Instead of selling scooters, the scooter company could have offered transportation on a per-kilometer basis. The French tire company Michelin adopted precisely that strategy for its tires for trucks and industrial vehicles. Michelin now sells tire performance and charges a price per kilometer. We will take a closer look at this and similar pay-per-use schemes in Chap. 8.

---

[32] Hart CWL (1988) The Power of Unconditional Service Guarantees. Harvard Business Review pp. 54–62.

Success Factors for a Premium Price Strategy

What are the common factors behind successful premium pricing strategies? What recommendations can I give?

1. *Superior value is a must:* Premium pricing will work over time only if a company offers superior value to customer.
2. *The price-value relationship is the decisive competitive advantage:* In contrast to luxury products, which depend heavily on the prestige effect, the successful premium products derive their true competitive advantage from their high value (in objective, absolute terms), translated into an appropriate price-value relationship.
3. *Innovation is the foundation:* In general, innovation provides the foundation for a successful, sustainable premium price position. This applies to groundbreaking innovations as well as continual improvements, such as Miele's under the motto "Forever Better."
4. *Consistent, high quality is a must:* This prerequisite comes up time and again. Successful premium suppliers maintain high and very consistent quality levels. Their service must also meet the same requirements.
5. *Premium pricers have strong brands:* One function of these strong brands is to transform a technological advantage—which is often temporary—into a long-lasting image advantage.
6. *Premium pricers invest heavily in communication:* They know that they have to make the value and advantages of their products perceptible and understandable to consumers. Remember: only perceived value counts.
7. *Premium pricers shy away from special offers:* They are hesitant to offer promotions and special offers. If the promotions they offer are too frequent or too steep, these instruments can endanger the premium price position.

The key challenge in premium pricing is the balance between value and costs. The emphasis here is on high value to customer, which includes not just the core product itself, but also the extensive "envelope" of other benefits which surrounds it. Nonetheless, costs must remain within acceptable levels.

Success Strategies for Luxury Goods Pricing

Beyond premium lies the land of luxury. There are no clear demarcations which say "premium only goes up to here" or "luxury begins here."[33] But the price scale for luxury goods has no upper limits. Some experts even claim that "the price for luxury goods can't be high enough." The prestige, snob, and Veblen effects are in full force in this product category and are more important than objective product quality, even though true luxury goods must nonetheless meet the highest quality standards. There is no excuse for poor quality.

---

[33] For a comprehensive look at pricing for luxury goods, please see Henning Mohr, Der Preismanagement-Prozess bei Luxusmarken, Peter Lang-Verlag, Frankfurt, 2013.

How Much Does a Luxury Watch Cost?

Global production of wristwatches, including illegal knockoffs, is about 1.3 billion units per year. The average price per watch is under $100. But watches are a category in which luxury models play a special role. Fig. 4.3 shows a selection of watch models and prices shown at the 2013 Geneva Watch Salon (Salon Internationale de la Haute Horlogérie).

Is the Chronograph Racer, priced at €5,000 ($6,500), already a luxury watch? The answer depends on whom you ask. The Grand Complication from A. Lange & Söhne, priced at €1.92 million ($2.56 million), turned the most heads at the Geneva Salon.[34] It costs 384 times as much as the Chronograph Racer. This gigantic difference illustrates how much pricing latitude is available to producers of luxury goods. The Grand Complication reveals another fundamental characteristic of luxury goods: as price rises into the stratosphere, the number of units available also seems to disappear into ever-thinner air. A. Lange & Söhne only manufactured six units of the Grand Complication.

One key secret to the art of pricing luxury goods is mastering "limited editions." The supplier must strictly abide by its own limit; otherwise it risks losing its credibility and reputation. The limited number of units determines the scarcity and thus the value of the luxury good. A prerequisite for successful luxury goods pricing is the skill to simultaneously set both the price and volume *ex ante*.

I use the words "prerequisite" and "skill" here, because attempts to do this can fail miserably, as the following story shows. At the watch trade fair Baselworld[35] a manufacturer displayed a redesigned model. Its predecessor was priced at $21,300. Because the watch was very popular, the manufacturer raised the price of the new model by 50 % to $32,000. Volume would be limited to 1,000 pieces, reflecting the

Model	Manufacturer	Price in €
Grand Complication (only 6 limited pieces)	A. Lange & Söhne	1,920,000
Royal Oak Offshore Grand Complication	Audemars Pignet	533,700
Tourbillon G-Sensor RM036 Jean Todt Ltd. Ed.	Richard Mille	336,000
Emperador Coussin Ultra Thin Minute Repeater	Piaget	187,740
Rising Hours	Montblanc	26,900
Luminor 1950 Rattrapante 8 Days Titanio	Panerai	13,125
The Calibre de Cartier	Cartier	8,110
Sporting World Time	Ralph Lauren	7,135
Chronograph Racer	IWC	5,000

Fig. 4.3 Selected luxury watches and their prices

---

[34] The Grand Complication is not the world's most expensive watch. That title belongs to a watch from Hublot, presented at Baselworld 2012 and priced at $5 million.

[35] Baselworld is the world's largest trade fair for watches, with 1,800 exhibitors and over 100,000 visitors. The Geneva Watch Salon positions itself is more exclusive. It has only 16 exhibitors and 12,500 visitors.

maximum capacity the manufacturer had available. At Baselworld, the manufacturer received 3,500 orders for the watch. The price should have been much higher; the foregone profit is enormous. Had the manufacturer sold the 1,000 pieces at $40,000 instead of $32,000, it would have cleared an additional $8 million in profit.

Swiss Watches

Luxury watches are a useful category for showing the difference between "volume" and "value." Watches manufactured in Switzerland represent just 2 % of the world's annual watch production. Yet on the back of this tiny volume, the Swiss watches altogether account for an incredible 53 % of the global watch market on a value basis.[36] The difference between their volume-based market share (2 %) and their value-based market share (53 %) is dramatic. The average export price of a Swiss watch is around $2,400 and the average end-consumer price is around $6,000.[37] Swiss watchmakers generated export revenues of $23.2 billion in 2012. Watchmaking ranks as the third largest industry in Switzerland behind pharmaceuticals/chemicals and machine tools. Rolex has annual revenues of around $4.8 billion, Cartier roughly $2 billion, and Omega $1.9 billion. These numbers show the potential that the production of luxury goods holds.

LVMH and Richemont

The luxury segment has experienced strong growth in the last two decades. Even the global recession put only a temporary dent in the ability of major luxury goods companies to grow and achieve enviously high profits. The recent financial performance from some of the world's leading groups reinforces this point. The global market leader, France's Louis Vuitton Moët Hennessy (LVMH), saw its revenue rise by 17 % in 2011 and again by 19 % to $36.0 billion in 2012. It earned an after-tax profit of $5.0 billion, for a return on sales of 13.9 %. Revenue increased by 29 % to $11.9 billion for Switzerland's Richemont Group in the 2011/2012 fiscal year. Richemont posted an after-tax profit of $2 billion, for a return on sales of 17.4 %. Hermès, another important player in the luxury goods market, showed even stronger profitability. Its revenue rose by 23 % to $4.7 million and its net profit came to $987 million, for an eye-popping net return on sales of 21.3 %.

It makes sense for companies with strong brands and a reputation for high quality to take a closer look at the luxury segment. People have begun to accumulate tremendous wealth in countries such as Russia, China, and India. These *nouveau*

---

[36] Große Pläne mit kleinen Pretiosen. Frankfurter Allgemeine Zeitung March 12, 2012, p. 14.

[37] Revill J (2013). For Swatch, Time is Nearing for Change," The Wall Street Journal Europe, April 11, 2013, p. 21. The data on this question are contradictory. Another report placed the average price for a Swiss watch at 430 Euros, while the CEO of a Swiss watchmaker put the average price at around 1,700 Euros.

riche are channeling a large portion of their enormous purchasing power toward luxury goods, and many industries now offer a good jumping-off point for luxury goods and services. American Express sells its luxury Centurion card in the USA for $2,500 per year, after a one-time in initiation fee of $7,500. In Germany the annual fee is $2,600, and in Switzerland it is around $4,600. In Los Angeles, you can rent a Bentley convertible for $900 per day. In the Burj Al Arab Hotel in Dubai, a one-bedroom suite costs $1,930 per night, plus 10 % for tax and another 10 % for service. The Ritz Carlton in Dallas has created a new 5,500-square-foot "privacy wing" to accommodate VIP entourages which may include a nanny, a chef, and a security team. The price: $7,500 per night.[38] The price per hour for a flight in a private jet ranges from $2,400 in a Citation Mustang to $8,700 in a Gulfstream G550.[39] In other words: there is plenty of supply and demand for luxury goods.

Stumbling Blocks in Luxury Goods Marketing

The previous cases may lead you to assume that luxury goods offer the ultimate path to price nirvana. Even when you "get it wrong" like the Swiss watchmaker prior to the Baselworld trade fair, you are still in pretty good shape. After all, after the price increase of 50 % that company's misjudgment of supply and demand still left it with a much higher profit.

That assumption about price nirvana is wrong, as the following case shows.

Maybach

It is flattering but very frustrating when a company offers an exclusive limited edition, and demand outstrips supply. In the world of luxury goods, it is not just frustrating, but also very unpleasant when the opposite happens: a company offers a luxury product, and hardly anyone buys it.

That was the fate suffered by Maybach, a Mercedes luxury car, which sold for around $650,000. After record sales of 244 cars in 2004, the number of vehicles sold dropped steadily to two-digit levels in 2010 and 2011. In contrast, Rolls Royce sold 3,575 cars in 2011. The last Maybach rolled off the Mercedes assembly line on December 17, 2012.

I once had the pleasure of riding in a Maybach. Liang Wengen, the wealthiest man in China and the founder of the construction machine manufacturer Sany, sent one to pick me up. At the time of my visit he owned four Maybachs and would eventually own nine of them. Unfortunately, Maybach found far too few customers such as Mr. Liang.

---

[38] Boom time ahead for luxury suites. The Wall Street Journal, March 21-23, 2014.

[39] See Aviation-Broker.com.

Was the price the problem? Or is a car such as the Maybach simply a relic from a bygone era? Volkswagen avoided a similar failure with the Bugatti Veyron, which it sold for a little over $1.7 million, because it limited production from the outset to 300 vehicles. And Volkswagen actually sold them all. The Veyron didn't make any money, but that was also not the objective. This "rocket" got worldwide attention and thus contributed to the fame of Bugatti and, indirectly, of its parent Volkswagen.

One wonders whether it would have made sense to continue producing the Maybach as the flagship of Mercedes. The Maybach's halo effect on the primary brand (in this case Mercedes) could have a lot of value. But there is another aspect of luxury goods that poses a problem on the cost side: their buyers expect not only products of extraordinary quality, but also service at the same level. The costs of providing exceptional service worldwide for a limited-edition automobile are far more than any company will reasonably bear. One should keep that in mind before bringing a service-intensive luxury product to market. For a luxury watch, providing service is not a big problem. For a luxury car, providing service is a Herculean task that can drive a business deep into the red.

The marketing and pricing for luxury goods face a number of obstacles. Obviously, luxury goods need to meet the highest expectations and the most stringent standards with no room or excuses for mistakes. That applies to more than just product quality in the narrow sense. It applies equally to service, design, packaging, communication, media, and distribution channels and last but not least to the employees who support these activities. The marketing of luxury goods requires a very intense level of commitment.

Luxury goods manufacturers need to attract highly qualified staff, engage the best designers, and invest large sums in communication and distribution. Only when you have no weaknesses across that entire performance spectrum will you be in a position to get customers to accept the high prices you want to charge. This makes luxury goods a high-stakes game. The barrier to entry is enormous, and once you are in, the slightest sustained weakness can cause irreversible damage and cost you the game.

Luxury goods companies also need to resort to all kinds of marketing "tricks" you might expect from more mainstream companies. In luxury watches, some models are in high demand, and others less coveted. In the diamond market, De Beers, the global market leader, has stones of better and lesser quality. What does one do in that situation? De Beers' answer was to offer a bundle of desirable and less desirable stones, rather than offering each stone individually. Customers used to have no choice in this matter: they could accept or refuse the bundle. If a customer refused, however, De Beers would not invite that customer to the next auction. In the meantime, De Beers' de facto monopoly in the diamond market has started to crumble. It can no longer employ such hardball tactics.

This kind of bundling also occurs in the luxury watch market. Dealers occasionally need to buy a bundle which includes models that are hard to resell. These models often end up in gray-market channels, where original watches get sold at steep discounts. This kind of price erosion is toxic for luxury goods. A customer who has paid $25,000 for a watch does not like to see the same watch offered elsewhere for $15,000.

The luxury goods manufacturers go to great lengths to shut down these gray markets, even tracing individual items. They contract with special agencies who conduct mystery shopping to find out what products sell for what prices in different stores. This chronic problem in monitoring channels, which results in part from the high reseller margins, has motivated luxury goods companies to take distribution in-house. The number of company-owned specialty stores in airports, hotels, and exclusive shopping malls has risen sharply in the last few years.

Owning its own stores gives a company complete control over prices, but this approach also has a dangerous downside. It takes what used to be variable costs—the commissions formerly paid to dealers and resellers—and converts them into fixed costs for rent and store personnel. This can drive up the break-even threshold. In a downturn that spells trouble for luxury goods companies.

In October 2009, at the high point of the global recession, I took a walk through the lobby of Singapore's Raffles Hotel, where dozens of luxury goods stores line the hallways. There was hardly a customer anywhere. I was virtually alone, except for the salespeople who stood idle at the store counters. The luxury goods companies were very fortunate that the downturn in their industry lasted only a few months.

Are There Limits to Prices of Luxury Goods?

Cartier's Trinity gold bracelet costs $16,300. Is that expensive? Perhaps it is when you compare it to $11,000, which was its price five years ago. And that huge price increase is nothing compared to a Chanel quilted handbag, whose price has jumped by 70 % to $4,900 in the same period. These increases clearly outpace inflation—which was close to zero in the recent past—and cannot be entirely explained by rising costs. That means they must have another motivation: to continue to tap into the wealthy's willingness to pay for luxuries.

In early 2014, some market observers began to feel that these prices have begun to "wear thin with Western customers," especially as competition from more affordable brands increases.[40] Manufacturers also face the risk of turning off some customers if economic growth sputters or stalls. This happened in the depth of the recession, as my walk through the Raffles Hotel in Singapore showed. And it can happen again any time.

The Challenge of Creating Enduring Value

When a customer pays a very high price for a product, he or she expects that the product will hold its value. This makes the creation of enduring value another challenge for luxury goods manufacturers. It also means that a luxury goods company cannot resort to special offers or discounts to create short-term growth. Such promotions would tarnish the company's image and water down the value of the product

---

[40] Soaring luxury-goods prices test wealthy's will to pay. The Wall Street Journal, March 4, 2014.

in the eyes of previous buyers. Luxury goods companies cannot afford to use price as a means to increase volume, even in times of crisis. Wendelin Wiedeking, the former CEO of Porsche, repeatedly pointed out that his company's prices, value, and reputation precluded offering high discounts. Doing so would lower the residual value of used cars. This is a particularly important argument for Porsche, because around 70 % of all Porsche vehicles *ever built* are still in use. Wiedeking explicitly prohibited cashback offers. When the chief of Porsche's US operations didn't observe this rule, he was fired.

The electric vehicle manufacturer Tesla is offering an interesting residual value guarantee on the Model S sedan, which it introduced in 2013. A buyer can sell the car back to Tesla after three years at the same relative residual value as a Mercedes S class (measured in percentage terms).[41] This price guarantee allows Tesla to project the high image of the Mercedes brand onto its own, in an effort to provide potential buyers more certainty that the Tesla Model S will retain its value. Managing the aftermarket, and occasionally buying back products, can help a company maintain the high-perceived residual value of its products. Ferrari takes this approach.

Observing Volume Limits

Self-control is another challenge which luxury goods companies face. Even when business is going well, a luxury goods company must resist the temptation to aim for big volumes. The combination "high price–low volume" (the exact opposite of the "low price–high volume" strategy discussed earlier in this chapter) is elementary for luxury goods. Placing upper limits on the volume is the only way to preserve exclusivity.

When the American Peter Schutz led Porsche in the 1980s, he liked to say that "the second Porsche on the same street is a catastrophe." Wiedeking, his successor, expressed a similar sentiment when he asked us the question: "How many Porsches can the world bear?" This was not an easy question to answer. But if a company wants to maintain a high-price position, such a number is not very big, and self-control is mandatory, lest the company exceed the feasible volume number and jeopardize its luxury position.

Ferrari's volume reached an all-time high in 2012. It sold 7,318 vehicles, not a very large number in the context of the automotive industry. If you divide Ferrari's revenue of \$3.24 billion by that number, you get an average price of \$442,732 per car sold. That gives us a rough idea of the price level for a Ferrari, even though the number is not an exact average price. Ferrari also generates revenue from service and spare parts, so its total revenue does not come solely from sales of vehicles. In any event, the air is very thin when a company charges around \$400,000 for a car. Porsche moved 143,096 vehicles in 2012, making it an automotive giant relative to Ferrari.[42] The "average price" for a Porsche, based on total company revenue, is just

---

[41] Tesla misst sich an Mercedes. Frankfurter Allgemeine Zeitung, April 4, 2013, p. 14.

[42] Porsche verkauft so viele Autos wie nie zuvor. Frankfurter Allgemeine Zeitung, March 16, 2013, p. 16.

over \$93,000, which is high but still at an entirely different level than where Ferrari finds its customers.

Lacoste may be the most famous example of a once highly prized brand which fell victim to "massification," the degradation of an exclusive brand to mass or mainstream status. Something similar happened decades earlier to the shirt brand "Schwarze Rose" or "Black Rose." In the 1950s, Opel, which is part of General Motors, had a strong position in the high end of the market with models such as Admiral and Kapitän. The gradual decline began when it introduced the mass-market Kadett model in 1962. At the end of the 1980s, Simon-Kucher & Partners examined whether Opel could reenter the upper end of the market. The chances did not look promising for the Opel brand, so Opel's parent company General Motors followed the recommendation to acquire the Swedish Saab brand, well positioned at that time. General Motors was, however, unable to reposition Saab in the high-end segment with any sustained success. GM sold Saab in 2010 to a Dutch company, which resold it in 2012 to the Chinese car Company Geely.

Success Factors for Luxury Goods Price Strategies

As we have done with the other price-positioning concepts, here are my recommendations for pricing luxury goods:

1. *Luxury goods must always deliver the highest level of performance:* This applies across all dimensions, including materials, product quality, service, communication, and distribution.
2. *The prestige effect is a big driver:* In addition to the dimensions above, luxury products need to convey and confer a very high level of prestige.
3. *Price contributes to the prestige effect and serves as a quality indicator:* A higher price does not usually come at the expense of volume. In fact, sometimes the opposite is the case.
4. *Volume and market share must remain within strict limits:* Observing volume and market share limits—especially if limited editions have been promised—is a must in the luxury goods market. Companies have to resist the temptation to go for a "bigger" volume or market share, no matter how attractive this may seem in the short term.
5. *Strictly avoid discounts, special offers, and similar actions:* They will tarnish a product, brand, or company's image (if not destroy it) and will diminish the products' residual value.
6. *Top talent is essential:* Every employee must meet the highest standards and perform on a high level. This applies to the entire value chain, from design and production down to the appearance of salespeople.
7. *Having control of the value chain is advantageous:* Luxury goods companies should strive to control the value chain, including distribution, to the greatest degree possible.

8. *The primary factor in price setting is the customers' willingness to pay:* Willingness to pay is decisive, while variable costs play a relatively smaller role than they do for lower price segments. More problematic are fixed costs, which can rise quickly as a company increases its vertical integration. Higher fixed costs drive up the break-even volume, which runs counter to the exclusivity and limited volumes which underpin a luxury price position.

What Is the Most Promising Price Strategy to Pursue?

If you are now wondering which of the price strategy options explored in this chapter—low, premium, or luxury—is the most promising, I would answer by saying that none of them is easy. As we have seen, a company can become a tremendous success or a miserable failure with any of the three price positions. There is generally no right or wrong strategy.

The price positionings we have discussed reflect the different mix of buyers in a specific market. In every market you will find customers who have seemingly limitless purchasing power and at the same time demand the highest standards. If a product meets these standards, those customers are willing to pay a very high price. The "middle-class" customers weigh the trade-offs between value to customer and price. They have demanding standards and can afford premium products, but not luxury goods. At the low end of the price scale, you find customers who must be extremely frugal and careful in how they spend their money. These customers are satisfied with acceptable, consistent quality and look for the lowest prices, so that they can stay within their financial means. Purchasing power is even more limited in the world's poorer countries. Here the challenge lies in offering the lowest acceptable product performance at ultra-low prices.

Of course, customers do not always fall into such nice, neat segments in every market. So-called hybrid consumers are supposedly becoming more common. These consumers buy their food and groceries at the deep discounters, so that they can afford to go out to dinner at a three-star restaurant. In order to find the right place within the highs and lows of pricing, a company also needs to understand these kinds of consumers, to the extent that they really exist in relevant numbers.

Selling to each of these segments places different demands on managers and requires different skill sets. The skill set and personality that work well for a company in one price segment can actually become an impediment in another. Luxury goods companies need the highest levels of competence in design, quality, and service, and the ability to maintain a consistent image and set of standards across all parts of the business. That in turn demands a certain kind of corporate culture. The skills and ability to control costs, in contrast, are not a success factor in that segment.

A premium price position moves the trade-off between cost and value to the forefront. A company needs to offer high-quality products, but without letting costs run amok. Success with a low-price position and especially an ultra-low price position requires the skills and abilities to keep costs as low as possible throughout the entire value chain. The corporate culture in those companies is often just as relentless and unforgiving as a luxury goods culture, but with the opposite focus. In contrast to the world of luxury goods, the culture of the low-price companies must be modest and frugal, if not outright stingy. This kind of working environment isn't for everyone. But even in low and ultra-low price segments, a company needs sophisticated marketing know-how and needs to attract the right talent. Companies in these price segments must know precisely what they can leave out without causing the customer to refuse the product or switch to a competitor.

These brief thoughts should suffice to show how difficult it is to execute both a high-price and a low-price strategy within the same company. The cultural requirements are radically different, though a company might overcome them if it can achieve a decentralized corporate structure. A company that pulls off that difficult trick is Swatch. One observer notes: "Swatch is well-positioned, because its brands range from inexpensive Swatch watches to the ultra-expensive Breguet and Blancpain lines."[43]

We can also try to answer the "what is the most promising price strategy?" from a more quantitative perspective. Michael Raynor and Mumtaz Ahmed recently undertook that challenge, analyzing more than 25,000 companies which were listed on US stock exchanges between 1966 and 2010 and thus needed to make comprehensive financial data available publicly.[44] The two researchers used return on assets (ROA) as their measure of success. To make it into the top category, which the authors referred to as the "Miracle Workers," a company needed to rank among the top 10 % in ROA in every single year it was publicly listed. Only 174 of the more than 25,000 companies, or 0.7 %, qualified. The second category, the "Long Runners," needed to be among the best 20–40 % performers in ROA in every single year. They found even fewer of these companies, a mere 170. The rest of the companies ended up in the category "Average Joe."

The authors then compared one Miracle Worker, one Long Runner, and one Average Joe from nine different industries. Their research revealed two success guidelines, which they referred to as "better before cheaper" and "revenue before cost." "Miracle Workers compete on differentiators other than price and typically rely much more on gross margins than on lower costs for their profitability advantage," the authors explained. "Long Runners are as likely to depend on a cost advantage as on a gross-margin advantage."

These interesting findings imply that the share of companies which are successful with a premium price strategy is greater than the share of companies which have achieved sustained success with low-price strategies. As we have seen, the business world has some extremely successful companies with low-price strategies, but they are few and far between. This must be the case, simply because most markets have room for one and at the very most two successful "low price–high volume" companies. This is also consistent with another finding of Raynor and Ahmed: "Very rarely is cost leadership a driver of superior profitability."

[43] Revill J (2013) Swatch boosts profit, forecasts more growth. The Wall Street Journal Europe, February 5, 2013, p. 22.

[44] Raynor ME, Ahmed M (2013) Three rules for making a company truly great. Harvard Business Review online, April 11, 2013.

In contrast, most markets can support a larger number of premium-price companies who achieve sustained success. All in all, I consider the results of Raynor and Ahmed's to be both plausible and valid. After 40 years in the pricing game I am convinced that only very few companies will achieve long-term success with a low-price strategy. These companies must become very large and extremely cost competitive. Many more companies can achieve sustainable success with differentiated offerings and premium-price positions, but they will not grow to the size of the low-price contenders. For luxury goods we see again a relatively low number of successful companies, and they are the smallest of the three categories.

In the first four chapters of this book, we have learned that everything in the economy revolves around prices, that the strange psychology of prices plays a key role with amazing new findings, and that different price positions can lead to sustained profits. After this bird's eye view on pricing, we will look more closely at the inner mechanics of pricing in the next three chapters.

Prices and Profits

5

It amazes me how often small business owners show an iron-clad grasp of prices and profits that seems to elude managers at large companies.

A couple of years ago I hired a gardener to do some work in my backyard. I told him that if he gave me an additional discount of 3 %, I would pay the entire bill immediately. These kinds of "early payment discounts" are common terms in many business contracts.

"No way," he said with calm self-assurance.

Surprised and curious, I asked him to explain.

"My net profit margin is about 6 %," he said. "If you pay me immediately, that will obviously help my cash flow. But if I give you that 3 % discount, I'll need to hire twice as many people and do twice as much work to make the same amount of money. That's why I can't agree to your offer."

I was speechless. Rarely I have seen managers and executives explain a price decision so succinctly and so correctly. Perhaps that understanding comes from the fact that those dollars are all his. He has the same visceral connection to earning a living that I felt at the farmers' market in my childhood.

How much profit do you think the average company really earns? Think of it in terms of a percentage like the gardener does. For every $100 in sales, how much remains on average in a company's coffers as profit?

Consumers tend to come up with some pretty wild estimates if you ask them to give a quick top-of-mind answer. In one study, US consumers estimated these profit margins or return-on-sales numbers at 46 %. In a similar study in Germany, the estimated margin was 33 %. The truth lies much closer to what my gardener earns than what people generally think.

Wholesalers and many retailers are happy when their margins are between 1 and 3 %. In its 2012/2013 fiscal year, Walmart's consolidated net income as a percentage of total revenues was 3.8 %.[1] An industrial company with a margin at 10 % would be above average.

---

[1] Walmart 10-K filed March 2013.

© Springer International Publishing Switzerland 2015
H. Simon, *Confessions of the Pricing Man*, DOI 10.1007/978-3-319-20400-0_5

Of course, exceptions to this rule do exist. For its 2014 fiscal year, Apple's net margin stood at 21.6 %.[2] Let's put that in context. If the *average* company were as profitable as Apple, we would all live in an entirely different world, a utopia beyond our ability to imagine. But we can leave that world to the philosophers and science-fiction writers. In the 21st century, where single-digit margins are the norm, businesses must care about their pricing. Every percentage point change in prices can have a stunning impact on profitability. The lower your margins, the greater the need for caution. If a company has a margin of just 1 % and wants to cut prices to grow market share, managers must realize that they are very likely to sacrifice all of their profits if they proceed.

The pursuit of profit is both a driver of excellent pricing and an outcome of it; there is no way to separate the two topics. Profit is ultimately the only valid metric for guiding your company. The rationale is simple: profit is the only metric which takes both the revenue side *and* the cost side of a business into account. A company which wants to maximize its sales neglects the cost side. A company which wants to maximize its market share can distort its business in many ways. After all, the easiest way to maximize market share is to set one's price at zero.

The example of Best Buy in Chap. 2 shows what happens when a company takes its eye off profit and focuses instead on one of those secondary goals, such as market share. But that example is mild compared to the fate that television makers recently suffered. The big, flat-screen TV is becoming a fixture in our living rooms, and we marvel at what these impressive and valuable devices can do. But in 2012, their manufacturers collectively lost $13 billion. How can this happen? The trade association's president attributed it to "too many companies focusing on market share instead of profitable results."[3]

Unfortunately, the word "profit" raises a red flag for many people. Hollywood movies over the last 30 years link profit and money making to excess and self-indulgence. I can't deny that these situations occur. After all, many of those movies are based on real people or composites of them. In my opinion, however, defending "profit" is not tantamount to defending greed and excess. It is a defense of corporate survival and growth. Let's remember the comment by Peter Drucker, one of the most respected and widely followed management experts of our time: "Profit is a condition of survival. It is the cost of the future, the cost of staying in business."[4] Or as the esteemed German economist Erich Gutenberg once remarked, "no business has ever died from turning a profit."

Profit transcends other corporate goals because it ensures a company's survival. Businesses cannot afford to treat profit as a "nice to have" or a "pleasant surprise" at the end of the year. Put another way: if the company you work for makes no profit—or takes actions which puts profits in grave danger—your own job is at risk. It is only a matter of time before the cuts come. My favorite example for this is Motorola at the end of 2006. The handset maker described its sales in the fourth

---

[2] Apple 10-K, filed September 2014.
[3] TV-Hersteller machen 10 Milliarden Verlust. Frankfurter Allgemeine Zeitung, April 20, 2013, p. 15.
[4] Drucker PF (2001) The Essential Drucker. Harper Business, New York, p. 38.

quarter of 2006 as its best quarter ever after it made steep cuts in the price of its Razr phone. That comment was a weak and ultimately unsuccessful attempt to distract from a cascade of bad news. Profits plunged by 48 % in that quarter. Market capitalization shrank by billions of dollars. And a few weeks after this news broke, Motorola announced that it would lay off 3,500 people.[5]

Because profit is an indispensable condition of survival, it follows that excellent pricing is a means of survival. Companies need to take prices into their calculations with the same intensity and rigor they apply to costs. For as many negative examples of poor pricing decisions presented in this book, there are also success stories which all followed another path: they created valuable products and services, and then priced them at levels which ensured both healthy sales and healthy profits.

Chasing the Wrong Goals?

Countries show significant differences in how profitable their companies are. I have tracked data on this topic for many years, and attribute some of the results to cultural norms. Figure 5.1 compares the average profit margins for companies in 22 countries.[6] US companies are in the middle of the pack at 6.2 %. German companies have an average after-tax profit of 4.2 %, placing them in the lower half despite their improved performance in the recent past. Japanese companies have assumed their

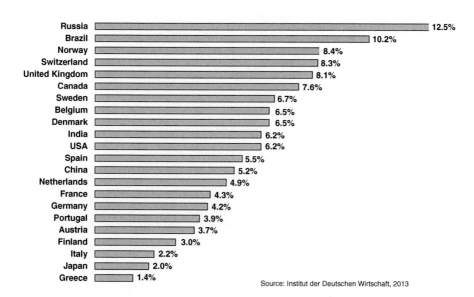

Source: Institut der Deutschen Wirtschaft, 2013

Fig. 5.1 After-tax profit (percentage of revenue) for private and publicly traded companies

---

[5] Motorola Plans to Lay Off 3,500. Associated Press, January 20, 2007.
[6] Data from the Institut der Deutschen Wirtschaft, 2013.

customary place near the bottom, with a meager 2.0 %. The average across all countries works out to 6.0 %.

What causes these sharp differences? To a large degree it is a matter of having the wrong goals. While I wouldn't say these numbers are completely self-fulfilling prophecies, they do reflect the priorities that companies set. Too many companies have given higher priority to goals other than profit. In the midst of one Simon-Kucher & Partners project, a top manager of one of the leading global automotive companies summed up the prevailing attitude nicely: "Let's be honest. Officially, yes, profit is our corporate goal. But in reality, if profit goes down by 20 %, no one really cares. If we lose even a tenth of a point of market share, though, heads will roll."

The executive vice president of a major international bank managed to express the same sentiment without actually using the term "market share." He wanted to use pricing for the express goal of increasing profits, but with one nonnegotiable condition: "We can't lose any customers. Not a single one."

For many years I served on the board of an engineering company which made a habit of signing large contracts which made them no money. One executive proudly announced one day that he had just received an order for $10 million from a large customer. Eager to hear more about a deal of that size in such a competitive marketplace, I asked what concessions he needed to make after the initial bid.

"We needed to give them an additional discount of 17 %," he said.

"And what was your original margin calculation?" I asked.

"Fourteen percent," he responded, without even being aware of the simple arithmetic which would tell him how much that concession would cost the company.

Deals such as this one were common in this company, despite my appeals to reconsider or even walk away from unprofitable business. Their dominant concern was always to have enough work for their people. Profit never governed their thinking and their actions. This was a shame because this company employed so many talented engineers with great ideas on how to improve their customers' operations. Eventually I resigned my board membership. The words of Peter Drucker turned out to be prophetic: the company's attitude toward unprofitable business sealed its fate, and it didn't survive. It filed for bankruptcy five years later.

In my decades as an academic, businessman, and consultant I have heard such statements and witnessed such actions often enough to know that these are not isolated cases. The tendency continues to this day. In 2013 the leading companies in Germany's wholesale market for pharmaceutical products waged an all-out price war. The primary opponents were Phoenix, the market leader, and its "attacker" Noweda. A third large player was Celesio. The outcome was predictable. Despite some temporary shifts back and forth, overall market shares barely changed once the dust settled. The victim was profitability, in a market with historically low margins. In December 2013 Phoenix announced ongoing declines across all profit metrics.[7,8] In January Celesio was acquired by McKesson, the American market leader.

---

[7] Rabattschlacht im Pharmahandel. Handelsblatt, March 20, 2013, p. 16.

[8] Q3 2013/2014 results releases for the company.

No country has a monopoly on emphasizing goals such as market share, sales, or capacity utilization at the expense of profit. In Japan, market share is a kind of national obsession, which certainly plays a role in Japan's perennial presence at the bottom of the profitability list in Fig. 5.1. I can't count the number of times that Japanese executives ended a discussion about pricing and profitability improvements with the comment "but then we would lose market share." With that motto, they would politely decline any recommendations to rein in their aggressive pricing and discounting policies, because a loss of market share is taboo in Japan. The loss of face associated with a loss of market share carries a significant social stigma. In Japanese culture, retreating is frowned upon. The country's topography allows no room for manoeuver, which may explain the roots of this belief. In China, however, a retreat can be an honorable tactic. The country's vast geography permits such a manoeuver. It will be exciting to see what strategic goals Chinese companies emphasize as they start to market more of their domestic brands internationally. In Germany, preserving jobs plays a similarly strong role as market share does in Japan. Among the larger countries, the UK and the USA are doing relatively well in terms of profitability. I attribute this to the influence of capital markets, which is stronger there than in most other countries. In my opinion, American companies, however, more strongly pursue market share goals. Market share still plays a strong role and its pursuit may explain the margin difference between the two countries which is almost two percentage points.

It is also surprising in Fig. 5.1 that companies in smaller countries tend to have higher profit margins than those in larger countries. At first glance, one would expect the opposite, namely that companies in larger markets profit from economies of scale. How can the opposite outcome be explained? Based on my experience I suspect two reasons. First, companies in larger markets are more strongly market share driven. Second, competition in larger markets is more intense, thus making it more difficult to implement higher prices. This is usually easier in small countries.

Fortunately, many companies have begun a reorientation toward profit in recent years. One compelling story comes from the German chemical company Lanxess AG, which introduced the motto "Price before Volume" in 2005 and has stayed on that successful course ever since. The company's EBITDA has increased from $600 million to $1.5 billion, a compound annual growth rate of over 14 % since 2004. This demonstrates the effects of consistent, value-oriented price management.[9]

There is nothing inherently wrong with having sales, volume, and market share targets. Most companies have them and work hard to strike the right balance. These three secondary goals, however, offer you no useful guidance for price setting. Price setting requires a thorough understanding of two things: how your customers perceive your value and the profit level you need to sustain or improve that value. If market share is your primary goal, why don't you just give away your product for free? Or even pay customers to use it? Of course such a strategy makes no sense. The reality in almost all companies is that goal setting is not an "either-or" exercise.

---

[9] Lopez-Remon L. Price before Volume-Strategy—the Lanxess Road to Success. Presentation, Simon-Kucher Strategy Forum, Frankfurt, November 22, 2012.

Balance is paramount. The central problem is that most companies are not balanced. They still underemphasize profits relative to such goals as market share, revenue, volume, or growth. And they misunderstand the often dire consequences of that prioritization. This imbalance results in bizarre pricing strategies and ineffective marketing tactics.

Does Amazon want to grow revenue forever without sufficient profit margins? Shareholders continue to believe in the strategy. In 2015 Amazon's share price increased by more than 50 %. But eventually even Amazon must turn a profit. What sense do the results of a ceramics company make which for the year 2013 reported revenue growth of 4 % and a profit decline of 28 %?[10] As Amazon, this company priced its products very aggressively. Very often, questionable pricing is one of the root causes when revenue increases and profit declines.

How Does a Price Increase of 2 % Affect Profits?

How would a price change of 2 % affect a company's profits? In order to keep the analysis simple, we will change only the price and keep everything else constant. For a small price increase the assumption that volumes would remain constant is not as farfetched as you might think. Companies have many means at their disposal— even in highly competitive markets—to effect a price increase of that magnitude with little or no loss in volume.

A major industrial company with around $14 billion in annual revenue asked us for recommendations on how to raise prices. We didn't recommend an outright change in prices. Instead, they changed the incentive system for the sales people, specifically by including an "anti-discount" incentive. The lower the discount sales-people offered, the greater the commission they would earn on that sale. The new system proved to be attractive and effective almost immediately. The average discount the company had to accept declined from 16 to 14 % within the first three months, with no noticeable loss in volume and no customer defections. This change amounts to a de facto price increase of 2 %.

How would the profits of selected companies from the Global Fortune 500 change, if they raised their prices by 2 %? Figure 5.2 shows the changes in profits for 25 companies, based on data for their 2012 financial years.[11]

A relatively small price increase of 2 % would have a dramatic effect on the profits of many of these companies. If Sony succeeded in raising its prices by 2 % without any loss of volume, its profits would increase 2.36-fold; that is, they would more than double. The profit increase for Walmart would be 41.4 %, and for General Motors 36.8 %. Even highly profitable companies such as Procter & Gamble, Samsung Electronics, or Nestle would see profits grow by more than 10 %. The most profitable companies in this selection, IBM and Apple, would see more

---

[10] Hoeherer Verlust bei Steinzeug, General-Anzeiger Bonn, May 1, 2014, p. 7.
[11] Global 500, The World's largest corporations. Fortune, July 22, 2013, pp. F-1–F-22.

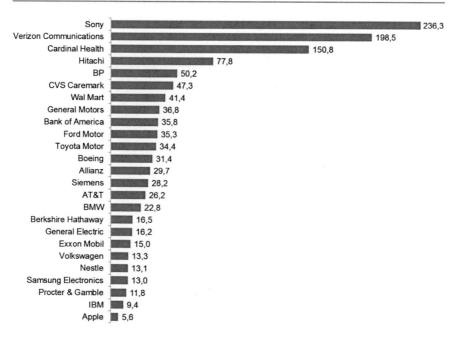

Fig. 5.2 Leverage effect on 2012 profits from a price increase of 2 %

modest but still significant profit increases. These numbers clearly demonstrate that
it pays to optimize prices.

Price Is the Most Effective Profit Driver

Revenue is the product of price and volume. Profit is the difference between revenue and cost. This means that every business has only three profit drivers: price,
volume, and cost. All of these profit drivers are important, but they affect profit to
different degrees. Anecdotal evidence, studies, and my own experience have told
me that managers dedicate most of their time and energy to cost cutting—you could
alternatively call it "efficiency improvement"—as a means for increasing profits,
especially in tougher economic times. I would estimate that managers allocate 70 %
of their time to cost issues, 20 % to volume, and only 10 % to price. The second
most "popular" profit driver among managers is volume or unit sales. They are
willing to invest in better sales tactics and support, building their sales forces, and
refining their competitive strategies. Price typically comes in last place, and in
some cases comes into consideration only as the handmaiden of managers waging
a price war.

The irony is that this prioritization runs in the opposite order of the effects
these drivers have on profits. Prices get the least attention, but have the greatest

Fig. 5.3 How improvement in profit drivers affects profit

impact. Let's look at a company that makes and sells power tools. The numbers derive from a Simon-Kucher & Partners project, but I have rounded and altered them to make the math simpler. It costs $60 to make the tool, which is sold to dealers and wholesalers at a price of $100. The fixed costs are $30 million. The company currently sells one million power tools per year. This turns into revenue of $100 million and total costs of $90 million. Thus, the company earns a profit of $10 million and a good margin of 10 %. The cost structure of this case is somewhat typical of industrial products. Now let's look at what happens if we improve each of the profit drivers—price, variable costs, volume, and fixed costs—by 5 % in isolation.

A price increase of 5 % boosts profits by 50 %. A 5 % increase in volume, in contrast, increases profits only by 20 %. The profit improvements from 5 % reductions in variable costs and fixed costs come in at 30 % and 15 %, respectively. Improving any of these profit drivers has a significant impact, which makes it worthwhile to invest in them. The point is that improving prices has the greatest leverage on profits. It's a power which managers typically underestimate (Fig. 5.3).

Now … Let's Change Your Prices and See What Happens

If you cut prices by 20 %, how many power tools would you need to sell to achieve the same level of profit before the price cut? The most common spontaneous answer from managers is "20 %." If only it were that simple. Getting 20 % is far below the volume you would need. Figure 5.4 shows what happens and how many units you would need to sell to keep profit constant.

Even if your sales force succeeds in selling 20 % more power tools after the price cut, you are still losing money. The contributions from your sales are not sufficient to cover your fixed costs. When your price goes from $100 to $80, you cut your contribution margin in half because it still costs you $60 to make each tool. The hard truth is that you need to *double* your volume after the price cut to keep your profits at $10 million. Anything less will reduce your profits.

	Starting situation	20% price cut, constant profit	20% price cut, volume rises 20%
Price ($)	100	80	80
Volume (units)	1 million	2 million	1.2 million
Revenue ($ mill.)	100	160	96
Variable costs ($ mill.)	60	120	72
Contribution ($ mill.)	40	40	24
Fixed costs ($ mill.)	30	30	30
Profit ($ mill.)	10	10	-6

Fig. 5.4 How price cuts affect profits

Fig. 5.5 The consequences of volume discounts and free shipping

	No discount, and shipping charged	20% discount, and free shipping
Price ($)	10	8
Volume (pairs)	10	10
Shipping ($)	5.90	
Revenue ($)	105.90	80
Variable costs ($)	50	50
Shipping costs ($)	5.90	5.90
Profit ($)	50	24.1
Profit index (%)	100	48.2

The calculations above are rather simple. Yet many managers are startled to learn that a 20 % increase in volume—which sounds like a success—would have catastrophic consequences for their bottom line.

Volume discounts and free shipping are common incentives for online businesses. One study by Simon-Kucher & Partners showed that consumers list "free shipping" as one of their main reasons for shopping certain categories online instead of going to the store. These incentives may indeed appeal to us as customers. But they can have an insidious effect on the company's ability to earn money. As you will see in the example below, the math is simple once you see it on paper, yet not immediately intuitive until you do.

Let's look at a company that sells socks online. If you order ten pairs, they will give you 20 % off your purchase price. When I asked one of their executives whether that makes sense, he said that he marks up the socks by 100 % from the wholesale price, so he can afford to offer customers that incentive. As an added sweetener, he also waived the shipping costs ($5.90) if you ordered more than $75 worth of socks.

Figure 5.5 shows the consequences of those decisions. To keep things even simpler in this case, and make things look even more favorable for the sock seller, we will assume that the business has no fixed costs.

The decision to offer the discount and the free shipping cuts the sock seller's profits by 51.8 % compared to the base scenario in which he offers no discounts and charges for shipping. Now you argue that the volume numbers should be higher in the scenario in the right-hand column, because of the intrinsic appeal of discounts and free shipping. You're right. How much higher must the volume be to achieve the same profit as without discounts?

To achieve the same amount of profit, the sock seller would need to more than double his volume in the "discount and free shipping" scenario. To be exact, he would need to sell 107 % more pairs of socks. This is highly unlikely for two reasons. First, consumer products such as socks are not so sensitive to price changes. Second, this kind of discount often leads to what consumer goods companies refer to as the "pantry effect." People will stock up on socks solely to get the discount and the free shipping, which results in fewer orders in the future. These discounts train customers, even the most loyal ones, to buy only when there is a deal or in a way that gives them a discount. In this case, most will order ten pairs of socks to get the discount and free shipping. But they will not buy more.

Big numbers make great stories. If the sock seller's volume was 50 or 60 % higher in the "discount and free shipping" scenario, that would probably make him happy. The problem is that big numbers are not enough. You need gigantic numbers for these schemes to pay off, sometimes impossibly gigantic ones.

Let's look at another online business, this time one that sells pet food and pet supplies launched an aggressive pricing strategy. The volume numbers gave management plenty of opportunities to dazzle investors. Sales jumped by 30 % in the first quarter and by another 34 % in the second quarter versus the prior year. The problem was that these attention-grabbing numbers overshadowed one key fact: the company posted a loss in the second quarter.

A similar situation happened when a large European retailer with revenue of more than $20 billion took part in a "tax-free" weekend and offered to waive the 19 % sales tax for its customers. "The traffic we generated is incredible," one of their executives told me. "We had 40 % more customers in our stores over the weekend!" I know of no retail manager or executive that would complain about having every aisle in the store overflowing with customers on a weekend. The problem is that the incentives which drew in those customers were far too generous. Using the same calculations in the previous tables, the retailer would have needed 113 % more customers to break even on that "tax-free" weekend.

The obsessive pursuit of the wrong goals—customer counts, revenue, and market share—leads even the sharpest managers to neglect the effects that discounts and promotions have on profits. It is hard to determine how many of the customers these promotions draw in will become repeat buyers at regular prices. But this doesn't change the simplicity and elegance of what my gardener knew: when you grant customers appealing and addictive goodies in the form of discounts, rebates, tax-free shopping days, free shipping, and on and on, you will typically see increases in interest, traffic, sales volume, and most of the time (but not always) revenue. That is what makes these discounts so alluring and so tempting. They look like successes.

But that success is often only an illusion.

Back to the Future: The General Motors Employee Discount Program

Business didn't look good for General Motors in the spring of 2005. In April, the company sold 7.4 % fewer cars than in the year-earlier month. May showed a slight improvement, but still trailed the previous year by 4.7 %.

Something needed to change.

The marketing teams at GM hit upon a revolutionary idea. They wouldn't just offer discounts or cashback incentives, the standard tools of the trade. They would offer their vehicles at the deeper discount normally reserved for its employees. The action began with much fanfare on June 1, 2005, and ran for four months. The company did not quantify the discount, as it normally would have. Instead, it declared that "GM's employee price is what a dealer actually pays for a vehicle."[12]

To call what happened in the next two months a "boom" may be underplaying the results.

This unprecedented marketing action yielded a volume increase so instantaneous and so large that it may have even taken GM and its dealers by surprise. In June alone, GM sold 41.4 % more cars than it did in June 2004. In July, sales increased by another 19.8 %, forcing GM to worry that it may literally run out of vehicles to sell. Ford and Chrysler launched their own radical versions of the employee discount program in July, which started to siphon off some of the attention and the demand.

The first important question after two tremendous sales months is this: Where did those customers come from? Aside from a house or a college education, a new car is probably one of the biggest purchases consumers ever make in their lives. It is not a casual spur of the moment decision. We are not talking about pantry loading for socks or potato chips. You will see the answer to the question in Fig. 5.6. Almost all of those customers came from one place: the future.

GM extended the promotion through the end of September, even though sales began to plunge in August. They fell by 23.9 % in September and declined by 22.7 % year on year in October; growth remained negative for the remainder of the year.

Instead of generating additional demand, GM borrowed customers from its future sales and sold those people cars at deep discounts. The solid line in Fig. 5.6 shows just how dramatic the volume declines were. They dropped from a peak of almost 600,000 units in July to fewer than 300,000 units in October.

The second important question is the following: How much did all this cost? GM's average discount per vehicle came to $3,623 in 2005. The company posted a loss of $10.5 billion. The market capitalization shrank from $20.9 billion in August 2005 to $12.5 billion in December. One year later, GM Chairman Bob Lutz offered his view of the program: "We're getting out of the junk business, like employee pricing sales that boost market share but destroy residual values. It's better to sell fewer cars at higher margins than more cars at lower margins. Selling five million

---

[12] GM's Employee-Discount Offer on New Autos Pays Off. USA Today, June 29, 2005.

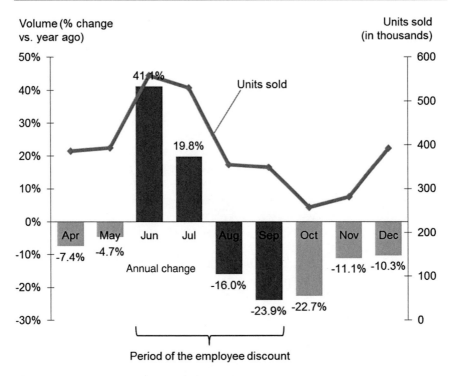

Fig. 5.6 GM's employee discount program results

vehicles at zero profit isn't as good a proposition as selling four million vehicles at a profit."[13] This is absolutely correct, but one wonders why clever Bob Lutz realized it so late.

General Motors led the world in car sales for 77 consecutive years, starting in 1931. It fell to second place in 2008. The company filed for Chap. 11 bankruptcy in June 2009.

Prices, Margins, and Profits

When I emphasize that price is the strongest profit driver, I am referring to total profit dollars and not to profit *margin*. Contribution margin is the difference between price and variable costs. In retail, this margin refers to the difference between the wholesale price and the retail price. In the base scenario for the power tool business, the contribution is $40, because the products were made for $60 each and sold for $100. If your total contribution exceeds your fixed costs, you make a net profit.

---

[13] www.chicagotribune.com, January 9, 2007.

People pay a lot of attention to contribution margins but this alone does not provide sufficient information for you to optimize your prices. Embedded in this thinking is what marketers refer to as "cost-plus" calculation. You figure out the price you want to charge by looking at your costs and "mark them up" by adding a certain percentage.

Having a high margin offers no guarantee that you will be profitable. One major reason is that this "cost-plus" approach has little or nothing to do with the value perceived by the customer, the most critical determining factor for setting a price. The "cost-plus" process takes neither the value to customer nor the resulting effects on volume into account. Cost-plus can lead you to set your prices too high, which can cause volume to collapse. Yes, you make a lot of money per sale, but if sales fall sharply your overall profit is minimal. This is the textbook definition of "pricing yourself out of the market."

The opposite effect is also true, in that a company can underprice its products. How many of you have heard the fateful phrase "don't worry, we'll make it up on volume" after someone makes a margin-slashing price cut? This kind of outcome, as several of my previous cases showed, sounds aspirational, but is more often than not an illusion.

The simplest method to understand these effects and guard against the ensuing margin deception is a break-even analysis. Let's use the data from our power tool business. The price is $100, the variable cost to make the tool is $60 (variable unit cost), and the fixed costs are $30 million. We can calculate our break-even volume, the minimum number of units we need to sell, as follows:

$$\text{Break} - \text{even volume} = \frac{\text{Fixed costs}}{\text{Price} - \text{variable cost}} = \frac{\$30,000,000}{\$100 - \$60} = 750,000 \text{ units}$$

We start making money after we have sold at least 750,000 units. If we start changing the price, you can see the big effect it has on the break-even amount. If we reduce the price to $80, we would need to sell 1.5 million units. At a price of $120, we would need to sell only 500,000 units to break even.

One question remains, though, when you set prices and figure out your break-even volume: Who wants your product? In other words, is the market large enough — and the perceived value sufficiently understood — to sell that many tools? We need to take the volume effects into account as well. The break-even analysis is a simple yet powerful way to see how price changes affect the likelihood of turning a profit. It also safeguards against making price cuts which have little or no chance of generating the huge volumes required to improve profitability.

Price Is a Unique Marketing Instrument

Most people, including managers, never think of the term "price elasticity" in their day-to-day lives. Yet we all have an intuitive sense of what it means and rely on it far more than we think when we make decisions. Whenever we need to decide whether changing something will make a difference, or how much of a change to make, we intuitively or subconsciously take elasticity into account.

All of us have encountered situations when we decided that proceeding is "not worth the effort" or "won't really make a difference." We have also experienced situations where a small adjustment or tweak has made an enormous difference.

An economist would refer to the "big effort, little change" as "inelastic" and "little change, big impact" as elastic. The same applies to prices. Price has a strong impact on volume and market share, and we use price elasticity to measure that impact. Price elasticity is the ratio of the percentage change in sales volume and the percentage change in price. It is usually a negative number, because prices and volumes normally move in opposite directions. But to keep things simple, it's customary to leave off the negative sign and just look at the magnitude of price elasticity.

A price elasticity of 2 means that the percentage change in sales volume is twice the percentage change in the price. Thus a 1 % price decrease would result in a 2 % increase in volume and conversely that a 1 % price increase would cause volume to fall by 2 %. Or, if we look at a price increase of 10 % volume would grow by 20 %, and vice versa.

We know from our investigations of tens of thousands of products that price elasticities usually fall into a range between 1.3 and 3.[14] The median is about 2, though price elasticities vary greatly depending on the product, region, and industry.

Other marketing instruments have elasticities as well. Advertising is a good example. In that case, we calculate the ratio of the change in sales volume and the change in advertising budget (both expressed in percentage terms). The same concept can be applied to sales force elasticity. On the average the advertising elasticity is in the range of 0.05 to 0.1 and the sales force elasticity is around 0.20 to 0.35. Thus the price elasticity being around 2 is on average between ten and 20 times higher than the advertising elasticity and roughly seven to eight times higher than the elasticity of the sales force investment. In other words, you would need to change your advertising budget by between 10 and 20 % or increase your sales force investment by 7–8 % to achieve the same effect you would get by changing prices by just 1 %.

Price elasticities are often—but not always—much higher when a special offer is in effect, such as the employee discount program offered by General Motors. Companies can amplify these effects even further when they combine the changes with more advertising and improved placement. In extreme cases, the price elasticity for such a special offer could be as high as 10, a rare example in pricing of "little change, huge impact." But as the GM example showed, you need to understand the source of demand. Have you attracted new customers? Have you won over customers from the competition? Or have you borrowed heavily against your own future sales, either by pulling sales forward at lower prices or, in the case of an inventory clearance, sold them something old now instead of something new later?

---

[14] Friedel E. Price Elasticity—Research on magnitude and determinants. Lang, Frankfurt, 2014.

Price has another big advantage over marketing instruments such as advertising or sales. Price changes usually can be implemented very quickly. In contrast, it can take months or years to develop or change a product. Advertising campaigns and budgets also require substantial time to implement and even longer to show their full effects.

You also see proof of this effect online. In December 2013, Delta Airlines made national headlines and became a hit on social media in a matter of hours after it offered outrageously low fares one morning. Customers snapped up deals such as Boston to Honolulu for $68 and Oklahoma City to St. Louis for just $12.83. Unfortunately for Delta but fortunately for the lucky buyers, the prices resulted from a computer glitch the company caught and corrected.[15]

You can change prices almost instantly to adapt to market changes, unless your contractual commitments or your published catalogs preclude it. Some retail stores now have the capability to change prices instantaneously on the shelf by algorithm or with a simple command. The same applies to e-commerce sites.

Pricing's high-speed, high-impact power has other downsides. Because prices are so easy to change, competitors can respond very quickly to neutralize any advantages you stood to gain from a price move. These competitive responses are usually swift and strong. This phenomenon alone helps explain why companies rarely win price wars. Unless you have an unbeatable cost advantage which prevents your competitors from responding in kind, it is almost impossible to establish a sustainable competitive advantage through lowering prices.

Finally, price is the only marketing instrument you can employ with no upfront investment. This makes it an especially powerful marketing tool for small business or start-ups with tight financial resources. The knowledge from this chapter alone can give anyone a head-start toward setting an optimal price, or at least weeding out dangerous options. Developing an advertising campaign, building a sales force, and conducting research and development are all essential parts of business success, but they all have a delayed payback and require substantial up-front investments. Optimizing these elements is critical, but is often not immediately financially viable for a small business or a start-up. Price can be set at the optimal level right from the start of a company.

All of these unique features make price an endlessly fascinating and interesting marketing instrument, but also one whose power is often misunderstood or neglected. Pricing can look like a daunting high-risk, high-reward activity if you approach it in a half-hearted way. One of my objectives with this book is to convince you to go "all in" on pricing, but in a way that lowers your risks and keeps the rewards attractive and achievable.

---

[15] http://money.cnn.com/2013/12/26/news/companies/delta-ticket-price-glitch/.

Prices and Decisions

6

Who, What, Where, When, Why … and How?

Who sets prices? It depends mainly on the structure of the market. Think back to the farmers' market from my childhood. In markets with homogeneous products and with many buyers and sellers, no individual player sets the price. Instead, the market sets prices through the interplay of supply and demand. The only way for sellers to influence their revenue and profit is to change the amount of product they decide to sell. That assumes, of course, that they accept the prevailing price and the process that created it.

More typically in today's world, however, we find markets in which the sellers have some leeway in setting prices. This leeway can be substantial if the product is innovative or even unique. It leaves the seller with room to increase his or her profit, but also with room for error. The same leeway also exists for what appear to be commodity products at first glance. Water is an example.[1] In most countries, the price of a bottle of Evian is many times higher than the price of local mineral waters. Even for products which have a commodity at their core, such as water, you can find a way to charge more. You can brand them (Evian), package them better (the ergonomic, resealable, plastic bottle), or provide better service. In those cases, you have transformed the supposed commodity into a differentiated good, as the price of Evian shows.

I use this example in speeches when someone asks whether it is possible for commodity or "me-too" products to command premium prices. Then, if the person who asked the question is not sitting too far away, I'll take a plastic water bottle from the podium and throw it to them. (Don't worry. No one has ever failed to catch it!) Many of those people call or write me later to say that they have never forgotten that lesson.

And who decides what the prices are? The "company" as an entity unto itself does not do that. Only people can make price decisions. That means these decisions are prone to habits, perceptions, and politics. Typically, pinning down a price

---

[1] A commodity is a substitutable, undifferentiated product, such as crude oil or cement.

© Springer International Publishing Switzerland 2015
H. Simon, *Confessions of the Pricing Man*, DOI 10.1007/978-3-319-20400-0_6

decision to one ultimate person is a surprisingly frustrating exercise. Prices have many parents, but hardly any single person ever takes full responsibility for the child. Many functions in a company have a voice in the price decision: marketing, sales, accounting, finance, and of course general management. Everyone has an opinion. Everyone is a pricing expert.

If you ask me which department in a company should "own" pricing I cannot give you a definitive, universal answer. Price setting has no natural home. From highly centralized, hierarchical companies to decentralized ones with flat hierarchies, price setting can take place anywhere in the organization. It is safe to say that a company's organization and product portfolio determine which of the departmental or functional voices carry the most weight in a price decision and who ultimately decides. In industries with very few key products—industrial machinery and aircraft come to mind—the top executives usually have the last word on prices. If a company has an extremely large and diverse assortment (retail, airlines, tourism, logistics), it means that their teams need to set hundreds of thousands of prices, if not millions of them. It is impossible for the senior executives to make these decisions. Teams or individuals further down in the organization rely on pricing processes and guiding principles to set the prices. If a company negotiates most of its prices, as practically all business-to-business companies do, it usually empowers individual salespeople to make price decisions on the spot within a predetermined range.

And *what* do these people decide on? What constitutes a price decision? In extreme cases, the answer is one single price. But I am not aware of any company that has just one price, even if it has only one product. We will always find variants, discounts or other terms, exceptions, and special charges for services such as shipping or travel costs. In general, companies have an assortment of products and services, all requiring price decisions. A carmaker doesn't just need prices for its vehicles, but also for hundreds of thousands of replacement parts. If a company serves different segments, its prices will also have several price parameters. Some companies use a combination of base prices and variable prices. Price differentiation can include a large number of components, conditions, and incentives. It should be clear that no matter how it looks at first glance, price is rarely just one number based on one decision. More often than not, it combines many numbers and an intricate web of decisions.

How do people make price decisions? As much as it may seem like an exact science, it is a wide open area. There is still a lot of truth in the words of advertising guru David Ogilvy: "Pricing is guesswork. It is usually assumed that marketers use scientific methods to determine the price of their products. Nothing could be further from the truth. In almost every case, the process of decision is one of guesswork."[2] He first made that statement over 50 years ago, and today it still applies to large parts of the economy.

---

[2] Ogilvy D (2004). Confessions of an Advertising Man. Southbank Publishing, London (Original 1963).

But as you might imagine, not everyone guesses. Some industries and individual companies set prices in a very professional way. These include life sciences and pharmaceuticals. I would also highlight the higher end segments of the automotive industry, where many carmakers capitalize very professionally on their leeway to charge a premium. Many online firms show a high level of professionalism. We need to distinguish between sophistication and professionalism. Airlines employ complex and very advanced pricing systems, but even they let themselves fall into devastating price wars.

To understand and appreciate the quantitative side of "how," we have to take a systematic look at price setting. Without a fundamental understanding of price decisions and the factors that go into them, it will be hard to categorize and evaluate the various pricing practices we observe in real life.

The Effects of a Price Decision

In the first five chapters I have tried to keep the stories and the math as simple as possible in order to make the messages easier to understand. In many cases, we made the assumption that the only thing changing in a given scenario is the price. If the price change is small, that assumption is acceptable. Larger price changes, though, will ignite a chain of interrelated effects that makes price management complicated. It's time for us to meet that complexity head on.

Price changes reverberate through an industry in many ways with positive, negative, and occasionally contravening effects. Figure 6.1 shows the most important of these interrelationships and demonstrates that the path from price to profit is neither singular nor linear. The dotted lines show definitional relationships: revenue is by definition the product of price and volume; profit is the difference between revenue and costs.

The solid lines show the behavioral relationships in this system. Price changes affect volume, and volume changes affect costs. You already know about the relationship between price and volume from the earlier discussion of supply and demand.

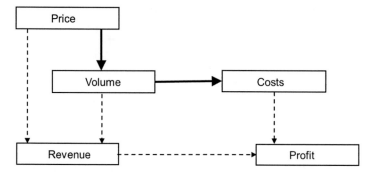

Fig. 6.1 The interrelationships of price management

The demand curve—or technically speaking, the price-response function—defines the direct functional relationship between price and volume. If you want to set price in a professional manner, you have to know what your demand curve looks like. The demand curve helps you estimate and quantify the impact your decisions will have.

The demand curve and the cost curve define the chain of effects through which price ultimately influences your profit. More specifically, as shown in Fig. 6.1, you have three paths that lead from price to profit:

Price → Revenue → Profit
Price → Volume → Revenue → Profit
Price→ Volume → Costs → Profit

Figure 6.1 illustrates the simplest case: one supplier and one time period. Missing from Fig. 6.1 are three factors which are common if not omnipresent in business: competition, time, and resellers such as distributors, dealers, or retailers. Adding them in puts even more complex chains of effects between price and profit:

Price → Competitors' prices → Market share → Volume → Revenue → Profit
Price (today) → Volume (future) → Revenue (future) and Profit (future)
Price (today) → Volume → Costs (future) → Profit (future)
Price (supplier) → Price (reseller) → Volume → Revenue→ Profit

These are only the most important and the most obvious paths. You will notice, however, that all paths to profit begin with price. There is no way around that. This is as deep as most pricing practitioners dive into the topic of price decisions. The reason for that is easy to appreciate: these paths are difficult to trace in the real world and even more difficult to quantify, which leads practitioners to fall back instead on their own experience or rules of thumb to make price decisions. The chances that they find the optimal price this way are low.

Price and Volume

Price normally has a negative effect on volume. The higher the price, the less you sell. That is the fundamental law of economics and we express that mathematically in a demand curve. You plug a price into that equation, and it tells you how many units you will sell.

A demand curve usually applies to an entire market or to a market segment. These curves are in reality the aggregation of many individual demand curves. The type of good you buy also matters.

- *Durables*: In this case the demand curves reflect a yes-no decision of each individual customer. People buy one washing machine, one smartphone, one camera, or one PC. Or they don't buy at all. The demand curve is the sum of the individual decisions.
- *Nondurables:* In this case, buyers often buy several units at a time, depending on the price. Think about how many cans of soda you have in your refrigerator or how many gigabytes in your smartphone plan. We call this the "variable quantity" case. Again the demand curve reflects the sum of the units bought by all customers.

The "yes-no" case is easier to quantify. Classical economics tells us that if the price is less than the customer's perceived value for the product or service, he or she will buy it. The highest possible price or maximum price corresponds directly to the product's perceived value. Economists sometimes refer to this as the reservation price. The reservation price reflects the customer's willingness to pay.

You can think of the "variable amount" situation as a series of separate "yes-no" decisions. The higher the price, the fewer units the customer will buy. In other words, a customer's willingness to pay generally decreases with each additional unit, because his or her perceived value for each additional unit also declines. The second, third, and fourth unit of a product brings less value (technically speaking, less utility) than the previous one. This is called the law of declining marginal utility.

If a company determines prices on an individual basis, as in a negotiated transaction, its salespeople will have different goals and different degrees of freedom, depending on whether they face a "yes-no" or a "variable quantity" situation. If the buyer's decision is "yes-no" the salesperson looks for cues and clues to try to determine the buyer's maximum price and try to make the sale as close to that price as possible. This information imbalance in favor of the buyer presents one of the biggest challenges in price setting in a negotiated transaction, especially when the salesperson has the power to make the decision.

In the "variable quantity" case, the sellers have at least two options. They can determine a fixed price per unit or they can vary the price depending on the number of units purchased, a technique known as nonlinear pricing. Mathematically speaking it is harder to derive a demand curve in the "variable-quantity" case than in the "yes-no" case, because you need a good estimate of the marginal utility of each unit.

The aggregated demand curve results from the sum of the individual purchase volumes of each buyer for a given price. Theoretically these buyers can be homogeneous. But in reality they are almost always heterogeneous, because the preferences and utilities of the different customer segments or individuals vary. In all typical cases, once again, the aggregated demand curve also has a downward slope. When you take many individual buyers into account, the demand curve will approximate a smooth line.

To make a well-founded price decision, managers need to take their company's own goals, costs, the behavior of its customers, and the behavior of its competitors into account. Taking all of those factors into account requires effort, trade-offs, and tough decisions. That's why managers often rely on only one of those inputs for price decisions. The two most common methods are (1) using costs or (2) following the competition.

Using Costs to Set Prices

As the name implies, this method of setting prices relies primarily on the costs and to a lesser extent on the company's own goals, while ignoring the behavior of customers and competitors, at least explicitly.

If you ask dealers, distributors, or retailers how price setting works in their business, they will probably say that they simply apply a markup to the costs of their product. If the product costs them $5, and the standard markup is 100 %, the merchant would charge customers $10 for that product. I criticize this method because it ignores too many important facets of the marketplace, but I admit that the approach has practical advantages. First, it depends on hard cost data, not on assumptions. It also guarantees the seller a positive unit contribution on every unit sold. Finally, if competitors use the same approach to set their prices, and also have similar buying power, this method minimizes price competition for the product and encourages the sellers to compete on aspects other than price. Cost-plus pricing can create a de facto price cartel, with the resulting stability and predictability. All these factors explain why this method is so popular.

However, this method also has very serious disadvantages. It does not take customer reactions into account, because the sellers only use costs. Staying with the example above, it is possible that only a few customers are willing to pay $10 for the product. If that's the case, a price of $10 is choking off the market's growth and probably encouraging customers to look for cheaper alternatives to satisfy their needs. Conversely, customers may be willing to pay $12 per unit, which means that the sellers have sacrificed a large margin.

The lesson here is that unless you get lucky and your cost-plus pricing happens to coincide with customers' willingness to pay, the cost-plus method of setting prices — despite its advantages — can either cost you customers or cost you profit. With cost-plus you have a good chance that your price is either too high or too low.

Following the Competition

Following the competition means that you set your prices based on what your competitors do. That can mean that you match your competitors down to the penny, or consciously price your products above or below the competition's.

Similar to the cost-plus method, one major appeal of this approach is its simplicity, as you can infer from the following comment.

"Setting our prices is easy," a marketing director at a safety products company once told me. "We just look at what the premium supplier in our market does, and come in 10 % below them."

This approach is not limited to business-to-business companies, either. I know one major retailer that sets the prices for its 600 top products by matching the prices of the hard discounter Aldi. They have teams which would scout Aldi stores for prices and keep an eye out for price changes. Those 600 products make up more than half of that retail chain's revenue. The senior executives were surprised, however, when I told them what this meant for their business. Yes, they had simplified their pricing process and positioned themselves as a head-to-head competitor of the hard discounter. But this pricing process also meant that they had delegated their price-setting responsibility to Aldi. You might say that they have outsourced the work of their pricing department. They essentially put Aldi in charge of managing more than half of their own revenue.

Of course a company needs to keep an eye on its competitors' prices and use them as input in setting its own. But a rigid, formula-based reliance on competitor prices as the basis of your own pricing will rarely lead to optimal prices. In the case of that major retailer, it is highly unlikely that the "follower" had the same cost structure and or the same demand patterns that Aldi does. So why should prices in each channel be identical?

Market-Based Price Setting

Managers can only avoid the disadvantages of cost-plus pricing or competitor-based pricing when they explicitly take the demand curve into account in their decision making. They can only find out what their profit-maximizing prices are if they know how customers will respond to specific price levels.

Let's revisit our power tool manufacturer, but this time use a demand curve to figure out what prices will maximize the company's revenue and profits. You will recall that the power tool division's fixed costs are $30 million and the variable unit cost for each tool is $60. The empirically derived demand curve for the tool works out to:

$$Volume = 3,000,000 - 20,000 \times Price$$

We know from our earlier discussion that a price of $100 results in sales of one million units and a profit of $10 million. But what is the optimal price, which in the spirit of this book would be the profit-maximizing price? To try to calculate that price, let's compare the key financial results for seven different prices, ranging from $90 to $120 per unit. Figure 6.2 shows the results.

The optimal price is $105 and the company earns a profit of $10.5 million at this price. You will also notice some patterns in how the results change as you look left and right of the optimal price. At lower prices, revenue increases, but total variable

Price ($)	90	95	100	105	110	115	120
Volume (mill. units)	1.2	1.1	1.0	0.9	0.8	0.7	0.6
Revenue ($ mill.)	108.0	104.5	100.0	94.5	88.0	80.5	72.0
Variable costs ($ mill.)	72.0	66.0	60.0	54.0	48.0	42.0	36.0
Contribution ($ mill.)	36.0	38.5	40.0	40.5	40.0	38.5	36.0
Fixed costs ($ mill.)	30.0	30.0	30.0	30.0	30.0	30.0	30.0
Profit ($ mill.)	6.0	8.5	10.0	10.5	10.0	8.5	6.0
Profit change (%)	-42.9	-19.1	-4.8	0	-4.8	-19.1	-42.9

Fig. 6.2 Calculating the optimal price

costs increase at a faster rate, resulting in a lower contribution and profit. At higher prices, revenue and variable costs both decline, but revenues fall faster than costs, again reducing contribution and profit. The same price change from $105—regardless of up or down—reduces profits by the same amount. The declines are indeed symmetrical. The company earns the same amount of profit by pricing the power tool at $90 as it does at $120.

This refutes the widely held belief among practitioners that when in doubt it is better to err on the high side rather than on the low side when you price your product. The Russian proverb I cited earlier proves true in this case: a price that's too high is as bad as a price that is too low. In both cases, you sacrifice profit unnecessarily. I will admit, though, that in practice it is easier to back off a high price than to raise a price which you have set too low. In that sense, it probably is better to err on the high side, as long as the error is not so large that it puts the profit of the product in jeopardy.

The numbers also show that relatively slight deviations from the optimal price do not result in severe profit declines. If you are off by $5 from the optimum, either too high or too low, your profit declines by 4.8 %. That is significant for a billion-dollar business, of course, but not as bad as missing the optimal price in this case by, say, $15. In that case you would sacrifice 42.9 % of the profit you get with the optimal price. This is an important insight. It means that it is not the end of the world if you don't have the optimal price figured out down to the last decimal place. It is more important to be in the right vicinity. The further away you are from the optimal price, the steeper your decline in profit.

Sharing Value Fifty-Fifty

So how do you arrive at the optimal price without building a table as in Fig. 6.2? Whenever you have a linear demand curve, as in this case, you can apply a simple rule to solve for it. The optimal price lies exactly in between the maximum price and the variable unit cost. The maximum price is the price which results in sales of zero. The maximum price for the power tool is $p^{max} = 3,000,000/20,000 = \$150$. You can solve for the optimal price with this equation:

$$\text{Optimal price} = \frac{1}{2} \times (150 + 60) = 105 \text{ Euro}$$

This simple decision rule leads to some other lessons and useful rules of thumb. Let's say that your variable unit costs go up. How much of a cost increase should you pass on? The equation above provides the answer. Because the optimal price lies halfway between the maximum price and the variable costs, you should pass on half of the cost increase to your customers.

If the power tool manufacturer's variable unit costs rise by $10 to $70, the new optimal price is not $10 higher, but rather $5 higher at $110. Similarly, you should pass along only half of any cost savings to your customers. This shows that cost-plus pricing is wrong, because it would call for you to pass along the full cost change to your customer. The price of \$110 is the midpoint between \$70 (the new variable unit cost) and \$150 (the maximum price, which remains unchanged). The same applies to reductions in variable unit cost. If it falls in this case from \$60 to \$50, the optimal price goes down by \$5 to \$100, not by \$10.

The same principle applies to exchange rate fluctuations. It is neither optimal nor wise to pass on exchange rate fluctuations to customers in full. If you export from the USA, it is also not optimal to set all of your prices in dollars instead of using a local currency. Your customers outside of the dollar zone will use their own currencies for their purchase decisions. If their currency undergoes a devaluation, the product becomes more expensive for them. This same principle likewise applies to increases of a sales tax. For every tax increase of 1 %, your price should rise by less than 1 %. The exact amount depends on the slope of your demand curve.

What if the customers' willingness to pay changes? If the maximum price increased by \$10 to \$160, the optimal price would rise by half that amount. You should never completely exploit that change in value perception and willingness to pay by putting it all in your own pocket. The rule of thumb, again, is to share the impact of the changes—whether positive or negative—evenly with your customers.

Common sense, not just mathematics, corroborates this principle. If your product delivers 20 % more value than the competitors' products, you should collect 10 % of that difference in price. If you demand more—or demand it all—the customer actually never gets to enjoy the difference in value. If your value difference is 20 % and your price difference is 20 %, the customer comes out of the deal empty-handed despite the greater value you provide. You offset the entire advantage for the customer by setting the product's price too high. This is a conclusive theoretical validation of what many experienced sales people know intuitively, that a form of "win-win" between you and your customers trumps the full extraction of value.

Figure 6.2 also gives some insight into the concept of price elasticity. If you set the price at \$100, you **sell** one million units. If you change the price by \$1, or by 1 %, your sales volume changes by 20,000 units or 2 %. The price elasticity at that price point is 2, which means that every percentage change in price results in a volume change that is double so high, in percentage terms.[3] If you raise the price by 5 %, your unit sales will decline by 10 %. I say the price elasticity is 2 at that price point, because the price elasticity is not constant when your demand curve is linear. It is the result of percentage changes, which means that it depends on where you start.

In the vicinity of the profit-maximizing price, the price elasticity must be greater than 1. Otherwise, volume would decline proportionally less than the positive price change, meaning that your profit would automatically rise. The price at which revenue reaches its maximum, in contrast, is where the price elasticity is exactly 1. If we project the table further to the left, we would see that company maximizes its

---

[3] Price elasticity, which is the percentage change in volume divided by the percentage change in price, is usually negative. But for simplicity's sake, one normally omits the negative sign.

revenue from the power tool at a price of $75. Volume reaches 1.5 million and revenue rises to $112.5 million. The problem is that a price of $75 completely wipes out the company's profit. It actually books a loss of $7.5 million at that price point. This underscores once again the danger of focusing too heavily on maximizing revenue versus maximizing profit, and the need for a balanced approach to goal setting, as we discussed in Chap. 5.

So far we have looked at one special case of the demand curves and cost functions, namely the linear case. Of course, in reality these functions are not always linear and the guidelines to deriving an optimal price not so straightforward. But my decades of experience tell me that within relevant price intervals, the linear demand curve is a sufficient approximation of reality and therefore a very useful tool. You can treat the recommendations we discussed in this section as broadly applicable lessons about taking pricing decisions.

How to Determine Demand Curves and Price Elasticities

If demand curves and price elasticity play an indispensable role in setting prices, where do they come from? How can you get the ones you need and ensure that they have enough validity? How do you turn your impressions and experience into hard numbers? The emphasis here is on the word "numbers." You may know intuitively that lowering your prices may boost sales by "a little" or "a lot," but that doesn't help you much. You need to express "a little" or "a lot" in numbers. Prices, after all, are numbers. So are costs and volumes. These are the three inputs you need to calculate revenue and profit, the hard financial metrics allow to judge the financial impact of your decisions and to determine whether a planned price decision is wise. Put most simply: you can't make good price decisions without numbers.

The good news is that we now have a comprehensive set of methods and tools at our disposal to build these curves and use them to answer essential business questions. Over the last three decades, Simon-Kucher has been at the forefront of a wave of research and real-world applications that has made considerable progress in quantifying demand curves and price elasticities. There is only a small number of proven, practical ways to derive a demand curve. Some require little more than back-of-the-envelope calculations, while others demand more sophisticated analyses. I will describe them in greater detail in the next section.

Expert Judgment: Making Direct Estimates of Price Elasticities

The simplest way to estimate price elasticity is to ask people. That may sound trivial, but if you ask enough people who are either close to customers or have enough market experience with a product, you can come up with some very useful numbers.

Of course you don't just walk into a meeting and say "how elastic do you think the demand for our product is?" You can, however, ask your team how much volume you would lose if you raised prices by 10 %. If the answer is 50 %, it means that your product has a price elasticity of 5. This gives you a clear indication that demand is very sensitive to price changes and you should proceed with caution if you plan to raise them. Conversely, if your team says that a price decrease of 10 % would cause volume to increase by 50 %, a price cut may be a very reasonable option. As simple as this method sounds, at Simon-Kucher we have used it very effectively as a discussion starter over the years. One of our clients in media even named the method "one up, one down" to remind themselves to check and discuss how price changes would affect volume, and then use the resulting price elasticities as a means to compare price sensitivity across different groups of products.

I would recommend that you gather these estimates for more than just a "one up, one down" scenario. This will reveal whether larger price changes—whether down or up—result in disproportionately higher or lower volumes, which in turn would show how price elasticity changes depending on the magnitude of the intended price change.

This approach works even better when you follow up your quantitative questions with two qualitative ones: Why? And what happens next? The "why?" question challenges the respondents to explain their estimates, particularly what happens to the demand if you cut prices and what happens if you raise them. The "what happens next?" question is another way of asking how your competitors will respond to your price change. Will they follow your move? If they match your price change, you will probably need to revise your estimates. Answering this second question is vitally important in competitive markets.

You might be wondering whether "expert judgment" is simply a euphemism for "guessing." It is a legitimate question, especially in light of the David Ogilvy quote at the beginning of this chapter. The two questions "why?" and "what happens next?" help take this approach beyond the realm of pure guesswork. You will notice that numbers often undergo revisions as people start to think through the consequences. Managers start to fall back on their experience, their meetings with customers, or similar cases they have seen. A lot of evidence, albeit often anecdotal, bubbles to the surface once you start this kind of exercise.

The results become even more insightful and useful when you ask these questions not only about changes across multiple price points, but also ask a range of people in the organization. Pull together the most knowledgeable and experienced people in your organization—executives, field sales, sales management, marketers, and product managers—and ask them. To mitigate the risk of group think or having one or two parties dominate the discussion, you can ask people to write down their answers individually before trying to establish a consensus.

The "what happens next?" question will lead you to play out scenarios with different competitive reactions. It helps to use computer support to track the answers and to derive sales and profit curves.

This expert-judgment approach is particularly useful for new products, because your "insiders" will be able to make better assessments than customers, who have yet to test the product. The "why?" will then prompt a discussion about the value of the product to customers and offer some guidance on what value messages you will need to communicate and reinforce.

You can use this method very quickly and at little cost. It also probably marks the first time that many of your team members have taken the demand curves in their heads and expressed them in hard numbers. These are the biggest advantages of this method. The "con" side is that these experts are all internal. You haven't asked any customers. Even the best experts can be off when they try to anticipate how customers will respond to price changes.

Asking Customers About Prices Directly

You can ask customers directly about how they will respond to price changes. More precisely, you can ask them how they will change their buying behavior. How you ask the question will depend on whether you have a "yes-no" situation, such as with consumer durables, or a "variable quantity" situation, in which the customers tell you whether they buy more or fewer units of a product. You can also ask at which point a price increase prompts a customer to switch to a competitor's product. This yields insights into the impact of relative price differences. Another approach is even more direct. You simply ask the customer what his or her acceptable price or maximum price is. There are very thorough, established sets of questions for this purpose, such as the Van Westendorp Price Sensitivity Meter.

The major advantage of these methods is simplicity. You can ask a large number of customers these questions quickly and generate a lot of data. The major disadvantage of these direct methods is that they make people unusually sensitive to price. When someone asks "in your face" questions about price, it makes the customer focus more on price at the expense of other product features and risks distorting the results. If a researcher asks a respondent whether he or she would buy a product at a higher price, will the respondent really give an honest answer? And what role does the prestige effect play in this answer? If you saw a price in a store in daily life and made a spontaneous decision, you may not be placing as much emphasis on price as you would if someone asked you directly about price in a survey.

These disadvantages cast doubt on the validity of these direct methods. I would not dismiss them entirely, though. Instead, my recommendation is that you do not rely solely on these direct methods as your input in determining a demand curve or setting your prices. You must complement this data with data from other methods.

Asking Customers About Price Indirectly

Indirect questions give you more valid and reliable insights into price sensitivity than direct questions do. "Indirect" means that you do not ask the customer about price in isolation, but rather about price and value at the same time. That makes price just one of several aspects of the customer's answer.[4]

---

[4] The most common method used for indirect questioning is called conjoint measurement.

The respondents face many different options and needs to indicate which of the options they prefer, and in some cases to what degree they prefer that option over the others. The options present a mix of product characteristics such as product quality, brand, technical performance, and also price. Each option has some stronger and some weaker features, which means that the respondents need to make trade-offs. Do I pick Option A even though it is not my favorite brand? Do I pick Option B despite its higher price, because I think it offers great value? The data from all these answers allow us to quantify what people would pay for certain product configurations and translate that into actual estimates of sales volumes. It gives us all the necessary data to make a robust, reliable price decision.

The general term for this category of research methods is conjoint measurement. Its first uses came in the 1970s. As you can imagine, it has undergone many transformative improvements as both knowledge and computing power increased. The advent of the personal computer was a watershed moment, because unlike a rigid paper questionnaire it allowed us to customize each survey to the individual respondent. The program which presents the options adapts to the customer's previous answers in order to make each successive set of trade-offs tougher. This adaptive approach also lets us come closer to simulating a real shopping experience and thus obtain data with even more reliability. Today these methods effectively help managers determine their demand curves and their profit-maximizing prices.

Price Tests

Sophisticated survey methods do an excellent job of simulating real buying behavior. But they are still simulations. There is always a margin of error in any model based on survey data. People don't always act as they say they will. This makes so-called field experiments appealing. A company changes the real prices at the shelf or online in a systematic way, and carefully tracks how customers respond to the price changes. The ability to collect real-life data is clearly the big advantage of this approach. In the past, though, conducting these experiments on a large scale was an arduous and expensive task, which meant that companies rarely used field tests for price setting. Modern technologies such as scanner data and e-commerce make these tests faster, easier, and less expensive than ever before. I expect them to become a more important method for price setting in the coming years.

The Big Data Myth: Using Market Data for Demand Curves and Price Elasticities

Headlines in leading business publications will convince you that we finally live in the era of "Big Data." I have immersed myself in the quantitative side of economics since college, so you might think that I welcome the dawn of this new and promising era. Instead, my reaction is more "déjà vu" than excitement.

Breakthroughs in econometrics in the 1970s and the rapid evolution and personalization of computer power marked the first burst of hope that "Big Data" will fundamentally change marketing and pricing. You could make precise estimates of demand curves and price elasticities, because you could finally track variations in price, market share, and volume in your market, analyze the data quickly, and use it to your advantage.

This great hope ended in disappointment.

The disappointment had little to do with the availability of data, its depth and richness, and the ability to "crunch" them. Instead, it had to do with the fundamental *relevance* of that data. Here we distinguish between the fresh market data from "live" market tests as described above and historical data sets collected in the normal course of business, not as part of an experiment.

As far back as 1962, Lester G. Telser, a professor at the University of Chicago, predicted that past market data has very limited relevance for predicting future behavior.[5] The reason is the amount of variation observed. In a market with a high price elasticity, you will probably observe little change in the differences of competitors' prices. Even without hard data, the competitors know that changes of the relative price position can cause significant shifts in volume. So no one risks a big change in the relative price position. If one firm changes its price, the others are likely to follow so that the relative position hardly changes. From an econometrics perspective, one would say that the independent variable (price) stays within too tight a range to allow you to make valid estimates of what the demand curve looks like.

In a market with low price elasticity, you may indeed observe significant variation in prices and price differences, but they yield very slight shifts in volume. Here the econometrics expert would say that the dependent variable (unit sales) moves in too narrow a range to permit valid estimates of what the underlying price elasticity truly is.

Simon-Kucher & Partners likewise had high hopes in this earlier "Big Data" wave and learned its lesson the hard way. When we started the firm in 1985, we planned to apply econometric methods to historical market data to help improve decision making about prices. Co-founder Eckhard Kucher devoted his doctoral dissertation to this realm. Since that time the firm has conducted over 5,000 pricing projects throughout the world in all major industries, and I would estimate that in no more than 100 of these projects we applied econometrics as the key method. Professor Telser was right.

I would supplement his observations with one of my own. I have noticed that companies pay less attention to pricing when times are good and markets seem very stable. It takes a major structural change in the market—the entry of a new competitor, the exit of a competitor, or the emergence of a new technology or new distribution channels—to force them to pay more attention to pricing, commission more analyses, or bring in a consultant. This happens when pharmaceutical patents expire and generics enter the market, when physical products become accessible in digital

[5] Telser LG (1962) The Demand for Branded Goods as Estimated from Consumer Panel Data. The Review of Economic Statistics No. 3, pp. 300–324.

form, or when companies aggressively enter new distribution channels such as the Internet. When such a structural change occurs, historical market data offer no valid insights into current or future customer behavior. A corollary of that observation applies to prices for new products, which also often represent a "structural break." If you are setting the price for a new product, such as an Apple iPhone historical data is of limited use at best, and in some cases offers no insights whatsoever.

What I have found over the years is that a *combination* of the methods I have described above produces the most reliable results. No one method, on its own, has so many compelling advantages that I would recommend you use it exclusively. Having one method cross-check the other gives you a range you can use to narrow down your options. When all methods show similar patterns and results, you can be fairly certain that you have correctly estimated how customers will respond to different prices, and thus have greater confidence that the price you ultimately set is optimal.

So ... What About the Competitors' Prices?

In most of the previous examples, I have kept things simple in order to get my basic points across. This required leaving out the whole topic of how competitors will respond to your price moves. In the context of a price decision, two complications arise when we include competitive reaction: the quantitative effect that competitors' price changes have on a company's own sales, and the qualitative challenge of trying to determine exactly how a competitor will respond. The former is relatively simple to explain and address, and the latter more difficult.

Let's begin with the effect that competitors' prices have on the company's own sales. It is obvious that competitors' prices influence customers' decisions. We can measure that influence by looking at the cross-price elasticity. The cross-price elasticity is the percentage change of our volume divided by the percentage change in the competitor's price. Let's assume that a competitor cuts price by 10 % and our sales fall by 6 % as a result. This gives us a cross-price elasticity of $6/10 = 0.6$. In contrast to the price elasticity of our own products, the cross-price elasticity is positive because our sales usually move in the same direction as a competitors' price change; that is, if they raise their price, your own sales should rise and vice versa. The absolute value of the cross-price elasticity tends to be lower than the price elasticity. The less differentiated the products are, the closer these two elasticities will be to each other.

It is evident that we need to incorporate competitors' prices into our demand curves. We can do this in a number of ways. Instead of using our own price as the independent variable, we can replace that with the difference between our price and our competitor's. We can also use the relative price, which would be our price divided by our competitor's price, as the independent variable. Finally, we can include our competitor's price as an additional variable in our demand curve. We can likewise use any of the methods described above to quantify the effects of changes in our competitors' prices on our sales volume.

The Prisoner's Dilemma: Let the Game Begin

Whenever you make a price decision, you need to ask yourself whether and to what degree your competitors will respond. This kind of interdependence—knowing their decisions will affect yours and vice versa—is characteristic of a market with only a small number of sellers, which economists call an oligopoly. Price changes by any competitor will have a noticeable effect on the sales of other competitors, who need to decide whether to react or accept the consequences without reacting.

If the competitors do respond, it creates a counter-effect on other competitors' volumes. It also risks starting the kind of chain reaction that leads us into the realm of game theory, established in 1928 by the mathematician John von Neumann, who also invented the computer.[6] Including competitive reactions in your decision making complicates your price decisions. The most common situation in pricing is the prisoner's dilemma, a specific situation in which you need to anticipate what another party might do, because your own fate depends on their decisions.

Let's assume that we want to make a significant price cut. If our competitors do not respond and instead leave their prices unchanged, we can expect an increase in volume. If our competitors follow suit, however, then our volume will probably change very little, certainly much less than if the competitor had left prices constant. Our price cut brought us no advantage, and even worse, saddled us with two financial problems: It cut our margins, and in the worst-case scenario, it may have gutted our overall profit. You might say we have spent a large amount of money (namely, our profit) in a high-profile, heavily marketed move for which we received nothing in return.

A price increase on our part creates a similar situation. If competitors do not respond, we may have a price disadvantage which causes our volume and our market share to fall. It is not unusual for the initiator of a price increase to rescind it if competitors do not follow. That happened recently to a major brewery after it raised prices for its premium products, and then withdrew the increase when competitors did not follow. If competitors do follow the price increase, the new higher prices may lead to only minor reductions in total volume, but all competitors realize higher profits.

If you want to take a more structured approach to anticipating competitive reaction and observing its potential effects, I would recommend either the expert-judgment approach or the indirect questioning approach (conjoint measurement) described earlier in this chapter. In the spirit of my earlier comment, it is wiser to rely on more than one method because, as discussed, all of them have their pros and cons.

This is especially true if you are in an oligopolistic market, where understanding and anticipating competitive reaction patterns is absolutely essential. Many modern markets are oligopolistic in nature so that understanding and anticipating competitive reactions is one of management's most important challenges. It also begs the question, from a standpoint of game theory, whether you can either influence another party's course of action or find clues *ex ante* which may reveal it. This next section brings up topics such as price leadership and signaling, which can raise

---

[6] von Neumann J (1928). Zur Theorie der Gesellschaftsspiele. Mathematische Annalen.

concerns with your legal counsel. Please always discuss any application of these approaches with your legal department or advisors to make sure that your company's policies comply with the law.

Price Leadership

The easiest way to understand and anticipate your competitors' reactions would be to ask them outright. But of course I am not recommending that. Price fixing and cartels are illegal. In the USA they are even criminal offences which carry stiff prison sentences.

A widely used method in the "game" of price setting is the concept of price leadership. Companies in the US car market practiced price leadership for decades, with General Motors in the driver's seat. Other competitors accepted GM's role as market and price leader in the days when its share stood at around 50 %. GM increased prices on an annual basis.

In Germany's retail market, Aldi serves as a price leader for key products. Many competitors will follow Aldi when it changes prices. One newspaper article acknowledges this leadership role exemplarily: "Aldi is raising prices for milk. It is expected that the entire retail sector will follow."[7] Another recent case of publicly acknowledged price leadership came up in the US beer market. Aggregating the shares of individual brands, the market-leading group is Anheuser Busch InBev (AB InBev), followed by MillerCoors. The American antitrust authorities determined that "AB InBev typically initiates annual price increases with the expectation that MillerCoors' prices will follow. And they frequently do."[8] *The Wall Street Journal* made a similar comment: "AB InBev has been steadily raising beer prices. And Miller Coors typically follows AB InBev's lead."[9] Price leadership can break down when new competitors enter a market and do not follow the leader. That is how the Mexican beer group Modelo behaved in the US market: "Modelo prices have not followed AB InBev's price increases."[10] Modelo eventually became part of AB InBev in 2013.[11]

Signaling

Changing prices is always risky. Will competitors undermine your price increases in an effort to grab market share at your expense? Or will they slash their prices — unilaterally or in response to our changes — and risk igniting a price war? These questions contain a high degree of uncertainty. The risk of making a mistake is significant, and getting these answers wrong can cut your profits. You can also

---

[7] Aldi erhöht die Milchpreise. Frankfurter Allgemeine Zeitung, November 3, 2012, p. 14.

[8] Bloomberg online, January 31, 2013.

[9] The Wall Street Journal Europe, February 1, 2013, p. 32.

[10] Bloomberg online, January 31, 2013.

[11] Grupo Modelo website www.gmodelo.com.

damage your reputation if you need to withdraw a price increase because the competitors do not follow.

One method to reduce that uncertainty is signaling. Well before taking its planned price move, a company sends "signals" to the marketplace. Then the company listens whether customers, competitors, investors, or regulators send signals back. You cannot rule out the possibility that a competitor bluffs, but competitors must also be careful if they communicate something and then backtrack or fail to follow through. In signaling, the credibility of the competitor is always at stake.

Signaling is not illegal per se. As long as companies keep their communication relevant to everyone in the marketplace, including customers and investors, and do not go overboard, they are usually on the safe side. The signaling must not have anything which implies or aims at an agreement or a contract, such as "if competitor X raises its prices, we will follow."

A price war plagued the German market for car insurance for years. In October 2011, the business press reported that "Germany's largest insurance group, Allianz, is going to raise prices drastically, effective January 1, 2012."[12] All other insurance companies publicly announced that they would raise their prices as well. In the course of 2012, prices rose by 7 % on average.

"In 2013, prices should rise again," said the chairman of HUK-Coburg, Allianz's biggest rival. The comment was prescient, as prices did indeed rise that year.[13] These developments showed a clear break from the downward price spiral of the previous years.

Companies also use signaling to announce a retaliation, in an effort to discourage their competitors from taking a course of action such as a price cut. Im Tak-Uk, the chief operating officer of Korean car manufacturer Hyundai, once claimed publicly that "… if Japanese car makers become aggressive in raising incentives and the red light comes on in achieving our sales target, we will consider raising incentives for buyers."[14] Incentives in this case mean price cuts in the form of discounts and promotions. The statement could not be any clearer: Japanese companies knew how Hyundai would respond if they raised their incentives.

Competitive Reaction and Price Decisions

How companies in a market anticipate and account for competitive reactions can have a massive influence on prices, and thus on the resulting profits companies earn. Failure to take these reactions into account—or making incorrect assumptions about them—can have dire consequences.

To understand this complex topic better and draw out some useful insights, let's start with the basic equation below. The market in question has two competitors,

---

[12] Financial Times Deutschland. October 26, 2011, p. 1.

[13] MCC-Kongress, Kfz-Versicherung 2013, March 20, 2013.

[14] Hyundai Seeks Solution on the High End. The Wall Street Journal Europe, February 19, 2013, p. 24.

	Starting situation	Chamberlin hypothesis	Cournot hypothesis
Price ($)	20	22.50	16.67
Volume (units)	500	437.5	583
Revenue ($)	10,000	9,840	9,718
Variable costs ($)	2,500	2,190	2,915
Fixed costs ($)	5,000	5,000	5,000
Profit ($)	2,500	2,650	1,803
Profit change (%)	0	+6.0	-27.9

Fig. 6.3 The effects of different competitive reactions

A and B, both equally strong and both with demand curves (price-response functions) that look like this:

$$\text{Own volume} = 1,000 - 50 \times (\text{own price}) + 25 \times (\text{competitor s price})$$

This is what economists would call a symmetrical oligopoly. One company's own price has twice the effect on volume as the competitor's price does. This means that A's own optimal price depends not only on B's price, but also on how B responds to A's price changes. Let's also assume that variable unit costs are $5 and each company's fixed costs are $5,000.

In the current situation, as shown in the second column of Fig. 6.3, the price stands at $20 and each company makes $2,500 in profit. Is it possible to increase that profit? That depends on how A and B behave as well as the assumptions they make about each other. There are two classical hypotheses for the potential competitive reactions: the Chamberlin Hypothesis and the Cournot Hypothesis.

Chamberlin Hypothesis: Under this hypothesis, A and B both assume that the other will follow price changes in full, and when one makes a price change, the other actually does follow. The third column in Fig. 6.3 shows what happens if one company raises its price to $22.50 and the other one follows: profit rises by 6 % to $2,650. Competitors A and B both behaved as if they were monopolists, despite the fact that their optimal price depends on the other's actions. This is the kind of result one would expect in a market characterized by price leadership. George Stigler, who won the Nobel Prize in economics in 1982, claims that price leadership is the best solution for companies in a highly competitive oligopoly.

Cournot Hypothesis: Under this hypothesis, A and B both assume that the other will not respond to any price changes. That assumption, however, typically turns out to be false. In reality, A and B almost always respond in a way that optimizes their own respective prices. In that case, the price drops to $16.67 and profit falls by 27.9 % to $1,803.

In my days as a professor, I often asked two groups to compete against each other using these same numbers. After each round, a group would receive two outcomes: its own sales results, and the price that its competitor charged. Which of the two results do you think came about more often?

It turned out that the Chamberlin solution occurred very rarely. The Cournot solution was far more common. Granted, one must be careful in projecting the results of such experiments to day-to-day business reality. But my experience tells me that real-life competition follows the same pattern. The Cournot solution or something similar happens much more frequently than the clearly more advantageous Chamberlin constellation.

This case shows in no uncertain terms that a company must be able to anticipate its competitors' countermeasures correctly. And that applies in both directions. Will competitors follow if you raise prices? Only then price increases make sense and bring the expected advantages. And how will competitors respond to a price cut? If you expect them to follow, it is often better to scrap your plans. The result is a decline in profit, often combined with only a negligible increase in volume. When you expect these asymmetrical reactions (competitors do not follow price increases, but do match price cuts), it seems wise to leave prices where they are. This conclusion helps explain why one often sees very rigid price structures in oligopolies, the business version of a staring contest as each waits for the other to blink.

If your company is part of an oligopoly, please keep these three points in mind:

– *No clear optimal price exists*: Instead, the optimal price emerges from the assumptions you make about competitors, the information you have at hand about them, and the actual behavior of the competitors.
– *Chamberlin outcomes are possible if certain conditions apply:* The competitors can achieve a Chamberlin price — essentially a monopoly price for the market — or at least get close to it, provided that they have similar cost structures and market positions and also have similar goals, and can back that up with a certain level of trust and strategic intelligence. The likelihood is higher when all competitors are smart enough to understand the interactions and behave accordingly.
– *It is wise to leave prices as they are if those conditions do not exist:* If those conditions mentioned above do not exist or one or more competitors face circumstances which make their behavior uncertain, it is wise to leave your prices as they are. Price cuts under such circumstances bring no sustainable advantage and will instead risk provoking a price war. The one exception is in the case of input cost increases, because they would probably affect all competitors to a similar degree.

So far in this chapter, we have looked at cost changes as one-off events. As a general rule of thumb, a company should not pass along cost increases in full, but rather share that burden with customers. But what happens when cost changes happen with greater frequency or over longer periods? A particularly challenging situation for price adjustments is the occurrence of inflation.

Inflation: What It Is and Why It Matters for Price Decisions

My grandfather used to tell me stories about life during the hyperinflation period in Germany in the 1920s. The moment he would get some money, he would immediately rush off to the store and buy something. If he had waited for a few days—in some cases even a few hours—the value of his money, and with it his purchasing power, would have dropped precipitously.

Hyperinflation is an extreme situation which still occurs today in emerging markets. But most of us know "inflation" in less severe forms. We generally associate the term "inflation" with a continual rise in prices. But what are the effects of inflation? And how should you take inflation—both actual and anticipated—into account when you set your prices?

Inflation harms people who hold onto money and people who receive nominal, fixed payments. At the same time, inflation benefits people who owe money.[15] You could describe it as a form of redistribution from savers and creditors to debtors. These general effects are well known, but inflation also has deeper and more far-reaching effects.

The main cause of inflation is the increase of money supply. The winners in that scenario are people who can get their hands on newly issued money quickly. They can still buy goods and services at relatively low prices. The later you gain access to money, the more you lose, because you need to buy at higher prices. This is known as the "Cantillon effect," named after the Irish economic theorist Richard Cantillon (1680–1734).[16]

Inflation also suppresses an important function of prices, namely their ability to signal the scarcity of goods. For consumers, price perceptions become distorted and confusing. It is hard to decide whether to hedge or hoard. For investors, inflation makes it much harder to recognize whether the prices they see reflect a real scarcity or a devaluation of the currency. This plundering money chases after certain forms of investment, causing prices to explode even though no underlying scarcity exists. This "bubble" effect has occurred time and again, from the Dutch tulip craze of the 1600s to the Internet bubble at the end of the 20th century and the US real estate bubble in the first decade of this century. At some point the bubble bursts, prices collapse, and it takes a long time before prices begin to reflect true scarcity again.

Inflation is also a gigantic redistribution mechanism. Inflation allows the quick, the clever, and the debtors to take advantage of the slow, the naïve, and the creditors. It goes without saying that sovereign governments, which issue and hold large amounts of debt, are among the biggest beneficiaries of inflation. When inflation threatens, you need to strike quickly. That is the time to buy or borrow. The longer you wait, the more you will pay, allowing benefits to accrue to those who "bought

---

[15] Polleit T (2011), *Der Fluch des Papiergeldes*. Finanzbuch-Verlag, München, 2011, pp. 17–20.

[16] Cantillon R (2010) Essai sur la nature du commerce general; 1755, in English: An Essai on Economic Theory. Ludwig von Mises-Institute, Auburn (Alabama).

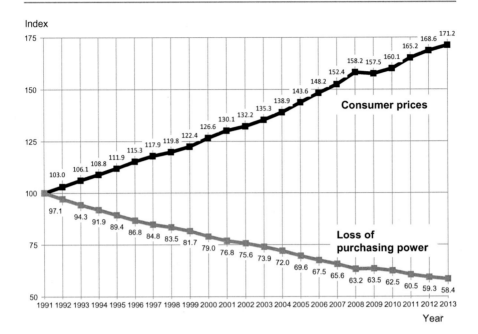

Fig. 6.4 Changes in the CPI of the USA, indexed, 1991 through 2012 (1991 = 100)

low" and can now "sell high." This is common sense. The art lies in seeing through the mass psychology at work and not interpreting the rising prices as a signal of scarcity.

The most common way to express inflation is the change in consumer prices, as measured by the consumer price index (CPI). Figure 6.4 shows the change in the CPI in the USA from 1991 through the end of 2013, a period of 22 years. I have set the index at 100 for the year 1991, to make it easier to see the percentage changes.

The upper curve shows the rise in price levels. At the end of 2013, the CPI was 71.2 % higher than in 1991, which corresponds to an average annual inflation rate of 2.47 %. If you have not increased prices in line with this curve, the real value of what you received in exchange for your goods and services has declined. You are among inflation's victims. What you paid $100 for in 1991 would cost you $171.2 at the end of 2013 reflecting your loss in purchasing power.

The lower curve is the flipside of the upper curve. It shows the loss of purchasing power since 1991. In these 22 years the purchasing power of the US dollar has declined by 41.6 %. If we go all the way back to 1971 the decline is much greater; the purchasing power of the dollar declined by 82.6 %.

Why did I pick 1971, which seems like an arbitrary year? That is the year the gold standard under the Bretton Woods system was abandoned by President Nixon, a move which opened the door to continuing inflation. You will hear politicians refer to an annualized inflation rate of around 2 % as "modest." Most conservative central bankers consider 2 % per year or a little more to be within an acceptable range.

The cumulative effect, however, is enormous and destructive for inflation's victims, who get dispossessed as their nominal dollars buy them less and less. The dollar has lost more than 40 % of its value in just over two decades and over 80 % of its value in the last four decades, despite this "low" level of inflation.

Relative to the price of gold the loss is even higher. On September 1, 2015 the price of one ounce of gold was $1,142. That's what you would have had to pay to get one ounce of the precious metal. Before August 15, 1971, the same amount of dollars would have bought you 37.1 ounces of gold. Thus, the loss of the dollar's value in gold terms since 1971 is 96.9 %.

I interpret the lack of discussion and attention on this topic as tacit acceptance of it, or perhaps resignation to it. Most people take this development for granted. The only effective way to stop it is to reestablish the gold standard. Such a move would remove some very powerful tools from politicians' toolboxes, though, which is why it is unlikely to happen. Unstable money which loses its value—whether slowly or quickly—will remain a fact of life in modern economies.

The high levels of government debt, combined with the relatively loose monetary policies since the Great Recession began, mean that a sharp increase in the inflation rate is unavoidable in the future. The only question is when it will come. Many companies will face do-or-die decisions when that happens. How they manage their prices will make a critical difference. In emerging markets we frequently see increasing rates of inflation.[17] Maybe we can learn something from the history of Brazil, a country that had very high inflation rates over several decades.

Price and Inflation: A Lesson from Brazil

In the 1980s, one of the world's largest pharmaceutical companies needed to make a high-stakes decision in Brazil, where out-of-control inflation reached a rate of several hundred percent per year. Their biggest product was an over-the-counter pain reliever. The company saw hyperinflation as an opportunity to increase market share through a combination of lower relative prices and more aggressive advertising. And that is exactly what they implemented. They intentionally raised prices below the rate of inflation, to make their product cheaper relative to the competition. They also increased their spending on advertising.

Management's confidence in these moves—and their odds of success—seemed to increase when the competitors continued to raise their prices at the rate of inflation or above. This widened the price gap in the favor of our client even more than they originally anticipated.

It turned out that this strategy was counterproductive. Why didn't it work? What happens to price perception during periods of inflation? Signals become confusing due to the constant flux of price changes. In Brazil at that time, the consumers did not recognize the price advantage that the pharma company had worked so hard to establish. It got lost in the noise, as did the increased advertising.

---

[17] Inflation Worries Mount. *The Wall Street Journal*, February 12, 2014.

Simon-Kucher & Partners recommended that the company not only pull back from its current tactics, but implement the exact opposite approach. They should raise prices at least at the level of inflation (or even a bit more) and cut back on advertising. Profits improved considerably with these new tactics, and market share barely changed as customers remained loyal to the brand.

I learned two lessons from this case. First, an attempt to establish a price advantage will not work unless customers notice and understand it. Price signals are harder to convey clearly in a period of high inflation. Second, under inflationary conditions I strongly recommend a series of small, regular price increases instead of fewer significant changes. The series of small changes allows you to keep pace and to avoid the need to overcompensate for lost time and money with a big price adjustment later. You should start these increases and establish the rhythm as early as possible when inflation looms.

In the last two chapters, we have looked at the fundamental economics of prices. Taking advantage of these principles is part "science" and part "art," and in the next chapter we will explore price differentiation, the high art of pricing.

Price Differentiation: The High Art

7

So far we have asked ourselves where the profit-maximizing price lies, meaning exactly one optimal price.[1] When we charge only one uniform price for a product, the left side of Fig. 7.1 shows what our profit situation looks like, with the numbers of our power tool business. Leaving fixed costs aside for simplicity's sake, the dark rectangle corresponds to our profit.

We can see from these comparative graphs that one uniform price—even when set optimally—exhausts only part of the available profit potential in the market. The right side of Fig. 7.1 shows the entire profit potential. It corresponds to the whole area bounded by the triangle A-B-C. It is much larger than the area on the left defined by the dark rectangle, which lies within the triangle A-B-C.

If we have a linear demand curve and a linear cost function, the area covered by the dark triangle on the right is exactly twice the size of the area covered by the dark rectangle on the left. If we have a nonlinear demand curve, the difference between the entire profit potential and the profit from a uniform price can be more or less than double. This depends on the distribution of consumers' willingness to pay, but still results in something close to double the profits. This realization—that a uniform price taps only about half of the profit potential—is dramatic. It says that even if a company succeeds in setting an optimal uniform price, it still leaves a large portion of its potential profits on the table. How can that be? The explanation is simple.

As we can see from the negatively sloped demand curve in Fig. 7.1, there are customers who are willing to pay more than the optimal uniform price of $105. Some would pay $115, and others would even be willing to pay $125. Until the price hits $150, there will be some customers who buy. Yet with a uniform price, we are asking all of these customers to pay only $105, even though they would be willing to pay more. They probably appreciate the bargain and gladly put the so-called consumer surplus, the difference of what they are willing to pay and what they have to pay, in their pockets. The shaded triangle at the lower right of the left figure

---

[1] A profit curve can also have two maxima. This can happen with the so-called double-kinked demand curve defined by Gutenberg.

© Springer International Publishing Switzerland 2015

H. Simon, *Confessions of the Pricing Man*, DOI 10.1007/978-3-319-20400-0_7

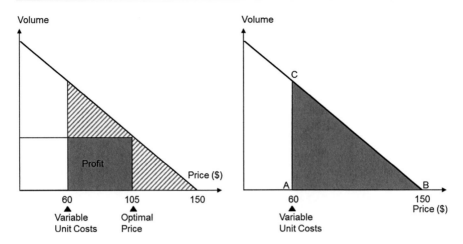

Fig. 7.1 Profit at a uniform price and profit potential from price differentiation

shows the profit that we are sacrificing from those customers who have a higher willingness to pay.

There is another group of potential buyers whose willingness to pay is below the optimal price of $105, but above our variable unit costs of $60. Those customers might be willing to pay $95, $85, or $75, but not $105. If we maintain our uniform price at the optimum of $105, these customers will not buy our power tool. Yet if we were able to offer these customers the product at $95, $85, or $75, they would buy and we would earn a positive unit contribution of $35, $25, or $15. That passed-up profit lies in the shaded triangle at the upper right on the left-hand side of Fig. 7.1.

Going from the Profit Rectangle to the Profit Triangle

The critical question is the following: How do we tap into the two areas of profit potential which elude us when we charge a uniform price? This is one of the most interesting, difficult, and potentially lucrative questions in pricing. How do we get from the profit rectangle on the left side of Fig. 7.1 to the profit triangle on the right side? I need to make one important remark before we answer that question: under normal circumstances it is impossible to completely exhaust the potential in the right triangle. That would work only if we managed to get every potential customer to pay his or her individual maximum price. This in turn would require that we are able to discern those maximum prices for each customer, and then segregate the customers to ensure that no buyer pays less than his or her maximum price.

There are situations in which sellers try to do exactly that. A trader at an Oriental bazaar asks a potential buyer all kinds of questions, in order to tease out his or her maximum willingness to pay and then ask for a price which exploits it. The questions can be rather innocuous, such as what kind of car they drive or what and where they studied. The objective of the trader at the bazaar is to obtain the maximum price from every buyer. These efforts can fail, of course, for a number of reasons, such as a bluff by a buyer or the exchange of information among buyers. If one buyer tells another how low the price was for a certain item, the revelation sets a price anchor that the bazaar trader will be hard-pressed to overcome.

Another method for tapping individual willingness to pay is auctions. The auction mechanism of eBay is set up so that every bidder submits his or her maximum price, but without the other bidders seeing it. If the bidder wins, he or she pays only the price of the next highest bidder plus a slight differential. This method is known as a Vickrey auction in which it is optimal for the bidder to reveal his or her maximum price.[2]

In order to get our profits closer to what the profit triangle promises, we need to charge different prices for the same product or for slightly different variants. The phrase "from profit rectangle to profit triangle" makes one point very clear: the profit increase that we can realize from differentiated prices is greater than the profit increases we can get from fine-tuning our way to an optimal uniform price. Comparing the rectangle to the triangle lets us easily visualize and understand this point.

What Does a Can of Coca-Cola Cost?

This harmless question defies a simple answer. It depends entirely on where you buy that can. Figure 7.2 shows the price of a 12-ounce can of Coca-Cola at different points of sale.

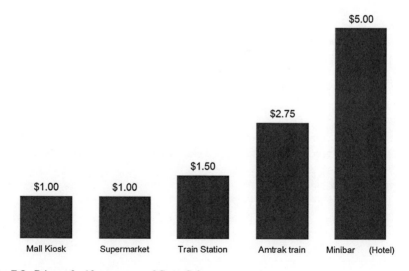

Fig. 7.2 Prices of a 12-ounce can of Coca-Cola

---

[2] Fehr B (1961) Zweitpreis-Auktionen – Von Goethe erdacht, von Ebay genutzt. Frankfurter Allgemeine Zeitung, December 22, 2007, p. 22; Vickrey W, Counterspeculation, Auctions and Competitive Sealed Tenders, Journal of Finance, 1961, pp. 8–37.

The price differences are enormous. We're not talking about differences of 5 or 10 %, but rather 400 %. The highest price is five times the lowest price. Maybe you were familiar with such price differences, but you probably weren't aware of how large they are.

It doesn't take much to figure out why these differences are so huge. The minibar at the hotel is a monopolist. Someone rushing to catch a train has no time for price comparisons or going out of their way, so the newsstand at the train station is their only alternative. The same applies to airports, although there one usually finds a 20-ounce bottle for as much as $3.00 per bottle. Everything at airports is more expensive anyway. The supermarket and the mall kiosks, in contrast, usually face heavy price competition.

Price differentiation is a sensitive area. In Japan, Coca-Cola had the idea of differentiating its prices according to the temperature.[3] When it is hot outside, drinking a cola provides greater utility. It seemed logical to charge more. From a technical standpoint, implementation was easy. One needed only to outfit the vending machines with a thermometer and program the machine to adjust prices accordingly. However, the plan became public and led to protests. Consumers felt that this kind of differentiation was unfair, and Coca-Cola tabled the plans. In Spain, the marketing agency Momentum tried the same idea in reverse. The price of a cola would drop as the temperature rose.[4] Can that be optimal? Yes, it can. Assume that with cold weather consumers buy just one can and are willing to pay $2.50. Even if the price was lowered they wouldn't consume more. The optimal price is then $2.50 and with 1,000 consumers Coca-Cola would earn a revenue of $2,500. Assuming unit costs of 50 cents and neglecting fixed costs a profit of $2,000 would result. Now let's assume that with hot weather people are willing to pay $3 for the first can, $2 for the second, and $1.40 for the third. What is then the optimal price? Coca-Cola could charge $3 per can and sell 1,000 cans. This would yield a revenue of $3,000 and a profit of $2,500—better than the cold weather profit. But is $3 the optimal price? No! If they charge $2 per can 2,000 cans will be bought yielding a revenue of $4,000 and a profit of $3,000. At the even lower price of $1.40 they would even sell 3,000 cans, and get $4,200 in revenue, but profit would decrease to $2,700—less than at the price of $2 which is the optimum in this case. At first thought it's counterintuitive, but it can indeed be optimal to charge a lower price in hot than in cold weather. This case shows how important it is to deeply understand consumers' willingness to pay under specific circumstances.

Here is another case of a weather-based form of price differentiation, employed by an aerial tramway in Germany. During good weather and good visibility, a ride costs 20 Euros; amid bad weather and worse visibility, the trip is 17 Euros because the ride is not as enjoyable, but the company still wants to draw customers. Lufthansa also has a weather-dependent offer for certain destinations and times, under the

---

[3] Hays C. Variable price coke machine being tested. New York Times, October 28, 1999.
[4] Morozov E. Ihr wollt immer nur Effizienz und merkt nicht, dass dadurch die Gesellschaft kaputtgeht. Frankfurter Allgemeine Zeitung, April 10, 2013, p. 27.

name "Sunshine Insurance." For every day that it rains at the given vacation destination, Lufthansa will refund 25 Euros, up to a limit of 200 Euros.

Extreme price differentiation is by no means an exception. The least expensive economy ticket for Lufthansa flight LH 400 from Frankfurt to New York on April 1, 2013, was $734, but for a first-class ticket one would have to pay $8,950.[5] That is a difference of 1,218 %. Granted, traveling in economy and first class is not the same experience, but the passengers still sit in the same airplane and arrive at the same destination at the same time. The basic service—air transport—is the same for all passengers. Up until 1907, Germany's rail service had four classes, and the price gap at the time was around 1,000 %, similar to air travel today.

As with Coca-Cola, the prices for millions of products differ by distribution channel. Massive amounts of fast-moving consumer goods and fashion items are sold on promotion, sometimes as much as 75 % off the regular prices. Hotels differentiate prices based on demand, and during conventions they often charge a multiple of the standard prices. In air transportation, some executives have the notion that every single seat should be sold at a different price. Electricity and telephone rates vary by time of day or day of the week. Restaurants offer lunch deals at lower prices; the same meals will cost much more on the evening dinner menu. Lower prices for advance purchases or early bookings are common. Rental car prices will depend not only on capacity utilization but on a thousand other factors. If you travel within the USA and can show your AAA or AARP card, you can get discounts from hotels, travel agencies, and even at outlet shopping malls. Cinemas and theaters offer lower prices for seniors and students. You can get a volume discount on almost anything you can buy in bulk. Look internationally and you can also see crass differences in prices for the same product. In short: price differentiation is a ubiquitous phenomenon in modern economies. Sellers who don't differentiate their prices run the risk of sacrificing a large amount of profit.

The Difference Two Prices Can Make

So the only motto can be: differentiate your prices! What happens in the example from Fig. 7.1 when we charge two different prices instead of one uniform price? Let us assume that we have a "yes-no" purchase decision; that is, each potential buyer wants only one unit. Then the demand curve results from aggregating the individual maximum prices. Using the data from Fig. 6.2 we know that at a price of $120 we would sell 600,000 units of the power tool and at a second price of $90 we would sell an additional 600,000 units. Figure 7.3 compares the results for the uniform price of $105 and the price differentiation with prices of $120 and $90. We assume that the buyers can be separated according to their willingness to pay.

We can increase our profits dramatically by charging two prices ($120 and $90) instead of the uniform price of $105. If we can find a way to sort the potential buyers

---

[5] Prices requested on www.lufthansa.com on March 15, 2013; the lowest economy-class price is for a restricted, round-trip ticket; the highest first-class price was for a flexible, one-way fare.

	Uniform Price	Price differentiation (two prices)	
		High price	Low price
Price ($)	105	120	90
Volume (units)	900,000	600,000	600,000
Revenue ($)	94.5 mill.	72.0 mill.	54.0 mill.
Variable costs ($)	54.0 mill.	36.0 mill.	36.0 mill.
Contribution ($)	40.5 mill.	36.0 mill.	18.0 mill.
Fixed costs ($)	30.0 mill.	30.0 mill.	
Profit ($)	10.5 mill.	24.0 mill.	
Profit index (%)	100	229	

Fig. 7.3 The effects of price differentiation with two prices

according to their maximum prices (= their willingness to pay), then everyone whose maximum price is at $120 or more will pay $120. The price of $90 will attract all potential buyers whose maximum prices lie between $90 and just under $120. With two prices, our profit in this example jumps to $24.0 million vs. $10.5 million at a uniform price, a huge difference of 129 %.

Are there risks in doing this? Yes! If the potential buyers with a willingness to pay $120 or more find a way to get the product at $90, our profits will look a lot worse than if we had a uniform price of $105. In the extreme case that all such buyers make their purchase at $90, we will sell 1,200,000 units, but our unit contribution drops to $30. That leaves us with a contribution of $36 million and a net profit of $6 million after subtracting fixed costs. That is 43 % less than what we would earn with the uniform price of $105, a disastrous profit decline. Price differentiation only makes sense when one succeeds in erecting a "fence" between the potential buyers with a higher and those with a lower willingness to pay. Without an effective fence, price differentiation is a dangerous endeavor. We will deal with the critical aspect of fencing later in this chapter.

Why the First Beer Should Be More Expensive

Price differentiation presents a different challenge when the consumer can buy more or less of the same product depending on its price. This is the "variable quantity" case. Let's imagine that a thirsty hiker shows up at a remote inn. According to the law of diminishing marginal utility, the first beer that this hiker drinks has a greater utility for him than the second, which in turn has a greater utility than the third one. The hiker may therefore be willing to pay $5 for the first beer, $4 for the second, $3 for the third, $2.50 for the fourth, and $2 for the fifth one. More beers than that bring the hiker no additional utility. He will not consume more than five glasses, even if the sixth were offered for free.

What is the profit-maximizing price structure for the innkeeper? The answer is simple: $5 for the first beer, $4 for the second, $3 for the third, $2.50 for fourth, and $2 for the fifth and final one. This kind of price structure is called "nonlinear"; each individual unit has its own price point. Under the nonlinear price structure above, the hiker drinks five beers and spends $16.50, or an average of $3.30 per glass. If the variable unit cost for each beer is 50 cents, the innkeeper earns a profit contribution of $14. So why shouldn't the innkeeper make things simpler and just charge a price of $3.30 per beer instead of using the complex nonlinear price structure based on marginal utility? At a uniform price of $3.30, the hiker would only buy two beers (because the price is less than his marginal utility). That leaves the innkeeper with a revenue of $6.60 and a profit contribution of $5.60, which is 60 % below the profit he would have gotten from the nonlinear price structure. What would have been the profit-maximizing uniform price in this case? It would be $2.50. At the price the hiker buys four beers and pays $10. That leaves the innkeeper with a profit contribution of $8, which is still 43 % less than he would have received had he differentiated his prices according to the nonlinear structure. If he had set his uniform price at $3 or $2 per beer, the profit contribution would have been lower, at $7.50 in each case.

This case provides us with several important insights. It confirms the huge profit potential that proper price differentiation can unlock. It also shows that a prerequisite for optimal price differentiation is detailed knowledge about the buyers' willingness to pay. Implementing this kind of price differentiation can be rather complicated. For example, the innkeeper needs to keep track of exactly how many beers each of his guests has consumed. He must also guard against arbitrage, which occurs when one guest buys as many beers as he can at low prices and then distributes them to other guests. Finally, the guests may resist such a price structure. If the innkeeper sets his prices to tap 100 % of each consumer's willingness to pay, their consumer surplus from drinking beer at the inn is zero. That can lead to serious dissatisfaction. These practical difficulties may explain why such nonlinear price systems—with prices differentiated according to a guest's marginal utility—have not established themselves in the restaurant and hospitality business.

Nonlinear Pricing for a Cinema

The law of diminishing marginal utility applies not only to consumer products, but also to services. The first visit to the movies in a given month has a higher utility than the second one, etc. In the case below, a cinema chain in Europe serves three customer segments, which we will call A, B, and C. Each segment is characterized by a different willingness to pay for the first, second, third, etc. visit in a given month. Figure 7.4 shows the data for this case.

The optimal uniform price is €5.50. At this price, Segment A's customers would go to the movies 2,000 times, B's would go 3,000, and C's would go 4,000 times. That works out to 9,000 visits in a month and a profit of €49,500.

To determine the optimal price differentiation, we use nonlinear pricing. The first step is to determine the profit-maximizing price for the first visit. This price is €9;

Visit	Maximum prices (€)			Optimal non-linear price structure (€)	Visits (in 1,000)	Profit (€) (in 1,000)
	A	B	C			
1	9.00	10.00	12.00	9.00	3	27.00
2	6.00	7.50	10.00	6.00	3	18.00
3	3.50	5.50	8.00	5.50	2	11.00
4	2.00	4.00	6.00	4.00	2	8.00
5	1.10	1.50	3.50	3.50	1	3.50
Total					11	67.50
Optimal uniform price				5.50	9	49.50

Fig. 7.4 Nonlinear pricing for a chain of movie theaters

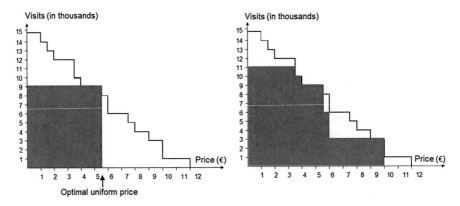

Fig. 7.5 Uniform vs. nonlinear pricing

customers from all three segments attend, and the profit is €27,000. If the price were €10, only customers from Segments B and C would attend, and the profit would fall to €20,000. If they charged €12 for that first visit, only segment C would visit and profits would be just €12,000.

Setting prices in the same manner for subsequent visits results in the nonlinear price structure shown in column 5 of Fig. 7.4. The prices range from €9 for the first visit to €3.50 for the fifth. In the spirit of the phrase "from profit rectangle to profit triangle," Fig. 7.5 illustrates just how dramatic the profit difference is between uniform and nonlinear pricing.

Price differentiation (shown on the right) does a much better job of exploiting the profit potential in the triangle than uniform pricing (shown on the left). The total profit from nonlinear pricing comes to €67,500, which is 37.7 % more than the €49,500 the cinema would earn from a uniform price. The number of visits rises as well, from 9,000 per month to 11,000, with an average ticket price of €6.14 vs. €5.50 in the case of a uniform price. Such simultaneous increases in volume and price are not possible with a uniform price and a normal (downward-sloping) demand curve. You can only accomplish such a result with this kind of complex price structure, which lets you eat into the two smaller profit triangles and strongly increase your overall profit. This structure does a much better job than a uniform price does in attracting buyers with a higher willingness to pay (over €5.50) and a lower maximum willingness to pay (under €5.50). The implementation in this case was simple. The customers who participated in the program received a card with their name on it. Upon each successive visit, the card would get stamped to indicate the first, second, third, etc. visit during the month. In contrast to the beer example, this card system prevents arbitrage, because the theater tracks each individual's actual usage.

Price Bundling

When a seller packages several products together and charges a total price less than the sum of the individual product prices, it is called price bundling. Bundling is a very effective way to differentiate prices.[6] Whoever buys multiple products at once rather than a single product receives a bundle discount. Widely known examples of such bundles are the numbered menus at McDonald's (burger, fries, and soft drink), the Microsoft Office suite, and the all-inclusive packages from travel agents, which include flight, hotel, and rental car.

The film industry was a pioneer in the use of price bundling through a tactic known as "block booking." The distributor didn't offer theater operators the movies on an individual basis, which would probably prompt the operators to pick only the most attractive titles. Instead they offered a block of films—usually a selection of attractive and less attractive titles.[7]

Why is price bundling so advantageous? We can answer that question using a simple example involving wine and cheese. Figure 7.6 shows the maximum prices (willingness to pay) of five consumers for both products. We assume that the maximum price for a bundle of wine and cheese equals the sum of the buyer's individual maxima for each product.

What are the profit-maximizing prices for wine, cheese, and the bundle? Let's assume that variable unit costs are zero. That assumption makes the math simpler without changing the underlying argument. The optimal price for cheese in isolation is $5. At that price, consumers 1 and 3 buy, and the profit (in this case equal to the revenue) is $10. If the seller charged $3 per piece of cheese, three consumers would buy, but the profit would be only $9. For wine, the optimal price is $4, with consumers 2 and 3 buying at that price. The profit (again, equal to the revenue) is $8. In total—with wine and cheese sold separately at their profit-optimal prices—the total profit is $18.

---

[6] For a comprehensive treatment of price bundling, please see Georg Wübker. Optimal Bundling: Marketing Strategies for Improving Economic Performance, Springer, New York, 1999.
[7] The US Supreme Court upheld a ban on block booking in 1962, citing price discrimination.

Consumer	Maximum price ($)		
	Wine	Cheese	Bundle of wine and cheese
1	1.00	6.00	7.00
2	5.00	2.00	7.00
3	4.00	5.00	9.00
4	2.50	3.00	5.50
5	1.80	2.40	4.20

Fig. 7.6   Maximum price for wine and cheese and for the bundle of both

Is it possible to make more money than $18 through bundling? Yes, one could offer a wine-and-cheese bundle for $5.50 and consumers 1 through 4 would buy. Only consumer 5 would decline the bundle at that price. The profit from the bundle is $22. This is so-called pure bundling, because the supplier offers only the bundle; that is, consumers can buy neither wine nor cheese separately. Even though the supplier offers a bundle discount of 39 % relative to the sum of the individual prices, his profit increases by 22.2 %. How can that be? The answer lies in the fact that the bundle does a better job at exploiting the consumers' maximum prices (willingness to pay) than the individual prices do. By charging individual prices, the seller sacrifices profit potential both at the high end and at the low end. Consumer 1 would have paid $6 for cheese, but only needs to pay $5. The same applies for consumer 2 and wine. The consumers with lower willingness to pay do not buy when the prices are $4 (wine) and $5 (cheese). But when the seller offers a bundle, the excess willingness to pay for one product gets transferred to the other product. Consumer 1 had a very low maximum price for wine, but when one adds in the higher maximum price for cheese, consumer 1 becomes a buyer of both products. The same applies for consumer 2 and consumer 4. Another way to interpret this transfer of excess willingness to pay is to say that the different levels of willingness to pay for the bundle are less heterogeneous than the levels of willingness to pay for the individual products. The high and low willingnesses to pay for the separate products balance each other out to some degree. This means that it is easier to segment buyers and non-buyers at the bundle level.

The profit increase from $18 to $22 is a big improvement. But the profit situation gets even better when the seller practices "mixed bundling," which means that buyers can buy either the bundle or the products separately. In our example, the optimal bundle price remains at $5.50 with mixed bundling. The optimal individual prices are $4 for wine and $2.40 for cheese. Consumers 1 through 4 would still buy the bundle, and consumer 5 buys the cheese. This increases the total profit to $24.40. Despite a 39 % bundle discount off the sum of the individual prices, the seller's profit jumps by 35.6 % when mixed bundling is applied.

Price Bundling for Optional Accessories

Car manufacturers offer a whole list of optional accessories at additional prices. For the individual customer, putting together one's own package of options can be a tiresome chore. It can also be a bit of a shock, once the customer tallies up the separate prices for each option and looks at the grand total. This can be a strain for the manufacturer as well; the extreme customization would create a burden because of the high logistics costs. One premium carmaker asked Simon-Kucher & Partners to configure optimal bundle packages for their optional accessories and then set the prices for them. We suggested to define three bundles (or packages): comfort, sports, and safety. Figure 7.7 shows the resulting profit.

Despite a bundle discount of 21 %, profits rose by 25 % compared to selling the optional accessories on an individual basis. This is another example of mixed bundling, which means that customers can either buy a package or buy individual options separately. The additional revenue from the packages offset the cost of the bundle discount by a wide margin. The car manufacturer saw other advantages from its mixed-bundling approach. The optional packages proved to be easier to advertise and sell than individual options. The higher level of standardization via the option packages also reduced the cost and complexity of internal logistics. This case again illustrates very clearly the kind of higher profits clever price structures can unlock.

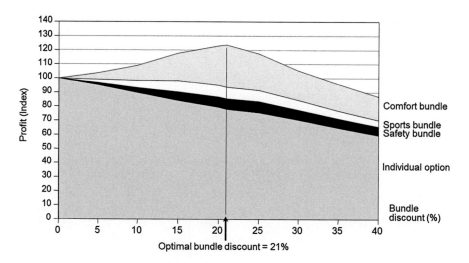

Fig. 7.7 Bundling for optional accessories

Unbundling

Despite the impressive profit improvements above, one cannot make a blanket statement that price bundling is always better. There are situations in which unbundling—the elimination of bundles by breaking them up into their constituent parts—can actually be more profitable. Similarly, there is no definitive answer to the question of whether pure bundling or mixed bundling will generate higher profits. The optimal solution always depends on the respective distribution of the customers' willingness to pay.

I recommend to consider unbundling under these conditions:

– *Opportunities for a higher margin:* This opportunity exists when the individual products have relatively low price elasticities. Such a situation comes about when the bundle price evolves over time and ends up becoming very high.
– *Market expansion:* The company can open new markets or market segments if it sells components on a stand-alone basis.
– *Increasing standardization and compatibility:* The more components become standardized and compatible, the riskier it becomes to pursue pure bundling, because each customer can put together his or her own individual package. The supplier faces a dilemma. It can fence itself off from the competition (through pure bundling) or it can unbundle and expand its market. In the course of a product life cycle and as the market matures, the balance tips increasingly in favor of unbundling.
– *A shift in the value <u>chain</u>:* In many industries there is a clear trend toward charging separately for value-added services which used to be included in the price of the product.

A well-known example of unbundling is the ongoing trend toward charging baggage fees and other surcharges in addition to the price of a plane ticket. Ryanair pioneered this trend. An interesting case is the television function in the BMW 7 series. The first generation of the navigation system in the 7 series included television at no extra charge. Subsequent generations offered television, but for a separate charge.[8]

Multi-Person Pricing

Multi-person pricing means setting a price for groups of people. The total price will vary by the number of people. Travel agents make offers which allow partners or children to travel at reduced prices or for free. Airlines sometimes will let a second guest or a partner fly at half-price or free. Some restaurants will charge half-price for a dish if one person pays full price. Northwest Airlines, now part of Delta

---

[8] www.bmw.de, as of February 23, 2013.

Airlines, once practiced a particularly original form of multi-person pricing: if a child paid the full price, an adult could fly for free. This tactic proved quite popular.

The profit increase from multi-person pricing derives from two effects, similar to price bundling: it does a better job of exploiting the consumer surpluses of hetero-geneous groups of customers, and it transfers excess willingness to pay from one person to another person. The following example illustrates these effects. For sim-plicity's sake, we will assume that both fixed and marginal costs are zero.

A wife is thinking about accompanying her husband on a business trip. The hus-band's maximum willingness to pay is $1,000. The wife's willingness to pay is $750. If the uniform price for the flight is $1,000, only the husband would go on the trip. The profit would be $1,000. If the airline offered a uniform price of $750, then both would fly. The profit rises to $1,500 ($2 \times 750), making $750 the optimal uni-form price. But it gets better. Using multi-person bundling, the airline sets the total price for the married couple to fly at $1,750, which in this simplified example is also its profit. This is a profit increase of 16.7 % relative to the optimal uniform price. Multi-person pricing takes advantage of the maximum prices of each individual in order to achieve higher profits.

Something which doesn't fall under multi-person pricing is the situation when consumers themselves bundle their demand, in order to press for a bigger discount. This method is somewhat common for the purchase of heating oil. Websites also exist to help individuals bundle their demand in order to extract lower prices. But in general this method is not very widespread.

The More, the Cheaper? Be Careful!

The most common form of volume-dependent price differentiation is the volume discount. The more someone buys, the higher the discount, which means that the customer pays a lower price per unit. Everyone knows this "universal law" and takes it for granted. But even with volume discounts, the devil is in the details. The result depends on how the volume discount is structured.

There are essentially two forms of volume discounts: full-volume and incremen-tal discounts. The full-volume variant means that the discount rate applies to the entire purchase volume. The incremental rebate means that the discount rate applies only to the incremental volume, not the full volume. This difference may sound harmless, but it is quite powerful. Let's look at the numbers in Fig. 7.8, which again uses numbers derived from our power tool case. We assume a list price of $100 and variable unit costs of $60. For simplicity's sake we assume fixed costs to be zero. Up to 99 units, the discount is zero. The discount is 10 % from 100 units onward, 20 % from 200 units onward, and 30 % for 300 units or more.

Using the full-volume discount—which applies to the total number of units purchased—the seller achieves revenue of $21,000 and a profit of $3,000 if he sells 300 units. But if he chooses the incremental discount—which applies a different discount rate to each portion of the 300 units—the seller earns $24,000 in revenue

Discount	Applies ...	Full volume discount		Incremental volume discount	
		Revenue	Avg. price	Revenue	Avg. price
0%	up to 99 units				
10%	from 100 units	$9,000	$90	$9,000	$90
20%	from 200 units	$16,000	$80	$17,000	$85
30%	from 300 units	$21,000	$70	$24,000	$80

Fig. 7.8 Full volume vs. incremental volume discounts

(an increase of 14.3 %) and a profit of $6,000 (an increase of 100 %). What looks like a relatively innocuous difference in the discount structure actually doubles the seller's profits. Sellers should choose incremental discounts whenever possible. For buyers the opposite advice applies. They should ask for full-volume discounts. In other words both buyers and sellers should focus not only on the percentage of discount they receive, but also the structure of the discount.

Differentiation or Discrimination?

A common form of price differentiation is person specific; different people pay different prices for the exact same product. Isn't that discrimination? The term "price discrimination" is often used synonymously with "price differentiation." In reality, person-specific price differentiation is a sensitive topic. If you were to find out that a friend of yours paid 25 % less for a product from the same seller as you did, you would not be pleased. Amazon suffered very negative publicity when it leaked that it was differentiating prices for DVDs according to personal profiles or browsers. Amid the intense public outcry, Amazon stopped the practice and reimbursed buyers.[9] The opportunities to conduct this kind of person- or user-specific price differentiation—and the temptation to actually act on them—multiply as Internet usage grows. One study showed significant behavioral differences among the users who booked hotels using an Apple Mac vs. customers who used another kind of PC.[10] The Mac users paid $20–$30 more on average per night. That makes a big difference when the average price for a hotel room booked online is $100. Mac users also made 40 % more reservations in 4-star and 5-star hotels. Such insights build a strong case for differentiating service and prices by user. But as the Amazon experience showed, sellers should be cautious in taking advantage of such insights.

It remains to be seen whether the following form of person-specific price differentiation becomes a standard. The airline Samoa Air Ltd. charges passengers

[9] Spiekermann S. Individual Price Discrimination—An Impossibility? Institute of Information Services, Humboldt University; see also "Caveat Emptor.com", The Economist, June 30, 2012.
[10] On Orbitz, Mac Users Steered to Pricier Hotels. The Wall Street Journal, June 26, 2012, p. A1.

according to their body weight. The price for a flight from Samoa to American Samoa costs 92 cents per kilogram. Samoa has the world's third highest level of overweight people. CEO Chris Langton is sticking to the plan, despite initial protests. "It's a pay by weight system and it's here to stay," he said.[11] The logic speaks for such a system. The weight of passengers is a cost driver for an airline. Why should the transport of freight be charged by weight, but not the transport of people? In the meantime, Samoa Air has adopted the slogan "A kilo is a kilo is a kilo" and continues to describe its pricing strategy as "the fairest way of paying for carriage."[12] Some US airlines have started to demand that extremely large passengers buy two tickets on a full flight. Personally I do not see this as a violation of their rights. Social acceptance of the approach is another matter. But who knows?

On the other hand, there are numerous person-specific price differentiation schemes which enjoy mainstream acceptance. These include all manner of discounts for children, students, veterans, and seniors. Nobody seems to mind that people who belong to certain organizations or clubs receive special prices or discounts. More critical from a consumer perspective, yet more interesting from a seller perspective are successful attempts to differentiate prices according to criteria such as buying power or price sensitivity. But in any situation in which buyers and sellers negotiate prices individually, that is precisely the goal. The list price forms just the starting point for individual price differentiation. When someone purchases a car, the degree to which willingness to pay gets exploited depends on the talent of the salesperson.

Person-specific price differentiation can also reflect the cost and risk differences among people. At the Italian bank UniCredit Banca, interest rates on loans depend on the past credit history and behavior of the person taking out the loan. The bank rewards loyalty and prompt payment with lower interest rates. The bank charges a spread of 100 basis points over the base interest rate in years 1–3. The spread then shrinks by 10 basis points each year (down to a minimum of 70 basis points) if the customer has made his or her payments on time. For a mortgage of $500,000, that can mean an annual savings of $1,500 per year.

More multi-faceted than in the traditional world are the attempts at person-specific price differentiation online. E-commerce suppliers learn a lot about their customers from all the individual transactions, and in extreme cases they can vary prices at the individual level. It has been said that online companies use a form of peak and off-peak pricing, charging more in the evenings than they do during the day. There are good arguments for this kind of time-based differentiation, which in reality is a form of person-specific price differentiation. During the day, it is more likely that price-sensitive teenagers and college students are online. Adults are more likely to be at work during the day, but tend to have higher purchasing power and lower price sensitivity. They also tend to order more online in the evenings. Doesn't it seem to make perfect sense to offer lower prices during the day and higher prices in the evening?

---

[11] Craymer L. (2013) Weigh more, pay more on Samoa Air. *The Wall Street Journal*, April 3, 2013.

[12] http://www.samoaair.ws/.

Recently I ordered a pair of shoes online from Zalando. Since then, it seems that every third webpage that I visit has some kind of advertisement for shoes. Zalando and others are able to place their ads on other websites and target me directly. If that is possible with advertisements, then it is possible with prices. This is one approach to go from the profit rectangle to the profit triangle, assuming that one has valid information about the willingness to pay of individual customers. "Big Data," the analysis of large amounts of data about transactions on an individual basis, opens up fantastic new opportunities for person-specific price differentiation. Interesting here is the question of whether consumers should occasionally order a very inexpensive product, in order to convey a high level of price sensitivity to the seller. This could trigger advertisements for special offers and attractive prices—a new kind of cat-and-mouse game.

Implementing person-specific price differentiation requires some effort. One needs to ensure that the potential customer belongs to the qualifying class (e.g., student ID card, proof of birth date) or issue the customer a special card (club card for BJ's, AAA card, or any number of retailer-specific cards).[13] For online businesses, the individual transactions of the customers must be stored and analyzed. Banks and insurance companies have collected since time immemorial every customer transaction, but the companies usually lacked the analytical competence to take advantage of this data and customize their offers for each client. The question remains relevant: To what degree can a company truly influence the behavior of individual customers? I have personally ordered several hundred books from Amazon, but have never received a recommendation from them for a book to buy which resulted in a purchase. In my case, whatever analytical work they did was all for naught. As for those annoying shoe advertisements from Zalando: they turned me off rather than increasing the chances I would make another purchase. Having said that, I don't discourage this practice. But I do believe that it needs to improve. One issue is that the data and the algorithms don't reveal the underlying behavioral drivers. With regard to prices, this is especially challenging, because the online seller knows only the price the customer has paid, but without additional information (e.g., from tests) they cannot be sure about the customer's price sensitivity.

Price and Location

Historically, a classic brand-name article had an identical price no matter where you purchased it. Manufacturers had the right to dictate the retail or end-user price for all resellers throughout the entire country. In most countries this ended in the 1960s and 1970s. After that only specific products fell under the so-called resale price maintenance. These rules differ from country to country. For most products, retailers are free to set prices. This led to regional and channel price differences. Unlike the manufacturer-prescribed prices of the past, the new prices reflect differences in purchasing power (in New York City, some prices are higher than in rural towns, but some are lower) as well as differences in competitive intensity and costs (gas gets

---

[13] BJ's is a club store in the USA; AAA is the American Automobile Association.

more expensive the further the gas station is away from a refinery and the lower the competitive density is).

Antitrust laws generally forbid manufacturers from exerting influence on the prices retailers charge, though a ruling by the US Supreme Court in 2007 overturned one long-standing pillar of the Sherman Antitrust Act.[14] The court declared in its decision on *Leegin Creative Leather Products, Inc. v. PSKS, Inc* that vertical price restraints were no longer *per se* illegal, but rather subject to the rule of reason. In other words, under certain circumstances a supplier could indeed justify setting minimum retail price requirements or pulling supplies from a retailer who prices the products too low. An intense discussion is going on in Europe because manufacturers are demanding some influence on the retail prices.

Prices can differ a lot between countries. This is partially due to institutional peculiarities, taxes, and differences in distribution systems. In Luxembourg, the price of gasoline is about 20 % lower than in Germany, which has resulted in Luxembourg having one of the world's greatest concentrations of gas stations along its German border. Some price-sensitive customers travel as far as 50 miles to fill up both their car gas tanks and their gas canisters. Cigarettes and coffee are also much cheaper in Luxembourg, and many people buy these products on their trips to get gas. That may have led to some absurd unexpected consequences. The rate of lung cancer in the German city of Trier (located near the Luxembourg border) is significantly higher than in the rest of Germany. So far no one has established the cause for this, but one hypothesis claims that the lower cigarette prices in Luxembourg and the ensuing higher rate of smokers in the Trier region are responsible. When the Euro saw a massive devaluation against the Swiss franc in 2011, eager Swiss consumers practically invaded southern Germany, because the prices there—expressed in Swiss francs—were so much lower than in Switzerland.[15]

The biggest advantage of regional or international price differentiation is effective fencing. If a product is only slightly cheaper at a store about 50 miles away from home, no one is going to drive that distance to buy it. On the other hand, as we learned in detail earlier, rational behavior is not always the norm. Does a trip to Luxembourg to get gas really save money, especially when one considers all the cost—both time and money—in driving anywhere from 25 to 50 miles? People often look only at their immediate "out-of-pocket" cost savings rather than at total costs of a purchase.

One study revealed irrational behavior regarding distances. It involved jackets and windbreakers. Test Group A saw a jacket with a price of $125. They also heard that they could buy the same exact jacket for $5 less from the same store chain, but they would need to drive 20 minutes to get there. Test Group B saw a windbreaker for $15, and then learned that they could buy the same windbreaker for $10 at the same store 20 minutes drive away. In both cases, the saving in absolute terms was $5. In Test Group B, some 68 % of participants were willing to drive the 20 minutes

---

[14] Century-Old Ban Lifted on Minimum Retail Pricing. The New York Times, June 29, 2007.

[15] Ohne Schweiz kein Preis. Frankfurter Allgemeine Zeitung, February 7, 2012, p. 3.

to get the lower price, but in Test Group A only 29 % were willing to make the same trip.[16] Apparently a saving of $5 on a price of $125 isn't worth the trip, but saving $5 on a price of $15 is something else. One can also interpret this in another way: the utility (in this case, negative) of the distance is not absolute, but relative. This has implications for regional price differentiation and for fencing.

Fencing of price differences by country is particularly effective. But there are exceptions here as well. If the price differences are large and at the same time the arbitrage costs (for transportation, customs duties, bureaucracy, and product adaptations) are low, one will see so-called gray or parallel imports, which is the flow of goods, unauthorized by the manufacturer, across borders. In pharmaceuticals, parallel imports play a major role. The company Kohlpharma generated revenues of $760 million in 2012 through parallel imports from other EU countries into Germany. International price differences are also substantial in the automotive market. It is estimated that the auto industry's profits in Europe would fall by 25 % if prices were uniform across the continent. Or put another way: one-quarter of the profits of car manufacturers in Europe comes from international price differentiation. Parallel imports do not play a major role in this market, though, because of difficulties in acquiring the cars (manufacturers control the number of cars they provide to each country) and because the arbitrage costs are rather high.

When the unified European common market came about, many companies responded by introducing uniform prices throughout the European Union. That is a simple strategy, but not a wise one by any means. Those companies sacrificed the profit potential that price differentiation across countries offers. One could even say that a uniform European price made less and less sense as the countries of Southern Europe slipped deeper into crisis, because of the growing gap in purchasing power between North and South. On the other hand, it remains impossible to maintain the once large price differences between countries, because they can cause significant market disruptions through gray imports. The solution is a compromise. For that purpose, Simon-Kucher & Partners has developed the so-called INTERPRICE model, which develops optimal international price corridors. The corridors take advantage of differences in markets while keeping gray imports at tolerable levels.[17]

Price and Time

Playing off an old Latin saying, one could say "Tempora mutantur et pretii mutantur in illis" which means "The times are changing, and prices are changing with them." Time-based price differentiation is one of the most important and widely used methods to go from the profit rectangle to the profit triangle. It comes in endless variations, from time of day to day of the week, to seasonal prices, advance booking discounts, last-minute offers, winter or summer clearance sales, Black Friday, and

---

[16]Trevisan E (2013) The Irrational Consumer: Applying Behavioural Economics to Your Business Strategy, Gower Publishing, Farnham Surrey, UK.

[17]Simon-Kucher & Partners, INTERPRICE-Model for the Determination of an International Price Corridor, Bonn, several years.

"special introductory offers." It also plays a role in "dynamic pricing," which adjusts prices as supply and demand fluctuate over time.

The driver behind successful time-based price differentiation—as with the other forms we discussed—is the fact that individuals at different times have different levels of willingness to pay. During a vacation period or a trade fair, people are willing to pay more for a hotel room than at other times. The sellers would be negligent if they failed to increase their prices in those situations. Closely related to this idea is the balance between supply and demand. The traditional peak-load pricing applied by electrical utilities pursues precisely that kind of balancing. Dynamic pricing emphasizes that same goal but combines it with an attempt to increase profits, not just control supply and demand.

Parking garages provide a good example of dynamic pricing. In their case, "dynamic" means that there is no set price per hour for a parking space. The price at any given time depends on availability. The garages at Heathrow Airport in London use this approach, as do other garages throughout the world. The price is adjusted so that a customer with the corresponding willingness to pay will always find a parking spot. On two occasions I have missed a flight because I couldn't find a parking space. My willingness to pay in each of those situations was extremely high, but because the garages charged a uniform rate, two things happened: the garages were full, and the garage also lost a chance to make a lot more money. Both the parking garage operator and I would have benefited from dynamic pricing.

It is not unusual, though, for a company to go completely overboard with the idea of time-based price differentiation. One downtown parking garage in my hometown has several hundred spaces that cost 2.50 Euros ($3.25) per hour on weekdays. On Sundays, the price drops to just 1 Euro ($1.30). Yet on Sundays the garage remains almost entirely empty. Where is the mistake? The garage operator mistook low demand for higher price elasticity. The garage isn't empty on Sundays because the weekday price of $3.25 per hour is too high. It is empty because very few people drive into the city center on Sundays anyway. The price cut to $1.30 is ineffective in attracting more demand. The operator is simply giving money away.

In a project for a large movie theater chain in England, Simon-Kucher & Partners discovered similar errors. The chain had offered discounts of 25 % on certain weekdays and at certain times, but saw no corresponding uptick in demand. We created a price structure that allowed the chain to capture higher profits in periods of higher demand. The chain offered a discount only on one day a week—it's so-called cheap day—but at a discount level so high that it actually filled the theaters. The new structure was tested at several locations prior to a broader rollout. As expected, the total number of guests declined slightly, but the chain saw a massive increase in profits. What is the lesson from the garages and the cinema chain? Not the demand level as such is relevant for optimal dynamic pricing; it is the way customers respond to different prices at different times, in other words: the price elasticity. Unless you know it you are just fishing in muddy waters.

Perishable Goods

Perishable goods present a tricky challenge for time-based price differentiation. How should a bakery or a fresh-fruit stand price its goods shortly before closing for the day? If they don't sell the products today, they become worthless. No one wants to buy day-old bread or spoiled fruit or vegetables. But "perishable goods" also include hotel rooms, seats on an airplane, or space on a tour. Every empty seat on a flight costs the airline revenue and profit.

Costs here are "sunk" and no longer play a role for the "last-minute" price decision. From a short-term perspective, the solution is clear. Every price above zero is better than letting a good spoil or let capacity remain unsold. This would imply that the seller should offer very favorable "last-minute" prices in order to fill seats or empty the shelf.

But this tactic has a catch. If last-minute prices become a rule customers will learn it and will increasingly attempt to do their shopping at the last minute in order to take advantage of the bargain prices. One housekeeper told me that she is usually buying her bread in a bakery which offers last-minute prices shortly before the store closes. The fencing between normal prices and last-minute prices breaks down, and the seller will then cannibalize his full-priced sales. That is precisely the reason why many companies let the goods spoil or leave the seats empty rather than resort to a predictable pattern of last-minute pricing. Of course in an individual case it is hard to quantify these two contravening effects—protecting higher price sales versus losing potential revenue by letting goods "spoil"—and weigh them against each other. But in my experience, in many cases it is wise to avoid the practice of last-minute pricing.

The possibilities for pricing in peak and off-peak periods are often asymmetrical. One can use price cuts to encourage someone to run a washing machine or a dishwasher in periods when electricity demand is low. And one can use higher prices to stunt demand in peak periods. With demand at restaurants or on the rails, however, the situation is different. Even if the restaurant or railroad offers low prices on a Monday evening, they will not have a full house or train. On the other hand, they do have opportunities to charge more in peak periods. But this is a sensitive issue, because consumers often react negatively to this price "gouging."

Patents for Dynamic Pricing

The following story shows what dimensions the battle for leadership in the area of dynamic pricing has taken on. Google submitted a patent application for dynamic pricing on September 30, 2011.[18] The summary of the patent refers among other things to "Methods, systems and apparatus, including computer programs for dynamically pricing electronic content ... adjusting a base price associated with

---

[18] US Patent Office, Application Number 13/249 910, September 30, 2011.

purchasing the item of electronic content, and providing the particular user with an offer to repurchase the item at the adjusted price." Google feels that it has a proprietary method for time-based price differentiation and wants to secure its rights to it.

What are the limits of dynamic pricing? It seems that some companies can be outright crass in the way they approach it online. The most frequent price changes occur for consumer electronics, apparel, shoes, and jewelry. It is not unusual for prices of these products to change several times an hour. Altogether the e-commerce world sees millions of price changes every day, a phenomenon we previously only witnessed with the airlines. In e-commerce, a primary goal is to make sure that one's site appears first in search-engine results.[19] When this effort relies primarily on price changes, which usually means lowering the price, it can become a profit-destroying pastime, creating behavioral patterns that drive prices ever further downward. It is a classic game-theory dilemma which favors only the buyers. It remains to be seen what kind of battles we will observe as companies fight for leadership in dynamic pricing and the first place in the search engines' lists.

Juggling Capacities and Prices

A particularly complex form of time-based price differentiation is what many companies refer to as "revenue management" or "yield management." Airlines practice this with great intensity and a high level of professionalism. Models, data analysis, and forecasting techniques play a key role. The goal is to generate the maximum revenue and return from each and every flight. To achieve this, the airlines combine product and price policies. For example, they increase or decrease their capacity in business class by moving the bulkhead wall forward or backward. Depending on the demand forecast, every price point will be allocated a certain number of seats out of the available capacity. Depending on how the actual bookings develop, airlines can adjust these assigned price-capacity combinations on an ongoing basis. This explains the phenomenon many of us have witnessed, sometimes to our benefit and sometimes to our chagrin. It can happen that we can book a flight at $59 at one point, and then see that the exact same flight costs $99 half an hour later. The revenue manager must make decisions like this: sell a seat now for $59 or hold that seat back in the hope—based on the adjusted models and the forecasts—that someone will buy that seat later for $99. In the latter case, the revenue manager takes the risk that the seat remains unsold.

Airlines, hotel chains, car rental services, and other similar business all practice some form of revenue management. It helps them to better manage their capacity and its utilization. But it is by no means a perfect solution, as shown by a conversation I once had with the revenue manager of the landmark Hilton Hotel in downtown Chicago.

"Tonight I have 13 empty rooms out of 1,600, even though the rest of Chicago is sold out," he said. "That is 13 rooms too many."

---

[19] Don't Like This Price? Wait a Minute. The Wall Street Journal, September 6, 2012, p. 21.

	13 empty rooms	50 empty rooms	200 empty rooms
Price ($)	100	110	110
Rooms sold	1,587	1,550	1,400
Revenue ($)	158,700	170,500	154,000

Fig. 7.9 Prices and rooms sold

"Are you sure about that?" I said asked. "Maybe it would have been better to raise the average price from $100 to $110 and have 50 empty rooms." Figure 7.9 compares two alternatives to what could have happened on that night.

If the average price were $110 and 50 rooms had remained unsold, the manager would have had a decent increase in revenue. This simple example reveals the core problem of revenue management. The unsold capacity is "hard" data which puts downward pressure on prices. The untapped willingness to pay of hotel guests on a given night is "soft" data with a high level of uncertainty. The Hilton Chicago manager knew "with certainty" that 13 rooms remaining empty at $100 meant $1,300 in foregone revenue. But he was unsure of whether 1,550 guests would have willingly paid the extra $10 and only 37 guests would have booked their room elsewhere. If only 1,400 guests would have paid the higher price, the revenue would have fallen to $154,000, as the fourth column in Fig. 7.9 shows. Revenue management is the best possible way to navigate all this uncertainty and achieve a desirable outcome. The better the forecasts are, the greater its profit contribution.

Price and Scarcity

A very sensitive issue is pricing during periods of scarcity or during an emergency. Hurricane Sandy provides a telling example. This storm struck the east coast of the USA in the fall of 2012, touching of a state of emergency which lasted for days, in some areas weeks. The demand for emergency electrical generators skyrocketed. What does a seller do in such a situation? He faces a dilemma. If he leaves his prices at normal levels, his supply will sell out in nothing flat. Clever buyers will buy up several units—the same way some people hoard food supplies—which leaves many people empty-handed or struggling to find alternatives. In the case of the generators, those buyers could turn right around and sell them online for twice what they originally paid.

The alternative for the dealer is to raise the price to a level at which his supply (which is fixed in the short term) comes into some harmony with demand. More buyers get the scarce good, but the supplier risks being labeled as a profiteer who is exploiting a disaster for his own advantage. Potential buyers with limited means may not be able to afford the more expensive generators anymore. Many people consider this "price gouging" to be unfair, and some countries ban the practice entirely.[20]

---

[20] Poundstone W. (2010) Priceless. Hill and Wang, New York, pp. 105–106.

A gas station operator in Florida, who raised prices in the aftermath of Hurricane Katrina because he had "too many customers" and was running out of fuel, was called before the courts under the state's anti-gouging laws.[21] Numerous tests show time and again that consumers resist price increases in emergency situations. Nonetheless, this form of time-based or, more precisely, event-based price differentiation is a hot topic.

Hi-Lo vs. EDLP

The "Hi-Lo" price strategy in retail is another form of time-based price differentiation. Under a Hi-Lo strategy, a retailer switches between higher regular prices and lower promotional prices on an occasional basis. The counterpart to Hi-Lo is the EDLP, or "Every Day Low Price" strategy. Under an EDLP strategy, a retailer maintains prices at constant, comparatively low levels over time. This means that consumers always see attractive prices, not just during promotional periods.

Retailers who use the Hi-Lo strategy often find that sales on promotion account for 70–80 % of their sales in categories such as beer, juice, and a wide range of household products. The true "normal" price in this case is the promotional price and not the regular price. The retailer supports its price promotions with advertising and flyers, and places the promoted products at several locations throughout the store. It is not unusual for sales to rise by a large multiple in the promotional period, relative to sales at regular prices. This is particularly true for strong brands, which have very high price elasticities when on promotion. That's why retailers prefer to use such brands for their promotions, a move which may conflict with the interests of manufacturers, who would prefer to have a more stable price image for their brands.

The effects of a Hi-Lo are extremely complex. Does the strategy generate real incremental sales? Or does the uptick in sales come at the expense of future sales, as in the case of General Motors' employee discount we discussed in Chap. 5? Does the steady stream of promotions under a Hi-Lo strategy train consumers to become bargain hunters? Does the product's price elasticity increase due to the promotions? What types of consumers prefer Hi-Lo vs. EDLP?

Among the few "converging results" on the questions above is the insight that low-income consumers prefer EDLP retailers and those with higher incomes prefer Hi-Lo retailers. A retailers' choice between the two strategies is often determined by competitive behavior. If relevant competitors employ one of the strategies, it can be wise to choose the other. Research also indicates that repeated exposure to Hi-Lo strategies really does make consumers more price sensitive. They learn that there is always a bargain price available somewhere, and that searching for it pays off. But overall the evidence remains unclear. One survey of the literature on Hi-Lo vs. EDLP concluded: "Existing research cannot give clear advice, which pricing

---

[21] Holman WJ (2012) Hug a Price Gouger. The Wall Street Journal, October 30, 2012.

strategy is better in terms of revenue, sales volume, store traffic or profitability."[22] This means that retailers have no other option than to look very carefully at their own situation and determine whether Hi-Lo or EDLP is the better fit. Based on current evidence, there is no clear-cut recommendation for one strategy over the other.

Advance Sale Prices and Advance Booking Discounts

Special variants of time-based price differentiation are advance sales prices, advance booking discounts, and "early bird" specials. These methods are common for events, air travel, and package tours. For flights, this method seems a logical form of differentiation. Price-sensitive leisure travelers tend to book early, while business travelers tend to be less price sensitive and also book on short notice. This seems like a relatively effective fence. With tours and events, the arguments in favor of these prices and discounts are less clear-cut. Are people who book early really more price sensitive? Or do people hold off and speculate that they can find a last-minute bargain? My impression is that an important motivation behind these tactics is the desire of the event promoter or tour operator to reach a certain level of sales as quickly as possible. The downside is that these early discounts can hurt profits because they prevent the sale of tickets or packages at higher prices as the event or the departure date draws near. Whether such opportunities will emerge is hard to assess in the early sales period.

An example of the preceding point can be observed in sports. The 2012/2013 season in Germany's premier soccer league, the Bundesliga, began on August 24, 2012. On that same day, the best team, Bayern Munich, announced that all of its home matches were sold out. That is not a reflection of an intelligent price strategy. Apparently the ticket prices were too low. It also confers an advantage to buyers who snapped up tickets early on and then sell them later on the secondary market. Bayern Munich's strategy would have made sense only if the team had a bad season and interest waned. They would have sold the bulk of their tickets when preseason hype was at its peak. It turns out that Bayern Munich had a very successful season in 2012/2013, winning the Bundesliga championship by a comfortable margin. In 2013, Bayern Munich also won the German Soccer Cup and the European Champions League final, as well as the unofficial world championship of soccer clubs. The fact that the club sold out in advance must make the successful season somewhat bittersweet for the club's management.

One should also heed this saying from the country of Montenegro: "If you want to get mad at yourself, pay in advance."

---

[22] ibidem.

Penetration Strategy: Toyota Lexus

Typical price strategies for new products are penetration and skimming. Penetration strategy means that a company sells the new product at a relatively low price, in order to achieve a high market penetration quickly and ignite a contagion effect as positive feedback about the product spreads. Penetration is also the recommended strategy if there are strong experience curve effects or economies of scale.[23] Toyota used a classic penetration strategy when it launched its luxury Lexus model in the USA. Although Lexus was an entirely new brand name and its advertising made no reference to Toyota, it became widely known that Lexus was a product from Toyota, which sells over one million cars annually in the US market. Toyota achieved strong sales with its Corolla and Camry models, which had a sterling reputation for reliability and high resale values. But this was hardly a basis to believe that Toyota would be able to produce and market a car for the luxury segment. Toyota introduced the Lexus LS400 in 1989 at $35,000 and sold 16,000 vehicles in the first year. Figure 7.10 shows the ensuing price increases for the LS400 in the USA.

The price increased by 48 % over the succeeding six years. In the second year, volume rose to 63,000 units as positive word of mouth from the early buyers started to spread. The LS400 was described enthusiastically in Consumer Report's annual review as a vehicle which "combines advanced technology with almost every conceivable form of comfort, safety, and accessories, which make this the most

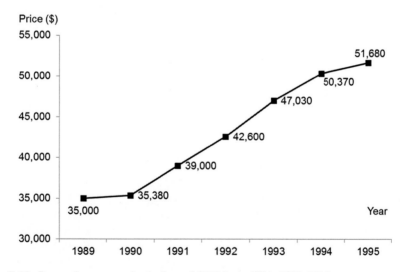

Fig. 7.10 Penetration strategy for the Lexus LS400 in the USA, 1989–1995

---

[23] According to the concept of the experience curve, unit costs fall by a certain percentage for every doubling of cumulative production volume. A low launch price leads to a more rapid doubling of the cumulative production volume and therefore to a more rapid reduction of unit costs. One speaks of economies of scale when unit costs decline as production volumes increase each period.

highly-rated car we have ever tested." The LS400 became the standard for a favorable price-value relationship in its segment and consistently appeared at the top of customer satisfaction rankings. The original uncertainty whether Toyota could build a true luxury car had vanished. Toyota continually raised the prices for the Lexus models. The low introductory price helped ease the Lexus's market entry and helped it both gain attention and start building its enviable reputation. This is a classic example of a penetration strategy. The price of $35,000 at launch was too low to maximize Toyota's short-term profits, but we can still interpret it as an example of shrewd pricing. In contrast to its success in the USA, the Lexus never established itself in Germany. One reason for that could be the fact that luxury car prices in Germany are a stronger indicator of quality and status than they are in the USA. In such a situation, a penetration strategy will not work.

The risk in employing a penetration strategy is that one sets the launch price too low. This is an easy mistake to make with a new product. At the beginning of 2006, Audi priced its new Q7 SUV model too low. It received 80,000 orders at the introductory price of 55,000 Euros ($71,500). The annual production capacity was only 70,000 units. One could argue here that the waiting list made the car more desirable, but it may have also led to impatient customers ultimately buying a competitive model.

The toy company Playmobil launched its model of Noah's Ark in Europe at 69.90 Euros ($90.87). The product was soon sold on eBay for 84.09 Euros ($109), which is proof that the launch price was too low.[24] Hewlett Packard introduced its innovative Series 4 printer at the start of the 1990s at a price significantly below the competitors' prevailing prices. Within one month, it had reached its sales target for the entire year. H-P withdrew the printer from the market and later introduced a similar model at a much higher price.

Another example of low prices being a downfall occurred in online data storage. The British firm Newnet introduced an "uncapped service" at 21.95 pounds ($36.50) per month in 2006. The first 600 customers exhausted the available capacity of 155 MB. The company then hiked the price by 60 % to 34.95 pounds ($58). The Taiwanese computer manufacturer Asus launched the mini-notebook "eee" in January 2008 at 299 Euros ($388). The product sold out in a matter of days. In the launch period, the company could only satisfy 10 % of the actual demand.

Using a penetration strategy is recommended for experience goods. These are products which require a consumer to gain some experience with them in order to understand their true value. A low price at launch motivates more customers to give the product a try, and can create a multiplier effect if customers have a positive experience and start to comment on or even evangelize about the product. One could interpret the popular use of a "freemium" model on the Internet as a form of penetration strategy. Under such a model, a customer receives a basic version of a product free of charge, in the hope that as many "free" users as possible decide to upgrade to a premium, paid version. We will take a closer look at freemium models in Chap. 8.

---

[24] Ebay, December 8, 2003.

Skimming Strategy: The Apple iPhone

Apple used a pronounced skimming strategy when it launched its revolutionary iPhone in June 2007. Figure 7.11 shows the price trend for the 8-GB version.

The introductory price was set at $599. After a few months, Apple undertook a massive price cut to $399. What could have been the reasons for the original high price? The price of $599 signals high technical competence and quality as well as prestige. And despite that high price, long lines formed outside the Apple Stores. Another reason could be that Apple wanted to limit demand in the introductory phase because it had limited production capacity. One can also not rule out that Apple made a mistake.

The massive price reduction to $399 led to a sharp spike in demand. There is a significant difference between offering the iPhone at $399 from the start and launching at a higher price, and then cutting it by $200 after a few months. Prospect theory says that the discount brings the buyer additional positive utility. The flipside is that some of the customers who purchased the phone for $599 became upset when the price suddenly dropped. They protested and Apple responded by issuing $100 gift certificates to these early buyers. The price of the iPhone continued to fall in the ensuing years.

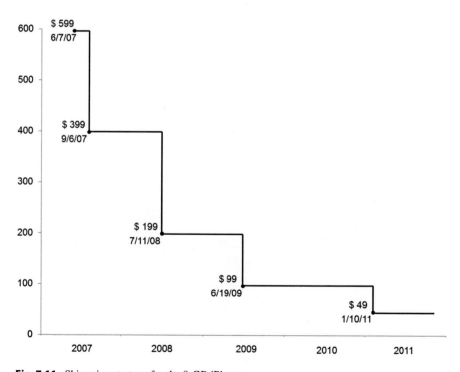

Fig. 7.11 Skimming strategy for the 8-GB iPhone

Apple's pronounced skimming strategy of tapping various levels of willingness to pay over time was driven not just by demand, but also by costs, which decreased due to technical advancements and also because of the veritable explosion in volume. Apple sold 125 million iPhones in its 2011/2012 fiscal year, generating revenues of $80.5 billion, or roughly half of Apple's entire annual revenue.[25] Dividing revenue by volume gives us an average price per iPhone of $640. Interesting here are the statements regarding costs. According to IHS iSuppli, the manufacturing costs in 2012 ranged from $118 for the 16 GB version to $245 for the 64 GB version. This enormous profit margin helps explain while Apple could earn an after-tax profit of $41.7 billion on revenues of $156.5 billion, which corresponds to an after-tax return on sales of 26.6 %. This temporarily made Apple the world's most valuable company, and the price strategy obviously played an essential role in the numbers and the outlook that drove that record valuation.

Apple supplemented its skimming strategy with continuous innovation and an expansion of its product line. This process is sometimes called "versioning," the ongoing introduction of new versions. Each new version offers superior performance compared to the previous generation, which allows Apple to keep the prices for its devices relatively constant. This is a common strategy for personal computers. The price level for a PC does not change all that much over time, but each new generation brings better performance. In terms of price-value relationship, one can speak of a skimming strategy in this case, because the customer pays less and less over time for a unit of performance.

Some price developments may look like skimming strategies in the launch phase, but are actually desperate actions resulting from poor decisions. Nokia introduced its new Lumia 900 smartphone in the USA in 2012. The introductory price was $99, in combination with a 24-month mobile contract with AT&T. Only three months later Nokia cut the price to $49.99 and justified it in a way that made it seem like skimming. "This move is a normal strategy that is put in place during the life cycle of most phones," a Nokia spokesman said.[26] Was that really the reason? The price cut followed what analysts described as a "lackluster" start. In the three months between the launch of the Lumia and the announcement of the price cut, Nokia's share price fell by 64 %. In 2013, Nokia's mobile phone business was sold to Microsoft, marking the end of the independence of a once proud company that was world market leader in mobile phones from 1998 until 2011.

This next case shows some other risks inherent in skimming strategies. In August 2012 the pharmaceutical company Sanofi introduced its oncology drug Zaltrap in the USA at a price of $11,063 per month. The Memorial Sloan-Kettering Cancer Center in New York, one of the world's leading cancer treatment centers, refused to buy it. "We are not going to give a phenomenally expensive new cancer drug to our patients," the hospital said according to a report in the *New York Times*.[27] Sanofi then reacted quickly with a heavy discount which essentially cut the price for Zaltrap in half.[28]

---

[25] Apple Annual Report 2012.

[26] Nokia Marks Lumia 900 at Half Price in the US. The Wall Street Journal Europe, July 16, 2012, p. 19.

[27] Cancer Care, Cost Matters. New York Times, October 14, 2012.

[28] Sanofi Halves Price of Cancer Drug Zaltrap after Sloan-Kettering Rejection. New York Times, November 11, 2012.

Misreading the market in that way is very unpleasant. The rapid reaction was probably the only response Sanofi could have made under the circumstances. Careful analysis ahead of time is the only way to reduce the risk of such a mistake.

In a letter to me in 2003, Peter Drucker revealed his views on skimming strategies:

> I had a few days ago a seminar with one of the world's largest branded consumer companies on pricing. They say that they find it easy to cut prices if they set them too high, but very difficult to raise them if they set them too low. And they think that this is enough for a pricing policy. It does not seem to have occurred to them that the wrong price impairs market and market share. Yet these people enjoy the reputation of most successful marketers.[29]

That is a reminder of an old saying: "One can make a price cut only when one charged enough to begin with."

Information and Profit Cliffs

After the cases in this chapter, no one should doubt that the high art of pricing lies in intelligent price differentiation. But it should also be clear that a company trying to practice this high art faces implementation hurdles and traps. So I will offer a stern warning: this topic should be handled with the utmost care. We'll now take a short look at the most severe challenges and problems.

Well-thought-out price differentiation requires much more detailed information than one needs to set a uniform price. This means information about willingness to pay at the individual level, or at least the segment level. In the case of nonlinear pricing, one must know the marginal utilities for each additional unit. Without knowledge of willingness to pay as a function of time, location, or other criteria which will serve as the basis for differentiation, managers are stumbling around in the dark. Reaping the rewards of price differentiation is a "micro" task and not a "macro" one. It requires a microscopic perspective, not a rough or back-of-the-envelope calculation. Gut feeling, no matter how much experience may back it up, hits its limits on questions of price differentiation.

The reason one needs so much information is that one must understand willingness to pay at the individual level as narrowly as possible, in order to take advantage of it through a differentiated price structure. Only that effort and diligence let one shift from the profit rectangle to the profit triangle. If a company overshoots its target even by a tiny amount, a lack of detailed information is usually the cause and falling off a profit cliff is usually the result.

Price differentiation requires a thorough understanding of the underlying theories, a very systematic collection and analysis of the right data, and the selection of the right differentiation models. Don't get too euphoric about the promise of data from online transactions or from "Big Data." These data contain information about actual transactions and their prices, but do not necessarily offer direct indications of

---

[29] Personal letter from Peter Drucker, June 7, 2003.

a customer's true underlying willingness to pay.[30] Yet this is precisely the knowledge which is critical for effective price differentiation. In line with this reasoning, equity markets are also showing a certain amount of skepticism toward the profit potential of Big Data.[31]

Fencing

As the cases have shown, successful price differentiation requires the ability to separate customers effectively according to their willingness to pay. If a customer with a higher willingness to pay finds a way to buy a product at a low price, the seller's attempt at price differentiation has backfired. Price differentiation makes sense only when fencing works. A classic fencing technique used by airlines was the Saturday night stay-over. One could get a low-priced ticket only by staying over at least one Saturday night at the destination. It worked as an effective fence because business travelers will rarely stay at a destination until Sunday. They want to be home on the weekend. Leisure travelers, in contrast, often don't mind staying the extra day or two.

Fencing is effective when the value difference between the two price categories is sufficiently large and the seller can control access. That means that the highest price category needs to offer correspondingly high value, and the value in the lowest price category is kept intentionally low. The French engineer Jules Dupuit noted this necessity way back in 1849. At that time, the lowest class passenger rail cars did not have a roof. "It is not because of the few thousand Francs which would have to be spent to put a roof over the third class-seats," Dupuit explained. "What the company is trying to do is to prevent the passenger who can pay the second class-fare from traveling third class; it hits the poor, not because it wants to hurt them, but to frighten the rich."[32] Effective fencing requires adequate gaps in value across the price categories. We see that same logic at work today when we look at the available legroom in economy class.

In order to erect an effective fence, pure price differentiation—which means charging different prices for the exact same product—is not sufficient. Product modifications (versioning), the use of different distribution channels, targeted messages to individual customers, access control, using different languages, and similar approaches are all legitimate options. Price differentiation needs to comprise several marketing instruments, which makes it more than pure pricing. It follows, then, that price differentiation also creates additional costs.

---

[30] There are exceptions. In a Vickrey Auction, similar to what eBay uses, the buyer has an incentive to reveal his or her true willingness to pay.

[31] Cukier K, Mayer-Schönberger V (2013). Big Data: A Revolution that Will Transform how We Live, Work, and Think. Houghton Mifflin Harcourt, New York; see also "The Financial Bonanza of Big Data", The Wall Street Journal Europe, March 11, 2013, p. 15.

[32] Dupuis J (1962). On tolls and transport charges. reprinted in International Economic Papers. Macmillan, London (Original 1849)

Pay Attention to Costs

In a perfect world, one would be able to ask each individual customer to pay his or her maximum price. This statement only applies, though, when we leave out the costs involved in price differentiation. It is realistic to assume that the costs for information, access control, or implementing an increasingly finer level of price differentiation rise disproportionately. At the same time, the profit growth from each incremental price differentiation gets smaller and smaller. In the numerical example at the start of the chapter, our contribution rose by 33.3 % when we charged two prices—$90 and $120—instead of a uniform price of $105, assuming that we had a successful way to fence the two segments. If we instead use three prices, whose optimal levels are $81.50, $105, and $127.50, our profit increases by only 12.5 %. The profit curve becomes flatter as price differentiation increases, but the cost curve becomes steeper. This implies that there is an optimal level of price differentiation. It is not the maximum price differentiation that is optimal, but rather the extent that strikes the best balance between value and costs. This also implies that when going from the profit rectangle to the profit triangle covering the entire triangle is not worth the effort, once we start taking the costs of differentiation into account.

Innovations in Pricing

8

Prices are as old as mankind. They existed long before the invention of money. They were not expressed in units of currency, but rather in exchange ratios among goods, a system we still know today as bartering. As children, my friends and I often played marbles, and we traded them. For a marble with a rare color, one would need to offer several marbles with more common colors. The price of a marble with a rare color was higher than the prices for the more common ones.

In light of the long history of prices, one would suspect that everything has already been discovered in this field, all possibilities have been exhausted, and innovations are few and far between. But in the last three decades, the exact opposite has been the case. New ideas, systems, and methodologies are sprouting up all the time on how one can gather information about prices and set them. Some of these innovative approaches have their roots in theory. These include new research methods such as conjoint measurement and the revolutionary approaches which behavioral pricing offers to explain economic enigmas. Furthermore, modern information technology and the Internet create opportunities for pricing which until only recently were the stuff of dreams.

In this chapter we look at a selection of pricing innovations which have either established themselves already or have the potential to do so. I expect this wave of innovation to continue.

Radical Improvements in Price Transparency

The most obvious price-related innovation on the Internet is the radical increase in price transparency. This may also be the innovation with the most far-reaching impact, because it affects every industry. In the "old days," one needed to visit a number of stores, call on numerous suppliers, ask for multiple bids, or read third-party reports in order to collect and compare price information. This process was tedious, difficult, and time consuming. It meant that many customers had only limited information about prices. Suppliers could implement and sustain glaring price

© Springer International Publishing Switzerland 2015

H. Simon, *Confessions of the Pricing Man*, DOI 10.1007/978-3-319-20400-0_8

differences which went largely unnoticed. With the advent of the Internet, anyone can go online and comfortably put together an overview of the prices from different suppliers in a matter of minutes at no or very low cost. The number of sites which offer these kinds of price comparisons seems endless.

In addition to those services, which gather prices across many industries, there is a multitude of industry-specific sites performing the same function. If you want to travel, you can visit expedia.com, hotels.com, kayak.com, and orbitz.com, among others. The penetration of smartphones into our daily lives has added a local dimension to this price transparency. Apps allow you to scan a barcode in a store and find out immediately what the same product costs at other nearby stores. This can severely restrict location-based price differentiation, which traditionally relied on spatial distance as an effective fencing mechanism. It will become more and more difficult to implement differentiated prices for identical products and services. Customers are simply too well informed and when in doubt they can buy the product elsewhere at a lower price. With the help of specialized sites such as alibaba. com, finding the lowest price supplier for a product is no longer a problem even in China. It is certain that further innovations will come, each improving the price information at customers' fingertips and increasing the competitive intensity and the cross-price elasticity.

Pay Per Use

The traditional price model is that one buys the product, pays its price, and then owns and uses the product. An airline buys jet engines for its aircraft, a logistics company buys tires for its trucks, and a car manufacturer installs a painting facility, buys paint, and paints its cars. Taking a needs-oriented perspective creates a totally different basis for setting prices. The needs of the customers often do not warrant owning the product; they would rather have the benefit, the performance, and the needs fulfillment that the product provides. An airline does not have to own jet engines for its aircraft. It needs thrust. Similarly, the trucking company needs the performance of the tires, and the car manufacturer needs a painted car. Instead of charging a price for the product, a manufacturer or supplier can charge a price for what the product actually does. That is the basis for innovative pay-per-use or pay-as-you-go price models.

That explains why General Electric and Rolls Royce sell thrust, not engines, to their airline customers. In this model, they charge by the hour for performance. For a manufacturer this can mean a completely different business model, as it marks the transition from a product to a service business. The company no longer sells products; it sells services. Taking it one step further, these companies now offer a system which creates the potential for even greater revenue than their previous product-based business did. In GE's case, the price per hour can comprise the operation of the jet engines, their maintenance, and other services. Their airline customers gain several advantages from this price model including reduced complexity, lower capital spending, and the elimination of fixed costs and personnel.

Michelin, the world market leader in car and truck tires, was a pioneer with an innovative pay-per-use model for truck tires, a model which can appeal to all kinds of trucking fleets from logistics to buses to waste management. The saying "imitation is the sincerest form of flattery" applies to this pricing model. Other tire manufacturers have started to offer similar systems. Under this model, customers with a truck fleet no longer buy tires. They pay per mile for the tires' performance. This can give the tire manufacturers a higher level of value extraction than with the classic sales model. In Michelin's case a new tire had a performance which was 25 % better than the previous model. It would be extremely difficult to charge a price that is 25 % higher. Customers are accustomed to certain price levels for tires, which form solid price anchors over time. Deviations from these anchors will meet resistance, even if the new products perform much better. The pay-per-use model overcomes that problem. The customer pays by the mile for use of a tire, and if the tires last 25 % longer, the customer automatically pays 25 % more. This model allows the seller to extract the added value of benefits to a greater degree. The customers also benefit: the tires cost them something only when the trucks actually roll, which means that the fleet is generating revenue. If demand is weak and the truck remains parked in the lots, the tires don't cost the company anything. This also simplifies the business calculations of the truckers' customers. They often charge their own customers by the mile, so it helps when their own variable costs (in this case, the cost of tires) are expressed in the same metric.

Similarly, Dürr, the world market leader in automotive paint plants, teamed up with BASF, the world market leader in automotive paints, to offer car manufacturers an innovative price model: they charge one fixed price per car painted. This arrangement provides the car manufacturer a firm basis for its financial calculations, because it transfers the price and cost risks to the suppliers. It also reduces complexity and the need for capital investment. EnviroFalk, a specialist for industrial water treatment, installs its units at its customers at no cost, and then charges them per cubic meter of water treated. These pay-per-use models give suppliers a cash flow they can plan on over time, and also allows them to find an optimal coordination between plants/installations and the input materials.

This kind of model would not immediately come to mind for some industries, such as insurance, but even there it has begun to establish itself. Norwich Union, an insurance company in England, offered young drivers a pay-as-you-go insurance option. Once the appropriate hardware was installed in the vehicle for a one-time charge of £199, the driver paid a monthly basic fee which covers fire and theft. The first 100 miles per month were free. The price per mile driven after the first 100 miles was 4.5 pence. For younger drivers between 18 and 21, the cost was £1 per mile in the particularly accident-prone hours of 11 pm to 6 am. The price difference was enormous and gave young drivers a very strong incentive to leave the car parked at night, when the risk of alcohol usage is high.

End-to-end solutions from one supplier can have a higher utility for customers because they offer more assurance and more efficiency. The Australian company Orica, the world market leader in commercial explosives, offers rock quarry companies a complete solution. Orica supplies not only the explosives, but also analyzes the stone formations and does the drilling and blasting itself. In this comprehensive solution, Orica provides the customer with blasted rock and charges by the ton. The customer doesn't have to take care of the blasting anymore. Each Orica solution is customer specific. It is hard for customers to compare prices and even harder for them to switch suppliers. For Orica, revenue per customer, efficiency, and safety all increase, in addition to repeat business that drives a continuous revenue stream.

If one broadens this needs-oriented perspective, one can imagine many other opportunities for pay-per-use models. But they would not be cost efficient to operate unless the supplier had information systems which can measure and relay usage data at low cost. For instance, there is no reason why someone needs to purchase a car or lease one at a fixed price per month. One can charge for driving—for instance as a function of distance driven and time of day—the same way one charges for phone services or electricity. Car sharing businesses such as Zipcar, now owned by the Avis Budget Group, already lean in this direction. Pay-per-use or pay-per-view is also penetrating the media business. In cable television, one can charge for actual usage instead of a flat monthly rate. The Korean company HanaroTV (now part of SK Broadband) quickly signed up one million customers with that kind of model. The pay-per-use model is also useful in facility management, for the operation of heating or air conditioning systems. Instead of daily or monthly rates, the facility management company could charge by actual usage or energy consumed. Similar to the model with truck tires, this system allows the suppliers to extract value more effectively and take a big step from the profit rectangle to the profit triangle.

Pay-per-use won't succeed in every situation, though. Simon-Kucher & Partners worked with a manufacturer to develop a pay-per-use model for elevators in office buildings. A very interesting question sparked the idea: Why do people pay for horizontal transportation (bus, rail, etc.) but not for vertical transportation? There is no inherent reason why they shouldn't. In the spirit of the pay-per-use model, the elevator manufacturer would install the units for nothing, but in return would receive the long-term right to charge for elevator usage. To implement this, the tenants in the building would receive special cards to track elevator usage, or have the usage tracking built into the security cards already in use in the building.

This pay-per-use model allocates the cost of elevator usage appropriately and more "fairly" than the typical lump-sum models, which are incorporated either into the rent or added as a surcharge. Whoever rides more pays more. One can even differentiate the prices by floor, usage intensity, or other similar criteria. Admittedly, this model has not seen widespread adoption. Maybe it is too innovative? Investors and tenants need time to get used to such pricing innovations.

New Price Metrics

A very interesting approach to pricing is to change the measurement basis for the price, or in other words, change the "price metric." Some of the previous cases in this chapter involve a new price metric (e.g., per mile vs. per tire), but in most of them the company changed the business model, not just the price metric.

One case from the building materials industry shows the potential that changing a price metric has. If a company sells cinder blocks for wall construction, it could charge by weight (price per ton), by space (price per cubic meter), by surface area (price per square foot), or for the complete installation (price per square foot of finished wall). For each metric, the company could charge very different prices and face very different competitive relationships. For example, with one new type of cinder block, a leading manufacturer's price was 40 % more expensive than the competitors' with tons or cubic meters as the price metric. But with square meters as the metric, the price difference was only about 10 %. Because the new blocks weighed less and allowed a team to build the walls faster, the price per square meter for a finished wall conferred a price advantage of 12 %. This makes it clear that the manufacturer should try to switch the price metric for these new blocks to square meters of finished wall. The problem is that it is not always easy to implement such changes. The more innovative the product is or the stronger the manufacturer's position is, the greater its chances to convince customers to adopt the new metric.

Hilti, the global leader for high-performance electric power tools, succeeded in changing the price metrics in an industry in which suppliers traditionally sell their products. Hilti introduced a "fleet management" model for its tools: the customer pays a fixed monthly price for its "fleet" of Hilti tools. Hilti ensures that the customer receives the optimal set of tools for its set of jobs, including loaners if tools are being repaired, and upgrades as job needs and technologies change. Hilti also takes care of everything from repairs, battery exchange, and comprehensive service, which saves time at the jobsite and eliminates the need for the customer to track down repair quotes or incur unexpected expenses. Instead, the customer can count on a predictable, fixed monthly price and can focus on its core competencies.

The advent of cloud computing has also given rise to new price metrics. Software is no longer sold on a license basis and then installed on-premise on the customer's own machines. The new trend is toward Software as a Service (SaaS), with software offered online and on-demand for a fee. Microsoft's Office 365 suite is no longer sold in the traditional way, but rather offered as a monthly or annual subscription. The Office 365 Home Premium costs 10 Euros per month or 99 Euros per year. In return the customer receives immediate online access to the latest versions and a range of additional services. The firm Scopevisio offers medium-sized companies its software under a similar model. It asks a monthly price per application and user. This allows the customers to combine the various online applications into a package which perfectly fits their needs, with the ability to manage the number of users on a monthly basis as needs change. The monthly price varies accordingly. This model will likely become the standard for cloud-based application software.

Introducing a New Price Parameter: The Case of Sanifair

Sometimes a company has a lucrative opportunity to introduce a price parameter and charge for a previously free service. The operation of toilets in a public facility or an office building requires considerable investment and results in high operating costs.

In restaurants, the usage of the restroom facilities is included in the price of the meal. So up until a few years ago, why was the use of bathrooms at a highway rest area free of charge as well, even when many of the guests never purchased any gas, food, or drink at the rest area? Who bears the costs when the customers, the users, receive the service free of charge? Decades ago in the USA, when pay toilets were common, customers themselves bore the costs, until some cities and states started to ban pay toilets in the 1970s and their installation in buildings fell out of favor. In Germany, the government was responsible for those costs at highway rest areas until 1998. A federally owned company managed the rest areas, whose toilets were in a condition I would like to forget. Then a private company called Tank & Rast took over the responsibility for rest areas from the federal government, massively upgraded them, and now licenses the operations for 390 rest areas, 350 gas stations, and 50 hotels along the German highway system, accounting for 90 % of such roadside services. In 2003 it introduced an innovative solution to the "toilet" question with the "Sanifair" concept.

First, Tank & Rast renovated all the restroom facilities to bring them to the most modern standards. Then they asked for a fee of 50 cents per use, but with a twist. Adults needed to pay the full amount to pass through a turnstile and enter the facility, but children and handicapped guests received a token to get in for free. This was a family-friendly form of price differentiation. But the 50 cents were not lost. The guests would receive a 50-cent coupon which they could spend at any store or restaurant at the rest area. This was an elegant way to differentiate among the guests who just wanted to use the toilet (and would now need to pay 50 cents for that privilege) and those who actually bought something. The latter group would still use the toilets for free. In 2010, Sanifair raised the price to 70 cents, and the guest receives a coupon for 50 cents.

Sanifair is innovative in a number of ways. First—and perhaps most importantly for the guests—it has improved the cleanliness and hygiene of the restrooms tremendously. Maintaining that standard results in costs, and the model does justice to that by asking the guests to pay a small amount for that leap in value. The prices are also differentiated in a number of ways. Children and handicapped users still have free access. People who solely use the restroom and drive away pay the full 70 cents. But those who buy something receive a rebate of 50 cents, effectively a reimbursement of 71 % of the price they paid. Their net price is just 20 cents. The operation of the payment and access process requires no personnel. Guests pay cash at the turnstile machine and receive their printed coupon, while the children receive a token. Many studies have shown that despite the fact that they need to pay something, the guests have a high level of satisfaction. Sanifair even received a prestigious award for its innovation. Considering that about 500 hundred million guests stop at the German rest areas every year, Sanifair's pricing and service innovations have made an essential contribution to the success of Tank & Rast. Companies within and outside Germany have begun to adopt the Sanifair system under license from Tank & Rast.

Amazon Prime

It seems as if every retailer in the USA offers some kind of loyalty card with perks. But few retailers charge a separate fee for the card or for access to the services and perks. Amazon offers its "Prime" program which guarantees delivery within two days with no separate shipping charges on over 20 million eligible items. The program today offers a range of other advantages and privileges, including unlimited access to over 40,000 movies and TV episodes with Prime Instant Video and a selection of over 500,000 books to borrow from the Kindle Owners' Lending Library.[1] The price for one year of Amazon Prime was $79 in the USA and 49 Euros (roughly $63) in the EU. The number of customers crossed the 10-million plateau in 2011. US customers in the program tripled their purchase volume with Amazon to $1,500 per year. In the USA, Prime customers generate an estimated 40 % of Amazon's revenue. Nonetheless, it is said that the revenue from Prime probably does not cover the direct costs Amazon incurs. The costs per customer are estimated at $90. Amazon views the program as an investment in customer loyalty. "If they can make customers more loyal, they can make more profit, even if they have to subsidize Prime," one former Amazon manager said.[2] In 2014, Amazon officially raised the annual price of Prime to $99, citing the fact that it hadn't raised the price in nine years despite increases in fuel and transportation costs during that time.

Industrial Gases

Two-dimensional and multidimensional price systems are commonplace. In industries such as telecommunications, energy, and water supply, prices regularly consist of a fixed base price and a variable price based on actual usage. In the case of industrial gases, which are sold in steel containers, there is a daily rate for renting the bottles, and a price per kilo for the gases. A customer who uses one bottle of gas per day therefore pays less per kilogram than a customer who takes 10 days to use up one bottle. In spite of offering the same scheme to each customer the actual price paid strongly differs significantly according to usage intensity: a very smart scheme for price differentiation.

ARM

Two-dimensional models are also common in licensing. ARM, the world market leader in intellectual property for semiconductors, issues a license in exchange for a one-time fee and then takes a royalty on every chip shipped. ARM chips are found

---

[1] E-mail to Amazon Prime customers in the US, March 13, 2014.

[2] Woo S (2012) Amazon increases bet on its loyalty program. The Wall Street Journal Europe, November 15, p. 25.

in 95 % of all smartphones. Since 2000, the company's sales have risen from $213 million to $1.12 billion in 2013.[3] In 2013 the average royalty per chip was 4.7 cents, not a high amount. But with about 12 billion chips per year this is adding up to a nice sum. About half of ARM's business comes from licenses and royalties.[4] An interesting alternative for them would be the BahnCard model, which means that they would collect an annual fee instead of a one-time upfront fee. All multidimensional price structures contain some form of price differentiation, because the fixed price gets allocated across different volume levels. An advantage of these systems is that a company makes the same price offer to all customers, but each customer pays a different amount according to his or her own actual usage.

Freemium

Freemium is a combination of the words "free" and "premium." It describes a price strategy under which a customer can either get a basic version of a service for free or can purchase a premium version of the service. On the Internet, the number of freemium business models has risen sharply. The marginal costs for many Internet services are zero (or close to it), which means that the free offer does not cause incremental costs. "Freemium-like" models also existed in the offline world. Banks lure customers in with free checking accounts, but if the customers wants anything beyond basic services, they must pay. Admittedly, the free offers for the basic bank account often came with conditions, such as a minimum balance requirement.[5] But such offers only look like freemium models. The customer pays because they earn little or no interest on their deposits. A similar hidden payment occurs with "zero-percent" financing offers from retailers or car dealers.[6] The financing costs are hidden in the purchase price.

The goal of a freemium model is to use the free price to attract the largest number of potential customers. The company hopes that if the user becomes comfortable with the basic functionality, he or she will have a growing interest in paying for a version which is more powerful, and more advanced, or offers additional functionality. Freemium fits very well to experience goods, whose full value only becomes apparent when customers have had a chance to use the good. One could interpret freemium as a specific form of penetration strategy. Freemium is becoming more and more popular. Typical industries include software (e.g., Skype), media (e.g., Pandora), games (e.g., Farmville), apps (e.g., Angry Birds), and social networks (e.g., LinkedIn).

---

[3] Financial Times, March 20, 2013, p. 14 and Fleissner L (2014) 'Internet of Things' gives ARM a boost. The Wall Street Journal Europe, April 24, 2014, p. 19.

[4] Fleissner L (2014) 'Internet of Things' gives ARM a boost. The Wall Street Journal Europe, April 24, 2014, p. 19.

[5] Direct mailing from Commerzbank dated March 26, 2013.

[6] Nicht jedes Angebot ist ein Schnäppchen. Null-Prozent-Finanzierungen werden für den Handel immer wichtiger. General-Anzeiger, Bonn, April 3, 2013, p. 6.

The key success factors for a freemium model are:

1. *An attractive basic offer*: which can attract a lot of users.
2. *The right fencing*: between the basic and the premium offer, in order to convert first-time buyers.
3. *A customer loyalty concept*: to turn the first-time buyers into repeat customers, who have the highest lifetime value.

There is a trade-off relationship between the first two factors. If the basic offer is too attractive, it will be hard to develop a clearly differentiated premium product and encourage customers to trade up to it. The company will definitely attract a large number of free users, but will struggle to convert them to paid users. On the other hand, if the basic version offers too little value, it may not attract enough free users at all. One may achieve a high conversion rate to the premium model in that case, but the absolute number of users remains small. The fencing between the basic and the premium versions is achieved through features, product versions, or differences in usage intensity.

In contrast, the communications software Skype offers a complete array of functionality, but restricts free calls to within its own network. It also offers instant messaging and file sharing free of charge within its network. If Skype users grow accustomed to the intuitive user interface, they are more likely to want to make calls to landline networks or cell networks, and also be willing to pay for those calls. When it began, Skype primarily sold individual talk minutes. Later on, it structured its service portfolio to resemble a classic telecommunications offering. The current paid offerings include bundles of minutes or flat rates for selected domestic phone networks.

Newspapers have introduced freemium models, after years of enduring the "free" culture for digital content. Newspaper websites used to earn their money online solely with advertising. In order to get money directly from readers as well, many publishers erected paywalls. The main fencing instrument here is not a better version of the product, but rather the reader's usage intensity. The *New York Times*, for example, allows a reader to access 20 articles in a month free of charge. Whoever clicks through more often needs to pay. But print subscribers receive free access to the online version. The German newspaper *Die Welt* is also experimenting with paywalls.[7] Each of those newspapers offers digital subscriptions for 99 cents per month, even though the list prices are between 4.49 and 14.99 Euros for *Die Welt* and between $15 and $35 for the *New York Times*. The Kindle version of the *New York Times* costs $29.99 per month. The offers of 99 cents for a monthly subscription are not too far from being truly "free," but the fact that these small amounts create a paid relationship makes a fundamental difference for the customer as well as the publisher. The largest hurdle in freemium models is getting customers over this initial price barrier, or getting them to cross the "penny gap." The challenge for the publishers is to draw customers away from the "free" culture and to establish

---

[7] Axel Springer glaubt an die Bezahlschranke. Frankfurter Allgemeine Zeitung, March 7, 2012, p. 15.

their digital content as a paid experience. IBM manager Saul Berman has called this "the challenge of the decade."[8] Stephan Scherzer, the head of Germany's newspaper publisher trade association, says that this is the "question which decides our future: How do the publishers get readers to pay for content online?"[9] Right now there are few media companies that make their money entirely from content. One example is the French investigative and opinion portal Mediapart, led by former *Le Monde* editor-in-chief Edwy Plenel. The portal charges a monthly subscription fee of 9 Euros, has 65,000 subscribers, and generates revenue of 6 million Euros. This is a small amount, but the company is profitable and achieves a margin of over 10 %.[10] Mediapart accepts no advertising at all.

When Simon-Kucher & Partners began a project for a social network, only 8 % of its users were premium customers. Using online price tests, we found out that price changes would barely affect revenue. Because the company faced many comparable competitors—some with completely free offers—the number of premium users fell quickly in the tests after a price increase. Price cuts, in contrast, did not attract many new customers. The price elasticities were roughly 1. That means that price changes would be more or less revenue neutral, as volume changes tended to balance them out. What did have an effect, however, were changes to the portfolio and to the offers themselves. On the strength of better, more content-rich offers, the share of premium customers rose from 8 to 10 %. That represents a growth of 25 % and corresponded exactly to the increase in revenue. It was the network's most successful project ever, and it confirms the central role that usage plays. The usage difference between "free" and "paid" must be large enough to get customers across the penny gap.

In online gaming, the freemium model has become so popular that even classic game manufacturers have started to offer many games online for free, with the goal of earning money with individual features. Based on its popular *Need for Speed* racing game, Electronic Arts has developed a freemium product called *Need for Speed World*. The player can use real money to purchase play money, which he or she can then use to buy additional cars or optional equipment to improve their cars' performance.

From a company's perspective, whether a freemium model is better than a conventional price structure or scheme depends on the competition, the target customers, and the product features.[11] The key metrics are conversion and the customer lifetime value of the premium customers. A company can get several hundred dollars from such customers, whereas users of the basic product generate no revenue at all.

[8] Berman SJ (2011) Not for free – revenue strategies for a new world. Harvard Business Review Press, Boston.

[9] Das nächste Google kommt aus China oder Russland. Frankfurter Allgemeine Zeitung, March 18, 2013, p. 22.

[10] Enthüllungsportal Mediapart bewährt sich im Internet. Frankfurter Allgemeine Zeitung, April 4, 2013, p. 14.

[11] A compact, good analysis of Freemium can be found in Uzi Shmilovici, The Complete Guide to Freemium Business Models. TechCrunch, September 4, 2011.

A systematic optimization of price and product using a freemium model typically increases revenues by about 20 %, according to Simon-Kucher & Partners' experience.

Media companies, however, can do very well without pursuing a freemium model. Simon-Kucher & Partners tested that hypothesis for a leading magazine in the USA, and ultimately recommended equal but slightly increased annual prices of $118 for its digital and online editions. The price for the bundle of digital and online was $148, a discount of 37 % against the combined price of $236, which is the sum of the two individual prices. After implementation, the average revenue per subscriber rose by 15 %, with no relevant loss of subscribers. One must note here, however, that this magazine enjoyed a very strong reputation. Customers are obviously willing to pay for it, and they perceive the combined access to the print and online versions as true added value.

Flat Rates

Flat rate is the modern term for a lump-sum price. A customer pays one fixed price per month or per year, and can then use the product or service as much as he or she wants in that period. Flat rates are very widely used today in telecommunications and Internet services. Cable television subscribers generally pay one flat rate per month to gain access to all available channels and watch them as often as they like. The BahnCard 100 is also a flat rate offer. Cardholders can ride the rails as often and as far as they would like. Flat rates are very effective tools for price differentiation. Heavy users realize huge discounts when they have a flat rate. For example, if someone travelled by rail so often that they would pay 20,000 Euros per year at regular prices, they would earn a discount of 79.6 % if they bought a second-class BahnCard 100. This heavy usage is precisely the risk that companies face when they offer flat rates. They should expect lower revenues from their heavy users, and potentially also higher costs (for example, additional investments in a telecommunications network).

Nonetheless, flat rates are among the most important innovations in pricing. We see monthly or annual passes to museums, theaters, and fitness studios all having a flat rate character. The all-you-can-drink offers for soft drinks at fast food restaurants follow the same principle. The "all-inclusive" offers in tourism combine flat rate elements (e.g., for food and drink) with price bundling. "All-you-can-eat" buffets are another example of flat rate pricing. The risk for the restaurant owner is limited, because guests can only eat or drink up to certain personal limits anyway. In Japanese bars, a popular price model is a flat rate which allows guests to eat and drink as much as they want during a certain period. The prices range from 1,500 yen (roughly $15) for one hour, 2,500 yen (roughly $25) for two hours and 3,500 yen ($35) for three hours. These flat rates are particularly popular among Japanese students. The time limit helps reduce the bar owners' risks. When I once tested this system in Tokyo I also had the impression that service was somewhat slower for flat rate guests.

For telecommunications and Internet companies, flat rates can present a problem. One European company offered its readers the following deal: for a flat rate of 19.90 Euros (around $24.70), they would have unlimited free calling and also have unlimited free Internet usage. They would also receive a Samsung smartphone.[12] What is the problem with these flat rates? One can only talk or surf for 24 hours in a day, but data amounts know no limits. They continue to increase. The discussions around flat rates in telecom and Internet businesses began in earnest in the late 1990s in the USA and soon spread abroad. Heavy users, who benefit the most from such price models, intensified their pressure on companies to offer more of them. On November 20, 2000, I made a presentation to T-Mobile entitled "Internet and Flatrate—Strategic Considerations." I presented two theses:

- *Thesis 1*: Flat rates mean that the vast majority of light users subsidize a small minority of heavy users.
- *Thesis 2*: Flat rates lead with a high probability to lower revenue and profits. From an economic standpoint, flat rates make no sense.

Whether one can still speak of a "small minority" of heavy users nowadays is an open question. As for the second and most important thesis, I still stand by those words today.

Data volume has been growing massively. Because of their flat rates, however, telecom companies have not participated in that growth the way they could have. Their revenues have stagnated. At the same time, they need to invest billions of dollars in new network infrastructure. They will not be able to harvest the fruits of these investments, though, because their flat rate price policies have capped the maximum amount of revenue they can receive from an individual customer. I am not claiming that any single telecommunications company could have withstood the flat rate wave on its own. The industry as a whole has done itself a disservice with flat rates. In recent years more and more telecommunications companies stopped offering their customers contracts with unlimited data usage. I expect that such price strategies will become a new standard in the industry and offer the telecom companies a way out of the flat rate trap. When I shared my two theses from above in 2013 with Rene Obermann, at the time CEO of Deutsche Telekom, the parent of T-Mobile, he admitted that such attempts to pull back "demonstrate that you and your team did in fact foresee this development in the year 2000."[13]

From a consumer perspective, flat rates offer many advantages. Some consumers opt for a flat rate, even when it is not their most economical choice. One reason is that a flat rate acts as a kind of insurance policy. It limits the consumer's out-of-pocket risk to the fixed amount. When one treats the flat rate as a sunk cost, the consumer's marginal cost for voice or data usage is zero. One has the perception that these services cost "nothing." They also avoid the "taxi meter" effect. From the perspective of prospect theory, every phone call or online interaction provides a

---

[12] *ADAC Motorwelt*, March 2013, advertising section from tema.
[13] Letter to the author.

positive utility. We have these experiences daily, and their sum is greater than the negative utility of the flat rate, which we pay once a month.

If consumption or usage is not constrained by some natural or artificial limits, companies should be very careful with flat rates. It is critical to have detailed information about the distribution of light vs. heavy users and to run rigorous simulations. Otherwise, one can experience a nasty surprise with flat rates. If the number of heavy users is large, flat rates put profits at considerable risk.

Prepaid Systems

Prepaid systems, which require users to pay for a service before they consume it, can be interpreted as a variation on advance sale or prerelease prices. Simon-Kucher & Partners supported the mobile phone service pioneer E-Plus with its pioneering launch of prepaid cards in the 1990s. Prepaid is now common at cafeterias and at shops such as Starbucks, which offers stored value cards and has built a loyalty program around them which also includes "gold" status that entitles the cardholder to discounts and free beverages. Starbucks does not publicize either the number of cards in circulation or the amount of money stored on them, but one indirect indication of their popularity is the amount of money Starbucks books as pure profit from cards deemed lost or permanently inactive. For the fiscal year 2013, it booked $33 million in extra profit from stored card money considered "dead."[14]

Typically with a prepaid card, a consumer either buys a card or loads up a free card (such as a Starbucks card) with a certain amount of money, and then draws the balance down with each purchase. The system has advantages both for seller and buyer. Because the customer has paid in advance (by loading money on the card), it eliminates the seller's risk of nonpayment. The buyer knows how much he or she is spending and this precludes the risk of exceeding one's budget. This is one reason why prepaid cards are popular in less affluent countries. One disadvantage for the seller is that the relationship with the prepaid buyer is looser than one governed by an actual contract for a specified time. One finds prepaid cards in unusual places in emerging markets. In Mexico, the insurance company Zurich offers prepaid car insurance. One can buy a card that offers 30 days of insurance coverage, starting on the day the customer activates the card.

Customer-Driven Pricing

During the first e-commerce wave in the late 1990s, there were big expectations for a new price model under which a customer would make an offer, and then the seller would decide whether to accept it. Whether it is called "name your own price," "customer-driven pricing," or "reverse pricing," the process rests on the hope that

---

[14] Starbucks fiscal 2013 10-K.

the customer will reveal his or her true willingness to pay. The price offered by the customer is binding for him or her, and payment is secured because the customer must supply a credit card number or allow their account to be debited. As soon as a customer's offer exceeds a minimum price threshold (known only to the seller), the customer gets the product and pays the offered price. One could describe the curve defined by aggregating these binding offers as the first ever "real" demand curve in history, an interesting side effect of this price model.

The pioneer of the customer-driven price model was Priceline.com, founded in 1998. Similar companies, such as IhrPreis.de[15] and tallyman.de in Germany, soon followed. In their early years, these companies offered a wide assortment of products. But it turned out that most customers named unrealistically low prices. Either these sites attracted only dedicated bargain hunters, or consumers intentionally hid their true willingness to pay and instead tried to get products at extremely low prices. Either way, the model was not a lasting success. IhrPreis.de and tallyman.de disappeared after a short time. Priceline survived, but evolved into a conventional Internet retailer and now has revenues of around $5 billion. The "name your own price" model plays only a very marginal role, as a means for suppliers to dispose of excess inventory. Or as Priceline.com describes it on its own website: "The *Name Your Own Price*® service uses the flexibility of buyers to enable sellers to accept a lower price in order to sell their excess capacity without disrupting their existing distribution channels or retail pricing structures."[16]

Despite their theoretically interesting potential to reveal consumers' real willingness to pay, these models did not fulfill expectations. One cannot rule out a comeback, though, or increased usage as a way for companies to clear inventories.

Pay What You Want

The "pay what you want" model takes customer-driven pricing one step further. Under this model, the buyer determines the price, but the seller is obligated to accept it. The music group Radiohead released its album *In Rainbows* online in 2007 with a "pay what you want" model. The album was downloaded over one million times, with 40 % of the "buyers" paying an average price of $6 apiece.[17] Occasionally one will see a restaurant, hotel, or other service business try a similar approach. After finishing the meal or checking out, the guest pays whatever price he or she wants to. From a pricing standpoint, the seller is entirely at the buyer's mercy. In such situations, the seller may indeed see a certain number of customers pay prices that cover costs. Other customers will take advantage of the opportunity to pay little or nothing.

---

[15] The author was a member of the board of IhrPreis.de AG.

[16] Investor relations homepage of Priceline, ir.priceline.com.

[17] van Buskirk E (2007) 2 out of 5 Downloaders Paid for Radiohead's 'In Rainbows'. Wired Magazine, November 5, 2007.

In contrast to zoos, museums, cinemas, or other facilities which also use such models, the hotels and especially the restaurants incur high variable costs which make the "pay what you want" model even riskier. In the worst case, some customers do pay absolutely nothing. I am not aware of any case in which this model has established itself as standard practice. I consider the "pay what you want" model to be a pipe dream. One could interpret a donation as a variant of "pay what you want." But in that case we are not talking about a "price," because the donation brings no tangible obligation or benefit in return.

There are two fundamental differences between the "pay what you want" and customer-driven price models. In the latter model, the seller can decide whether to accept or refuse the price the customer names, and that decision comes before any goods or services are exchanged. Under a "pay what you want" model, consumption can occur before payment is required or the price is set, or after payment, as in the entry to a zoo or a museum. And the sellers no longer have any decisions to make. One middle ground is the "suggested price," a practice used by some museums in New York and Washington, DC. This is "pay what you want" with a hint. New York institutions seem to be moving away from the model, but it is still popular at many places and is in practice at multiple sites around the National Mall in Washington, DC.

But even in those cases, the operators or owners depend entirely on a customer's goodwill. Whether a customer pays—and how much—is entirely up to that customer, with no other obligations or conditions. In short: businesses should avoid "pay what you want" systems.

Profit-Oriented Incentive Systems

In this book I have said on many occasions that over the long term, only a profit orientation can serve as a rational guideline for pricing. Other goals—such as those based on revenue, volume, or market share—lead to less-than-optimal results. The same holds true for incentive systems. Despite this insight, revenue-based compensation remains the most commonly used form of incentive for salespeople. This tends to lead to discounts which are too high and prices which are too low. Under normal circumstances, the price which generates the maximum revenue is much lower than the price which maximizes profit. If you have a linear demand curve and a linear cost function, the revenue-maximizing price is half of the maximum price, while the profit-maximizing price lies at the midpoint between the maximum price and the variable unit costs. For our power tool business, you might recall that we had a maximum price of $150 and variable unit costs of $60. This means that we have the following "maximizing" prices:

- Revenue-maximizing price: $75, with a loss of $7.5 million
- Profit-maximizing price: $105, with a profit of $10.5 million

The profit difference between the two prices is abysmal. If salespeople are rewarded for maximizing revenue, we can assume that they will naturally make that their goal. To do otherwise would be irrational from their perspective. If one also empowers them to decide on price levels, prices will tend to decline, taking profits with them. Of course, in the power tool case, managers should establish some floors or limits to prevent the company from slipping into the red. But the trend in prices is still downward. So why are sales- or revenue-based compensation systems so common? This may have several reasons, from sheer habit to simplicity, to the desire to keep knowledge about profits and profit margins out of the hands of salespeople.

Instead of perpetuating these revenue-based plans, I strongly recommend that companies switch to profit-oriented incentive plans. In making that switch, companies do not need to sacrifice simplicity or confidentiality. One simple approach is to link the commission or incentive to the level of discount. The lower the discounts a salesperson grants, the higher his or her commission. At Simon-Kucher & Partners we have developed numerous plans of that kind for companies from a diverse set of industries. Normally the realized discounts drop by several percentage points, without any losses in volume or any customer defections. It helps when the salesperson can actually see the changes to his or her commission during the negotiations on their PC or tablet. That enhances the effect of this kind of incentive. Modern information technology plays an important role in the creation and maintenance of incentives. The actual form of the incentive and its parameters matter less than the fact that measures of profit—not measures of revenue—are what determine a salesperson's variable compensation.

Better Price Forecasts

In a commodity market, the individual supplier has no influence on prices. As I described in Chap. 1 with the farmers' market and hog prices, the price reflects the interaction of supply and demand. Does that mean that one is powerless from a price perspective and must sit back and wait to see what happens? Not necessarily! If one is able to know in advance which way the price will move, one can pull forward or postpone a sale; that is, one can sell more at higher prices and less at lower prices.

A large chemical company faced precisely that challenge. The salespeople visited their customers in the textile industry on a weekly basis and could exert some influence on the timing of orders. Together with the chemical company, Simon-Kucher & Partners developed a forecasting model for prices, which incorporated data about supply and demand as well as estimates which salespeople provided after each of their visits. Figure 8.1 shows the forecasts for 30 and 90 days.

The company made these forecasts available to the salespeople. The key was understanding the timing in the forecasted price trends. When will the price rise? When will it fall? If the model showed a forthcoming rise in prices, the instructions to the salespeople were as follows: "Sell less now; push out the purchase dates." If the forecast showed a pending drop in prices, the advice was the opposite: "Sell

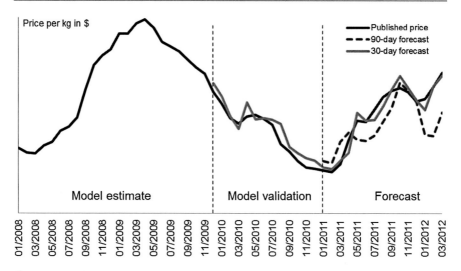

Fig. 8.1 Price forecasts for a commodity chemical

more now; pull purchase dates forward." The situation is similar to trading on a stock exchange. Whoever has better information over future trends will have an opportunity to make more money. These forecasts—and the resulting ability to improve transaction timing—were responsible for an increase of one percentage point in the company's profit margin, which is an enormous improvement in a commodity business.

Intelligent Surcharges

Many pricing innovations which we observed or initiated at Simon-Kucher & Partners over the last few years were based on surcharges. One can divide surcharges into several categories, depending on the form and the intent:

- *Unbundling*: A product or service previously included in the total price is now priced separately, in the form of a surcharge or an additional payment.
- *New price components*: A product or service which never had a price before now gets a stand-alone price. This creates a new price component. The Sanifair concept is a good example.
- *Passing on cost increases*: A company passes along cost increases to its customers in the form of a surcharge, usually tied to some form of index defined in the contract.
- *Price differentiation*: The surcharge is used as a means to differentiate prices, based on time, geography, personal characteristics, etc.

Ryanair is particularly creative in inventing and collecting surcharges. In 2006, the no-frills airline became the first airline worldwide to charge separately for checked baggage, at the time a radically new and controversial move. Back then customers needed to pay 3.50 Euro (about $4.50) for each checked bag; nowadays the price per piece (up to 20 kg) is 25 Euro ($32.50) in the slow season and 35 Euros (around $45) in peak travel periods. Ryanair does not provide a detailed breakdown of its net earnings from this surcharge, but the airline flies more than 100 million passengers per year.[18] Even if only a small percentage of passengers check their bags, Ryanair earns hundreds of millions. Ryanair chose a surprising way to communicate the introduction of the checked-bag fee: "This will reduce the overall ticket price for passengers not checking in bags by about 9 percent." Who can oppose a checked-bag fee after that? In addition to the low base fare, to which customers pay close attention and which has a high price elasticity, Ryanair has thought up a long list of surcharges, which people pay less attention to and which therefore have a lower price elasticity. They charge a credit card fee of 2 % and an administrative fee of 6 Euros. Reserving a seat costs 10 Euros, and bringing sports equipment or a musical instrument with you would cost 50 Euros. The list goes on and on. If a passenger does not book online, the surcharges are even higher. From time to time Ryanair CEO Michael O'Leary threatens to introduce even more surcharges, such as for using the toilets on the plane, but doesn't always follow up. Perhaps Ryanair passengers are very thankful for that.

Surcharges are an appropriate way to take advantage of higher willingness to pay in peak periods. A passenger railroad could introduce surcharges for travel on Friday afternoons or on Sunday evenings. These surcharges would have two effects: they would increase the company's profits and also damp demand, which lowers the chances that trains will be overbooked or overfilled in those peak travel times. Price cuts in off-peak periods often have little effect, but price increases in peak periods can have a significant effect. We see these kinds of asymmetries in time-based price differentiation in a number of industries.

When a company offers its customers additional value, surcharges provide a way to extract some of that value. If Air France passengers want a seat in an emergency exit row, they need to pay 50 Euros ($65) for that privilege. If the flight lasts longer than nine hours, the surcharge is 70 Euros (around $90). Air France waives the fee for its gold and platinum cardholders. Other airlines have adopted similar surcharges. The added value of more space is clear. Why shouldn't customers who want that added value pay something for it? This is also a wonderful fencing mechanism.

Often the value of a product depends on how quickly it becomes available or how quickly a customer can access it. If a dump truck at a mine has a damaged tire, the truck is unusable. Every hour that the truck stands idle, the mining company loses revenue. The faster the company can get a new tire delivered and installed, the shorter the downtime. This implies that the mining company would be willing to

---

[18] http://www.ryanair.com/en/investor/traffic-figures

pay for faster service. That is reflected in the price model for a leading manufacturer of tires for heavy-duty industrial vehicles. The standard delivery time varies by type of tire. Tires in high demand are stocked at warehouses and are always available. For those tires, the company charges nothing extra for immediate delivery. Delivery times for less common tires can be several days. If the customer wants faster delivery, the tire company charges extra. This example shows how surcharges can help a company use this model of availability to earn money from better or faster services.

Passing along higher costs through a change in the normal product price is often difficult. But if a company introduces a surcharge for certain cost parameters, that is usually more palatable for customers. Rising fuel costs prompted a pharmaceutical products wholesaler to tack on a fuel surcharge to its prices. Competitors followed. Margins in this industry are extremely tight, at less than 1 %, so this surcharge boosted returns by 30 %. A British ready-mix concrete company instituted a surcharge of £70 ($115) per delivery truck on weekends and £100 ($165) per delivery truck at night, on top of the base price of £600 (ca. $1,000). A German company in the same industry demands a surcharge of 8 Euros per cubic meter for deliveries when temperatures are below freezing.

Another interesting idea is to offer additional services in exchange for a surcharge. The luxury Jumeirah Beach Hotel in Dubai allows guests to use its executive lounge for a fee of roughly $50 per day. That price includes breakfast in the lounge, which would cost around $37.50 separately. That means that the net surcharge for a day's lounge usage is $12.50. The offer is popular and increases the hotel's revenue per guest.

We could view tips as a special form of surcharge, or even a variant of "pay what you want." In some countries, such as Japan and Korea, tipping is not customary at all. In other countries, it has the character of a de facto surcharge. One "must" tip 15 % in American restaurants, though one may pay more. Some restaurants make this tip obligatory, at 15 or 18 %, for groups above a certain size. Up until a few years ago, taxi drivers in New York accepted only cash, and the guest decided how much to add as a tip. The average amount was around 10 %. The drivers then began to accept credit cards. The guest now needed only to swipe his or her card in the reader, which is installed within easy reach. Then the guest can choose the amount of the tip manually, with three default options available to press on the touch screen: 20, 25, and 30 %. After the introduction of this system, the average tip rose to 22 %, which corresponds to additional annual income of $144 million for New York's taxi drivers.[19] Not bad, and all because of smart pricing!

Surcharges are also a way to make some alternatives less attractive and steer customers to others. In 2002, Lufthansa Cargo introduced a surcharge of 5 Euros for traditional bookings, and pushed electronic bookings with the slogan "e for free." These measures massively increased the share of electronic bookings. Once customers grew accustomed to making their bookings online, Lufthansa Cargo eliminated the surcharge for traditional bookings.

---

[19] www.slate.com/blogs/moneybox/2012/05/15/taxi_button_tipping.html. May 15, 2012.

Normally the price elasticity for surcharges is lower than the elasticity for the base price. But sometimes we see the opposite effect. As of 2010, all public German health insurance companies received a uniform amount per person/member they covered. Companies for whom those amounts were not sufficient to cover their costs needed to surcharge their members directly if they wanted more revenue. Some instituted monthly surcharges. Even though these surcharges—typically 8–10 Euros—were very small relative to the base contribution members paid each month via a payroll deduction, their introduction met with strong resistance. The insurers who added the surcharges lost so many members that they ended up in financial difficulties. The CEO of the largest public insurance fund said that "[t]he additional surcharges sent a strong price signal with little positive financial impact. Instead, they caused significant shifts in membership to competitors. As an instrument to raise revenues, the surcharges proved ineffective."[20]

There are psychological explanations for these strong negative effects. The members perceive the difference between a price of zero (no additional surcharge) and an additional price as something negative, even if the additional price is very small relative to the total price. Furthermore, members did not have a sense of the actual premiums they paid, because the public insurance companies expressed their "prices" for many years as a percentage of a member's income rather than in Euros and cents. That "price" was paid in part by the employee (member) and the employer. It then appeared as a largely inexplicable entry among many others on the monthly payroll stub. In contrast, the member would need to pay the surcharge directly, out of his or her own pocket. In terms of prospect theory, the perceived negative utility is high.

The rental car company Sixt also met with resistance when it tried to levy a surcharge on all kilometers driven beyond 200 (ca. 120 miles). After complaints and protests from customers, Sixt withdrew this surcharge. Deutsche Bahn has also misfired with surcharges. It tried to charge an additional 2.50 Euros for all tickets issued in person at a ticket counter. In this case, not only customers but also leading politicians complained, prompting the company to rescind the surcharge after two weeks Bank of America experienced a similar disaster when it tried to charge customers a monthly fee of $5 for their debit cards. Customers became so upset that the bank lost 20 % more customers than it had the previous year.[21] After a short time, the bank withdrew the surcharge. Only through carefully planned and executed market research does a company stand a chance of avoiding such damage to its image.

à la Carte Pricing

Whoever used to buy music on a CD needed to buy the entire album, with an average of 14 songs. This is an example of pure bundling. Unless a music company released a single, one could not buy a title individually. Much like film studios in the days of

---

[20] Wir müssen effizienter und produktiver warden. Interview with Christoph Straub. Frankfurter Allgemeine Zeitung, January 30, 2012, p. 13.

[21] Bertini M, Gourville J (2012) Pricing to create shared value. Harvard Business Review, June 2012, pp. 96–104.

"block booking," a typical album would have a mix of more attractive and less attractive songs. In this manner, the record companies transferred the excess willingness to pay for the top titles to the other tracks on the album, as described in our earlier section on price bundling. The customer usually had no other choice than to buy all the songs together. Many customers hated the fact that they had to buy 14 songs, even though they only wanted two or three. The desire for an alternative model was clearly there.

When Apple opened its iTunes stores on April 28, 2003, it used an innovative "à la carte" price model. Customers could now buy each track individually. It is said that Steve Jobs personally visited the heads of all the major record companies, in order to get the rights to sell the songs on iTunes and to use à la carte pricing. This led to an unbundling of music which later included price differentiation. The iTunes library offers 35 million titles, including music, ebooks, apps, movies, and other titles. Music tracks cost 69 cents, 99 cents, and $1.29. Other products and titles fall into different price categories, and iTunes also offers weekly specials. At one point, iTunes sold 24,000 music tracks every minute, around the clock, 7 days a week. It controlled two-thirds on the online music market, which in 2013 made up 34 % of the total market for recorded music.[22] In the first 10 years of the platform, customers had downloaded more than 25 billion songs.

The innovative price model played a significant part in the spectacular success of iTunes, but it offers no guarantee for future success. Spotify, Pandora, and Google have all offered music streaming services for a flat rate in the form of a monthly subscription. Apple has since countered with iTunes Radio, and has long offered an option called "complete my album" which allows users to add all the remaining songs from one album at a fixed price with a small bundle discount. This makes users feel like they are getting a deal.[23] But competition continues to grow. Sirius XM Radio had over 25 million subscribers in 2013 for its satellite radio service. Spotify had 20 million paid subscribers and 75 million active users in 2015. Beats Electronics, most famous for line of headphones, launched a music streaming service which offers over 20 million titles and has an exclusive family plan deal with AT&T Mobility, which is bundling the plan with its smartphone services. In May 2014, Apple announced plans to purchase Beats Electronics for $3.2 billion. Times and price schemes keep changing.

Harvard Business Review Press

The à la carte model fits well in many industries. Harvard Business Review Press sells individual book chapters and individual articles from *Harvard Business Review* (HBR) at a price of $6.95 each. Other publishing companies have adopted a similar model. This is a very attractive model for those customers with an intensive interest in one topic or aspect. That should give the publishers cause to rethink their overall price strategies. An annual subscription to *Harvard Business Review* costs either $89

[22] Theurer M (2013) Herrscher der Töne. Frankfurter Allgemeine Zeitung, April 20, 2013, p. 13.

[23] Apple's Streaming Music Problem. Fortune, April 8, 2013, pp. 19–20.

for print and online or $99 for "all-access" across mobile platforms.[24] If someone reads fewer than 13 articles in a year, it makes more sense for them to buy à la carte. If someone only needs or reads six articles, they save 53 % with the à la carte model vs. an annual subscription. The à la carte price model does carry risks and must be introduced carefully and with forethought.

Auctions

One of the oldest forms of price setting are auctions. This book began with the description of one, at a farmers' market. It seems as if prices for agricultural products, flowers, commodities, art, and public contracts have always been set with the help of auctions. Auctions come in many forms, each designed to fit a particular situation or challenge.[25] Their importance has grown in recent years, and they have also undergone a lot of innovation. This is due in part to massive government auctions of telecommunications bandwidth, energy rights, and exploration rights in the oil and gas industry. Companies are using them more often in procurement as well. Starting in 2013, Tank & Rast used a new auction process to sell the rights for fuel delivery at more than 100 of its highway gas stations.

The Internet has helped drive the usage and appeal of auctions. The most widely known example is eBay. The highest bidder wins the auction on eBay, but they pay the bid of the next-highest bidder plus a small differential. This is almost identical to an auction process already used by Johann Wolfgang von Goethe around 1,800. He would sell his manuscripts to the highest bidding publisher, who would then pay the price of the second-highest bidder. Columbia University professor William Vickrey proved that it is optimal for a bidder in these auctions to reveal his or her maximum willingness to pay. He won the Nobel Prize for this fundamental insight in 1996 and that form of auction now bears his name.

Google uses a clever auction system for selling advertising space, which takes into account the utility of the ad for the search-engine user as well as the willingness to pay of the advertiser. Google also provides the advertisers key data on advertising efficiency. The system was developed by the renowned economist Hal Varian, who has been Google's chief economist since 2007.

In auctions the idea is normally to extract the maximum willingness to pay from the bidder. For public contracts, other goals can take precedence, such as ensuring the financial viability of the participating companies, securing energy supplies, or avoiding capacity constraints. In order to achieve such goals, economists develop special "market designs."[26] Sometimes these auctions can lead to very high prices.

---

[24] Prices quoted in the HBR.org website in May 2014.

[25] Krishna V (2009) Auction theory. Elsevier Academic Press, London and Klemperer P (2004) Auctions: theory and practice. Princeton University Press, Princeton.

[26] Ockenfels A, Wambach A (2012) Menschen und Märkte: Die Ökonomik als Ingenieurwissenschaft. Orientierungen zur Wirtschafts- und Gesellschaftspolitik (4): pp. 55–60.

In 2000, mobile phone service companies in Germany paid a combined total of 50 billion Euros ($65 billion) for the rights to UMTS bandwidth in a government auction. In the Netherlands, a bandwidth auction in 2013 netted 3.8 billion Euros (ca. $5 billion), much more than expected. In the Czech Republic, regulators broke off a bandwidth auction in the spring of 2013 after they started to worry that the winning bidders may lack the funds to make the necessary investments in new infrastructure. Mobile phone network operators are now fearing bandwidth auctions, and the CEO of one of the largest players did confirm to me that these auctions represent a very difficult problem for his industry. Auctions and market designs are some of the most innovative areas in modern economic research. We can assume that more and more prices will be set through auctions tailored to the unique circumstances of a market at that time.

Pricing in Crises and Price Wars

9

Crisis: What Does That Mean?

In the context of this book, we consider a crisis to be a collapse in demand. This has several consequences for pricing. Unlike a market with a balance between supply and demand, a crisis induces a "buyer's market." The balance of power has shifted in favor of the buyers. Basic indicators of such a situation are the following:

- *Capacity utilization*: Internally, a company's production capacity and its employees are underutilized; this can result in furloughs, job cuts, or wage cuts.
- *Inventory*: Unsold goods pile up in warehouses, factory lots, or at resellers.
- *Price pressure*: Arises when customers try to take advantage of the new balance of power or when competitors start undercutting each other. Price pressure also increases internally as the urge grows to clear out unsold inventory.
- *Selling pressure*: The sales force gets pushed harder and harder to sell more units at the same time when buying resistance from the customers grows. It becomes more difficult for salespeople to meet their targets.

These developments of supply and demand lead to massive effects on prices. A crisis causes one or more profit drivers—price, volume, and cost—to develop to the company's detriment. At prevailing prices, volume falls. The company may feel the need to reduce its own prices as a reaction either to reduced demand or to price cuts by competitors.

To show the negative effects on profit, let's return once more to our power tool case. This time around we are on defense instead of offense. Our starting situation is a price of $100, variable unit costs of $60, fixed costs of $30 million, and sales of one million units. Figure 9.1 shows how profit drops if either price or volume falls by 5 %.

Cutting prices by 5 % leads to a 50 % drop in profit, much greater than the 20 % profit decline we would see if volume fell by 5 %. From a profit perspective, it is better in a time of crisis to suffer a volume decline than a price decline. The reason for this

© Springer International Publishing Switzerland 2015
H. Simon, *Confessions of the Pricing Man*, DOI 10.1007/978-3-319-20400-0_9

A decrease of 5%.....   ... leads to a
                                                           profit decline of...

	Profit driver		Profit			
	Old	New	Old	New		
Price	€100	€95	€10m	€5m	-50%	
Volume	1m	0.95m	€10m	€8m	-20%	

Fig. 9.1 Effects of a price or volume decline

is easy to understand. The price decline has a full, direct impact on profit. The profit margin—which includes an allocation of fixed costs—falls by half, from $10 per unit to just $5. Because volume and variable costs do not change, and fixed costs don't change anyway, the profit likewise falls by half. The situation is much different, though, when volume falls by 5 % (or 50,000 units) but price remains constant. The drop in volume means that variable costs fall by $3 million (60 × 50,000), so that total profit decreases by only $2 million instead of $5 million.

Confront managers with the statements above as they need to choose between Alternatives A and B below, and you get an explosive debate.

Alternative A: Accept a price cut of 5 % and volume remains constant.

Alternative B: Accept a volume reduction of 5 % and price remains constant.

I have discussed these two alternatives with many managers at seminars and workshops. Almost all of them lean toward Alternative A, even though the profit is $3 million lower. The managers generally present the same arguments, namely that volume, market share, and staff utilization are higher in Alternative A. One avoids the need for furloughs or outright staffing cuts. We already examined this fundamental goal conflict between profit and volume in Chap. 5. Under normal circumstances, managers tend to show a preference for a "lower prices, constant volume" alternative, but this tendency becomes more pronounced in a time of crisis. The effort to keep sales and capacity utilization up, and keep people at work, takes precedence. But in a time of crisis, that can be precisely the wrong approach.

The case of our power tool business—where either price or volume drops, but not both—is bad enough. But it is relatively harmless when compared to a crisis in which both price and volume fall by the same percentage. Figure 9.2 shows this devastating impact.

If both volume and price fall by 5 %, revenue drops by 9.75 % and profit plunges by 67.5 %. If both price and volume drop by 20 %, revenue declines by 36 % and we post a loss of $14 million. If price and volume both fall by 30 %, revenue will plummet by 51 %. These declines may seem extreme at first glance, but such acute, life-threatening declines were not uncommon in 2009, the worst year of the Great Recession.

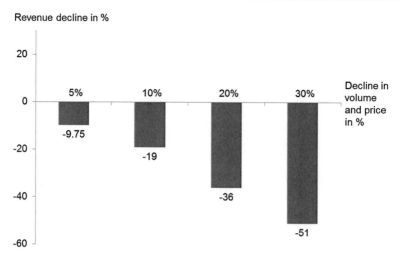

Fig. 9.2 Revenue impact of a simultaneous percentage decline in price and volume

Cut Volume or Cut Price?

How should one respond to a crisis? Is it better to cut prices or to accept a decline in volume? The statements below—from two CEOs in the automotive industry— show just how different the opinions are on questions of price and volume management in a time of crisis.

Richard Wagoner, the former CEO of General Motors, said: "Fixed costs are extremely high in our industry. We realized that in a crisis we fare better with low prices than by reducing volume. After all, in contrast to some competitors, we still make money with this strategy."[1] Former Porsche CEO Wendelin Wiedeking represented the exact opposite end of the spectrum with this statement: "We have a policy of keeping prices stable to protect our brand and to prevent a drop in prices for used cars. When demand goes down, we reduce production volume but don't lower our prices."[2] He went a step further when he noted: "One thing is clear to us: we are not going to pump the market full of cars when there is no demand for them. We always want to produce one car less than the market demands."[3]

Both executives spoke about a crisis-induced decline in demand and came to the exact opposite conclusions:

– General Motors lowers its prices, in order to prevent or lessen a decline in the production volume.
– Porsche lowers its production volume, in order to prevent or lessen a decline in prices.

[1] Statement at the International Automobile Show in Frankfurt in September 2003.

[2] Comment provided by Georg Tacke, CEO of Simon-Kucher & Partners, who told the author about his conversations with Wendelin Wiedeking.

[3] Sportwagenhersteller Porsche muss sparen. Frankfurter Allgemeine Zeitung, January 31, 2009, p. 14.

Our previous analysis indicated that from a profit standpoint, it is better to accept a volume decline than a price cut. Yes, managing volume is an important measure in times of crisis. But what is the right choice? The laws of economics show their merciless power here. If a company or an industry throws too much product into the market, lower prices and lower margins are unavoidable. The problem begins in the factory. If there is pressure to keep people working and to produce the corresponding amount of goods, this excess will suppress prices. Low variable unit costs and high fixed costs, which are a blessing in good times, become a curse in a crisis. High fixed costs need to be spread across the largest possible number of goods. At the same time, low variable unit costs mean that it is still possible to get a positive unit contribution despite low prices. All of these factors conspire to put formidable pressure on the sales force, which uses price concessions to try to move the required volumes.

One objective during a crisis must be to defuse this vicious volume and supply cycle as quickly as possible. Many companies in various industries did this in 2009, reacting in a calm and cool manner as the crisis deepened. They introduced shorter work shifts and closed factories. Almost all car companies reacted that way. The global chemical giant BASF shut down production at 80 plants around the world. Arcelor-Mittal, the world market leader in steel, reacted even sooner, curtailing production by one-third as early as November 2008.[4] US-based airlines followed suit in June 2009, when Delta said that it would trim foreign capacity by 15 % and domestic capacity by 6 %. American Airlines, in turn, reduced its capacity by 7.5 %.[5] The champagne industry in France saw demand fall by 20 % in 2009. But instead of cutting prices, the vintners in the Champagne region left one-third of their grapes in the fields. That allowed them to keep the price level relatively stable. Those are all intelligent moves. But sometimes a price cut is nonetheless unavoidable.

Making Intelligent Price Cuts

"One of the most important decisions in this recession is what to do about prices. In booms you don't have to get pricing exactly right. Now you do!" wrote *Fortune* editor and columnist Geoff Colvin in 2009.[6] During a crisis, price becomes an extremely important yet incompletely understood tool. An indispensable prerequisite for intelligent pricing is a precise understanding of the relationship between price and volume. What has changed since the crisis hit? Will price changes have different effects in the crisis than under more normal or stable circumstances? The most common reactions in a crisis are also the most incorrect ones: cutting prices or increasing discounts. How can we explain this counterproductive behavior? In most cases, again, the primary motivation is the desire to protect existing volume levels and keep employee utilization at levels which do not require furloughs or job cuts.

---

[4] Hoffnung an den Hochöfen. Handelsblatt, February 12, 2009, p. 12.

[5] The Wall Street Journal, June 12, 2009, p. B1.

[6] Colvin G (2009) Yes, you can raise prices. Fortune, March 2, 2009, p. 19.

A volume crisis means that a company sells fewer units at the same price. But by no means is the opposite true: it does not mean that a company can sell the same number of units as before if it cuts its prices. That is a grand illusion which is rarely fulfilled. Why is that true? There are two reasons. First, the crisis has altered the demand curve, shifting it downward, which means that a company doesn't sell as many units as it used to at a certain price. The previous demand curve no longer applies. Second, price cuts or steeper discounts do not yield the desired upturn in sales, because competitors are also cutting their prices. This fact alone dashes any hopes the company may have had of increasing its market share or defending its previous volume. It is not true that high prices discourage consumers from buying during a crisis; they stop buying altogether because they perceive high uncertainty and hoard their cash. A price cut within normal ranges does little to alleviate this uncertainty. It therefore stands to reason that one should refrain from using price aggressively during a crisis. The most likely consequence is that the company starts a price war which doesn't increase anyone's volumes, but ruins margins for a long time. On the other hand, it is also an illusion that one can navigate an entire crisis without making any price concessions at all.

If there is no way to avoid a price cut or a price concession any longer, then one should structure the price cut in such a way that it minimizes the negative margin effects and maximizes the positive volume effects. Suppliers have asymmetrical interests depending on whether they are raising or cutting prices. In an ideal case, a customer should not notice a price increase. For a price decrease, the more the customer notices it, the greater the positive volume effect will be. This places the onus on the supplier to use communications to increase the price elasticity of the product or service. Empirical studies have shown that a volume increase from a price cut is significantly higher when the action is supported with special price-oriented advertising, additional placements, or special signage. This volume increase is more necessary than ever during a crisis, but precisely in such tough times, communication budgets are also limited. This presents the company with a dilemma. The company might need to make more price reductions, but lacks the money to communicate them effectively.

The "cash for clunkers" program in 2009 is an example of a well-publicized price incentive which did indeed boost sales. The program offered consumers between $3,500 and $4,500 if they would trade in their old cars for new, fuel-efficient ones. Edmunds.com estimated that the average residual value of the cars traded in was $1,475. Thus, the subsidy created a significant benefit for US consumers.[7] The government-backed program ran out of its initial $1 billion in funding after two weeks, so Congress allocated an additional $2 billion to extend it. The same kind of program proved even more popular in Germany. The car makers added more incentives on top of the $3,500 the government provided, resulting in net price discounts of over 30 %. The German Government initially allocated $2 billion for the

---

[7] Congress Passes $2 Billion Extension of 'Cash for Clunkers' Program. ABC News, August 6, 2009.

program, but ultimately appropriated a total of $7 billion.[8] These massive price reductions clearly combined with high attention overcame the purchase resistance many people in the target group may have had. The programs showed how such large, well-publicized incentives can work, but not every industry will have the good fortune of getting government subsidies in a crisis.

For an effective example without government support, we can look at Hela, a regional home improvement store chain in Germany. Even to this day, German retail stores remain closed on Sundays, except for four designated "open" days throughout the year. On one such Sunday in the spring of 2009, one Hela outlet offered a 20 % discount on all purchases.[9] This created absolute gridlock in the parking lots and streets surrounding the store. Hela saw a run on its merchandise. The combination of a dramatic price cut and effective communication—buoyed by the open Sunday—encouraged consumers to set aside their uncertainty and go shopping. Whether Hela turned this enormous amount of traffic into actual profits is another story. Did the additional volume compensate for the "sacrifice" of 20 % on every sale? If we assume that Hela had a gross margin of 25 %, it would need to sell five times as much merchandise as on a typical day to earn the same level of profit. Even in crisis situations, and despite the potential in combining large price cuts with an intense communication campaign, one should still be wary of making such cuts.

Offer Cash or Goods Instead of Lower Prices!

Price concessions can come in the form of cash rebates, which reduce the transaction price, or in the form of additional goods and services. Offering goods and services instead of lower prices has several advantages during a crisis:

- *Price*: The nominal price level is not harmed.
- *Profit*: Assuming the same percentage, the supplier is better off profitwise by offering goods or services instead of a straight discount.
- *Volume*: This form of discount generates more volume and keeps people working.

To illustrate this, we will look at the case of a manufacturer of playground equipment. When the crisis hit, it reacted by offering resellers a special deal: buy five and get the sixth unit for free. At a price of $10,000 per unit this represents an effective price decrease of 16.7 %, because the reseller receives six units but only

---

[8] Driving out of Germany, to pollute another day. The New York Times, August 7, 2009.

[9] This action is reminiscent of the tagline of the home improvement chain Praktiker, which offered "20 percent off everything except pet food." Burnout is the main reason why Praktiker's permanent discount of 20 % had minimal effect on sales (see chapter 10). In contrast, Hela rarely offered discounts, so a discount of 20 %—especially during a crisis—proved very effective.

pays for five. The profit calculations show the effect of a discount via goods versus a straight-up discount. At a price of $10,000 with one unit for free, the manufacturer gets revenue of $50,000, has a volume of six units, and earns a contribution of $14,000. But if the manufacturer had offered the flat discount of 16.7 % instead, it would get a price of $8,330 per unit (reflecting the discount of 16.7 %). The manufacturer gets $41,650 in revenue, has a volume of five units, and earns a contribution of $11,650.

Using goods as a means to deliver a discount improves volume, employee utilization, and profit. This kind of offer has an additional advantage. If the manufacturer designates it as a temporary measure during the crisis, it is easier to rescind when the crisis ends. Trying to restore the "crisis" list price of $8,330 back to its pre-crisis level of $10,000 would be much harder.

A manufacturer of designer furniture also fared well with discounts in the form of goods during the 2009 crisis. This leading brand placed great emphasis on price consistency and continuity. Whenever customers argued for a price discount— which they did frequently and sometimes relentlessly during the crisis—any concession would involve an additional piece of furniture rather than a price discount. In most cases, the customers were satisfied with this offer. The tactic resulted in higher capacity utilization (they sold more units than they would have with a price discount) and also in a higher contribution. This higher contribution was based primarily on the different ways that the manufacturer and the customer perceive the value of the additional furniture. The customer perceives the value of the additional furniture based on its retail price, while the manufacturer looked instead at the variable cost. In other words, the manufacturer can offer a gift which has a value of $100 in the eyes of the customer, but costs the manufacturer only $60. In the case of a direct price discount, the manufacturer needs to give up the actual $100 in order to give the customer a "gift" of the same value.

The same principle applies to renting, not just to purchases. In general, it is more advantageous for a lessor to offer a new tenant several months of free rent instead of a discounted price per square foot. The valuation of a building depends on a multiple of the rent, and banks use a similar metric when they make decisions on financing. This gives a lessor an incentive to have a high nominal rent, even if one assumes that rent will be zero for the first few months. It is interesting to note that the tenants also place a high perceived value on the free rent. That may be due to the fact that in the initial period of their lease, they have other pressing obligations such as moving costs and buying new furniture.

Staying Off the Customers' Radar Screen

Despite the heavy price pressures, it is still possible to make selective price increases during a crisis. On the one hand, some price systems are so complex that customers never have full price transparency. That can stem from the sheer size of the product assortment, the number of individual price elements, or a complex and convoluted system of terms and conditions. On a price list of a bank, for example, many customers do not even notice some of the line items, never mind recall the actual prices. Normally the customer's eye falls only on certain prominent prices or price elements. In banking, this can be the monthly fee for basic banking services, transaction fees for investment funds, or the current interest rate on savings, certificates of deposit, or money market accounts. Business customers would more likely have their eye on key international interest rates and the fees for wire transfers. Private customers are less likely to know the management fees for investment funds, the interest rates charged for overdrafts, or even their exact credit card interest rates. That latter group of price elements offers opportunities for price increases.

During the recent crisis, a regional bank raised certain prices that would remain under the customers' radar screens. These increases yielded several hundred thousand dollars in additional revenue without any customer complaints. A prerequisite for this was a complete analysis of all price and product components regarding the number of transactions, assets, returns, and the sensitivity of customers to potential price increases. These aspects were researched through a survey of the bank's customer relations team, which was a quick and cost-effective process.

Selective price increase potential is buried in many places when you have a large assortment. This applies to retail, spare parts, or tourism. Their customers usually orient themselves on a few key products and know them well, but have little or no knowledge of the prices of the rest of the assortment. That is especially true for products customers rarely buy. You might recall my encounter with the padlock for my barn, when I had little knowledge of what a padlock should cost and chose one from the middle range of the assortment.

Spare parts offer several areas where a company can raise prices during a crisis without losing volume. First, customers still need spare parts, crisis or not. One area to focus on is differentiation of the parts by segment, based on the customers' different levels of willingness to pay. One category is exclusive parts, available only from the original manufacturer. Another category is commodities, which someone could buy from the original manufacturer or from a number of alternative suppliers. The challenge here is to set up the right price policy for each volume tier. In one such effort for a car manufacturer, Simon-Kucher & Partners helped implement an average price increase of 12 % for the spare parts business, resulting in a profit improvement of 20 % versus a base scenario. This came about because of selective price increases for spare parts which had very low price elasticities—the reward for a deep analysis of the buyers' needs and behavior.

Another aspect to consider is the changing nature of price differentiation, which creates new opportunities in a crisis as people change their habits. Studies have shown that people tend to dine out less during a crisis, but also read more because they spend more time at home or have more leisure time. These changes can manifest themselves in greater or lesser levels of demand and also increased or decreased price sensitivity. This means that I cannot make any blanket statements on how prices and price strategies should change when a crisis hits. Only a thorough understanding of the effects and their intensity and duration will lead you to the right answers.

The Arch-Nemesis: Overcapacity

The biggest challenge facing pricing in the modern world is overcapacity. This conclusion has become clearer and clearer to me over time, and received a lot of support during the last crisis. This problem confronts even new growth industries such as wind power technology or smartphones.

"The capacity in the wind power industry exceeds the global demand by a factor of two," said one trade association official in 2013.[10] We see overcapacity almost everywhere. In one of Simon-Kucher & Partners project in the building materials industry, overcapacity was the issue that preoccupied managers more than any other. The steel industry constantly bemoans the fact that it has too much capacity, and it also seems to be a chronic problem in the automotive industry. The industry saw record-high global sales of 80.1 million vehicles in 2011, but global manufacturing capacity was 100 million vehicles and continues to expand. Overcapacity is typical as a market enters its mature phase, as companies overestimate growth potential, and also typical for a market's decline phase, which companies often do not anticipate. Even emerging markets can get to a state of excess capacity relatively quickly.

"Global overcapacity for car makers is not only a problem in the saturated markets of Europe," said one expert. "The booming emerging markets—especially China—could become a problem sooner or later for carmakers who have quickly ramped up their production capacity."[11]

We can appreciate the effects that overcapacity has on prices and profits in this statement from the CEO of an engineering company, the global leader in its market, who got straight to the point with this comment: "No one can make any money in our business. Every single company has too much capacity. Every time a project comes up for bid, someone needs it desperately and offers suicidal prices. Sometimes it's us, sometimes it's a competitor. Even though four suppliers make up 80 % of the global market in our business, no one makes any money."

It didn't take long for me to formulate my answer: "As long as this overcapacity remains, nothing will change."

The Great Recession of 2009 forced one company to withdraw from that market, and the surviving companies all reduced their capacity. What happened next? The industry quickly returned to profitability. The share price of the engineering company whose CEO I spoke with also benefited from this fundamental shift in the industry. After languishing for years and sitting at just $13 in 2009, it rose to over $100 per share by 2015 after the industry got its capacity under control. No competitor in the industry could have eliminated the miserable overcapacity on its own. Prices in the industry rose to profitable levels only after several competitors reduced their capacity. The crisis was actually helpful because it eventually forced all competitors to adjust their capacity to demand.

---

[10] Frankfurter Allgemeine Zeitung, January 31, 2013, p. 11.
[11] Produktion, April 23, 2012.

The presence of overcapacity—and the pressure it puts on prices—does not always prevent investment in more capacity. The luxury hotel industry is a good example. Comments such as ""overcapacity is pelting the prices at top hotels" and "the higher the standard, the lower the profits" describe the state of the industry."[12] Despite the depression in prices, investment in new luxury hotels remains robust. This will only worsen the problem. In many companies and industries, I have witnessed many attempts and many discussions—some of which dragged on for years—as managers scrambled to implement the prices they needed to earn a reasonable profit or ensure the company's survival. But as long as overcapacity remains in such markets, most of the efforts to obtain better prices will not be very effective. The answer here lies not in vain attempts to raise prices, but in cutting capacity. This means that the complex interplay between price and capacity is a top management issue of highest priority.

What can a company do, though, if it reduces capacity and other competitors do not? Or even worse: What can a company do when a competitor seizes another's capacity reduction as an opportunity to increase its market share? Similar to the situation with a price increase, we have another prisoner's dilemma. If competitors do not follow the move, or counter it with their own capacity increase, then cutting one's capacity can be dangerous. One will lose market share or even put the company's long-term market position in jeopardy. For this reason—just as it is with price increases—a company needs to observe its competitors closely and within legal limits explain the need for lower capacity in the industry. Of course, antitrust law forbids any kind of coordination or contractual cooperation among competitors, be it about prices or capacity in the industry. Signaling, or the announcement of a company's intentions or plans, is one legal way to help determine the appropriate course of action in face of the prisoner's dilemma. One should therefore consider using signaling systematically as an instrument for capacity management and not only for price. Effective signaling can include announcements that a company will defend its market share, or that it will retaliate if competitors take advantage of a change in the supply situation.

As with pricing, it is important to maintain consistency between pronouncements and actions. In order to remain credible, a company needs to follow through on the changes and the timing it has publicly announced. Management also needs to make sure that the sales force complies with any changes in price, discounting, or other sales policies and remains disciplined. If management announces a more disciplined course of action, but salespeople continue to pursue aggressive prices, it risks drawing a severe counter-response from competitors, to the detriment not only of the company but also of the entire industry. The statements in the economics and marketing literature on price management in an oligopoly apply equally to capacity management.[13]

In a crisis situation, the chances are greater that competitors will understand the need to reduce capacity, as it is in their own self-interest. Many industries saw

---

[12] Unter einem schlechten Stern. Handelsblatt, March 20, 2013, p. 20.

[13] Simon H, Fassnacht M (2008) Preismanagement, 3rd edn. Gabler, Wiesbaden.

significant reductions in overall capacity from 2008 to 2010. The leading tour operators TUI and Thomas Cook reduced their capacity throughout Europe.[14] Many airlines eliminated flights to less popular destinations. Price pressures in a market always have root causes, and one of those is often overcapacity. As long as this root cause remains unaddressed or unresolved, any changes companies make are just doctoring with symptoms rather than finding lasting cures. The path to rational, reasonable, profitable prices often requires the elimination of excess capacity.

Price Increases in Times of Crisis

Crises change the supply and demand-situation in a market and therefore create an opportunity for companies to analyze and rethink their price propositions. One should not confine oneself to price decreases, but instead think more broadly and also consider the alternative. For example, the crisis period of 2008–2010 hit the restaurant industry particularly hard.[15] After all, dining out is more expensive than eating at home. But the Panera Bread chain, which operated roughly 1,300 outlets in the USA at the time, reacted differently than its competitors as the crisis struck. Instead of cutting prices or offering promotions, Panera upgraded its menu and raised its prices. This included adding a lobster sandwich to the menu at $16.99. Panera-CEO Ron Shaich explained the changes as follows: "Most of the world seems to be focused on the Americans who are unemployed. We're focused on the 90 % that are still employed."[16] Bucking the industry trends, Panera's revenue rose by 4 % in 2009 and profit by 28 %.[17] Apparently the people in Panera's target segment were willing to pay higher prices for higher value.

In June 2009, at the peak of the crisis, US stainless steel manufacturers raised their prices by between 5 and 6 %. The industry's capacity utilization at the time was only at 45 %, which automatically increased total unit costs. Because all manufacturers were affected more or less equally, the attempt to raise prices succeeded. "We are raising prices because of the increased costs of operating our mills at the current lower demand levels," commented Dennis Oates, the CEO of Universal Stainless & Alloy Products. He then added that "[t]he whole mindset has changed in the industry. Sometimes you have to accept the fact that raising prices is a risk. But you are better off not chasing that last sale at the bottom. Nearly all of our customers have accepted the price hike."[18] Even in hindsight, this price increase comes across as a wise move.

---

[14] Meitinger K (2009) Wege aus der Krise. Private Wealth, March 2009, pp. 26–31.

[15] Industry trends in a downturn. The McKinsey Quarterly, December 2008.

[16] Jargon J (2009) Slicing the bread but not the prices. The Wall Street Journal, August 18, 2009.

[17] Jannarone J (2010) Panera bread's strong run. The Wall Street Journal, January 23, 2010.

[18] The Wall Street Journal, June 11, 2009, p. B2.

Price Wars

Price wars happen in many industries everywhere across the world. In the Global Pricing Study of Simon-Kucher & Partners, some 59 % of all managers surveyed said that their company was involved in a price war.[19] The situation was worst in Japan, where 74 % of respondents reported being engaged in a price war. The rate in Germany was slightly below average at 53 %, while the USA (along with Belgium) had the lowest incidence at 46 %.[20]

Very surprising, however, were the answers to the question of who started that price war. An incredible 82 % of respondents said that a competitor had started the price war. As is often the case in life, the instigators are always "the others." Some 12 % of the respondents said that their own company had intentionally started the price war. The remaining 5 % admitted that their company had started the price war unintentionally, which can only mean that they had made a move without correctly anticipating the competitive reaction.

Price wars are one of the most effective ways to destroy profits in an industry for a long period. One remark from an American manager sums the situation up succinctly: "In a war, the atomic bomb and price are subject to the same limitation: both can only be used once." That statement may be somewhat of an exaggeration, but the parallels are clear. Starting a price war in an industry is easy, but a price war is hard to stop, creates tremendous mistrust, and leaves behind scorched earth. What factors precipitate a price war? And how much damage does it do to price levels? Figure 9.3 answers these questions.[21]

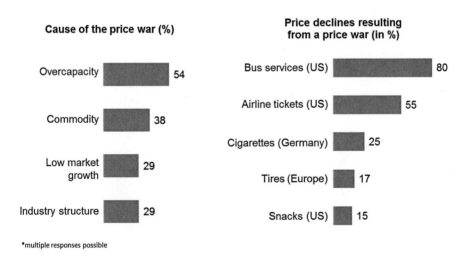

Fig. 9.3 Price wars: Their causes and the effects on prices

[19] The Global Pricing Study included responses from 2,713 managers from 50 countries.

[20] Simon-Kucher & Partners, Global Pricing Study 2012, Bonn 2012.

[21] Heil O (1996) Price wars: issues and results. University of Mainz.

Fig. 9.4 Industries with the highest incidence of price wars (in percent)

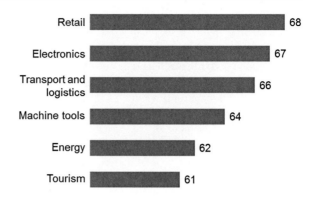

This study shows that overcapacity is the most frequent trigger for a price war. That is especially true for commodity products or services, i.e., those with little differentiation and for which price is often the decisive purchase criterion. Slow growth also increases the risk of a price war. As the right side of Fig. 9.3 shows, collapses in price levels can be catastrophic. Earning a profit after such price declines is virtually inconceivable.

If we look at the incidence of price wars by industry, the picture matches up pretty well with this diagnosis. Figure 9.4 shows the industries where price wars occur with above-average frequency around the world.[22] Noteworthy is both how high these frequencies are and how similar they are across different industries.

How can a company prevent a price war? And how can it end a price war? These are certainly not easy questions to answer. To make one point clear up front: there are no definitive, universally applicable solutions to those questions. In addition to the factors shown on the left side of Fig. 9.3, personal aggressiveness of managers plays a key role. Time and again I have met managers whose one and only goal seemed to be the complete and utter destruction of their competitors. I once witnessed a CEO turn to his Sales VP and ask point blank: "what would it cost to drive Competitor X from the market?"

"It would cost $2 billion," the Sales VP said.

"Then do it," the CEO ordered without a moment's hesitation.

When bosses infect their teams with that kind of attitude, especially the sales teams, it is no surprise that such a company comes across to the market as price aggressive. In the end, the company took no clear-cut action.

Unrealistic goals fall into the same category. For instance, General Motors was traditionally market share oriented. Business school professor Roger More says: "Historically, GM's financial metrics have focused on market share and revenue, rather than on cash flow and profit."[23] The managers at GM lived out that philosophy. At a sales meeting in 2002, the company's managers wore a lapel pin with the num-

---

[22] Simon-Kucher & Partners, Global Pricing Study 2012, Bonn 2012.

[23] More R (2009) How general motors lost its focus – and its way. Ivey Business Journal, June 2009.

ber "29" on it. The company's market share in the USA had fallen steady over decades, and at that time was well below 29 %.[24] The "29" on the pin represented the new market share goal. No one outside the company thought that GM could turn things around and achieve that goal. But even after real market developments showed that the "29" was an illusory goal, management still had faith.

"'29' will be there until we hit '29'," Gary Cowger, at that time the president of GM North America, said two years later. "And then I will probably buy a '30'."[25] Such unrealistic attitudes and goals lead to price aggression, price wars, and ultimately to bankruptcy, as General Motors itself proved in dramatic fashion. Since 2002, GM's market share declined continuously, falling to 19.9 % in 2009 and 17.9 % in 2012. The best methods to avoid a price war are to curtail aggressive statements and behavior and to set realistic targets for revenue, volume, and market share. I strongly advise managers to deal more peacefully with competitors and save their stubbornness and discipline for their negotiations with customers. I admit that such advice runs counter to what you will read in most management and marketing books.

But price wars are by no means confined to mature markets such as automotive. We observe them in young markets as well. In April 2014 the Wall Street Journal writes "Price War Erupts in Cloud Services."[26] Amazon, Microsoft, and Google cut prices on various services by up to 85 %, sparking a three-way price war. The ones who enjoy this are the customers. "It's terrific for my business," one customer said.

Communication and signaling are essential for avoiding or ending price wars. The following advice captures this sentiment well: "Companies that successfully avoid price wars consistently write and speak publicly about the horrors of price competition and virtues of value competition. They do this 'jawboning' in articles, in their in-house publications, at industry association meetings, and in every available public forum."[27]

Taking a softer stance toward competition is a path that leading companies have already followed, as this statement from Toyota Chairman Hiroshi Okuda shows. He told reporters that "Japan's auto industry needed to give Detroit time and room to catch its breath" and suggested that Toyota might increase its car prices in the USA. The move would still have a self-serving component, because higher prices would likely boost Toyota's profits. But it would also create an opportunity for US automakers to gain additional market share.[28]

Price communication should decrease the probability that customers and competitors misinterpret a price action or the motivations behind it. Misinterpreting prices and price changes can be damaging, regardless of whether the competitor or

---

[24] Sedgwick D (2002) Market share meltdown. Automotive News, November 4, 2002.

[25] GM is Still Studying the $100,000 Cadillac. Automotive News, May 17, 2004.

[26] Ovide S (2014) Price war erupts in cloud services. The Wall Street Journal Europe, April 17, 2014, p. 20.

[27] Presentation by the author: "How to Boost Profit Through Power Pricing" at the World Marketing & Sales Forum, Madrid, November 22, 2008.

[28] Sapsford J (2005) Toyota Sends Mixed Messages on Detroit Woes The Wall Street Journal, April 27, 2005, p. 22.

the company itself makes the error in the first place. Both cases can lead to a price war. Let's assume that Company A wants to introduce a new product that will replace an older model. Its warehouses still contain a large inventory of the old model. Perhaps the simplest solution would be to make a massive price cut and then support it with a heavy price communication campaign. Yet in its campaign, the company neglects to mention its intention, which is to replace that old model with a new one, nor does it mention the motivation behind the price cut, namely to clear out the older inventory.

If Company A is fortunate, customers will buy the products at the much lower price and empty the warehouse. But how will competitors respond to such an aggressive price cut, in the absence of additional information? The chances are high that competitors will perceive the price action as an attack and as an attempt to steal market share. Under such circumstances, the competitors are only a short step away from striking back with their own aggressive price cuts. If competitors really do cut their prices, then Company A suddenly has two problems. First, it will sell fewer units of the old products than originally expected, which means that it does not deplete its stocks. Second, it may have permanently destroyed the price level and may need to introduce its new version at a lower price.

The competitive responses would probably be much different if Company A instead announces that it will soon introduce a new version, and that its price cut is a temporary action to clear existing inventory. If competitors find these explanations credible (a function of Company A's previous behavior), the likelihood is greater that they will restrain themselves and avoid starting a price war. The exact same action—in this case a temporary price cut of, say, 30 %—can be interpreted in different ways by customers and competitors and can lead to entirely different responses. This makes signaling the method of choice if a company wants to reduce the risk of a price war.

I summarize my insights into price wars very simply: there are smart industries and there are self-destructive industries. What is the difference? The smart ones avoid price wars, and the self-destructive ones get stuck in them. The smart ones are profitable; the self-destructive ones incur losses or destroy profits. The problem is that it only takes one self-destructive competitor to render an entire industry self-destructive. That's why it is better to have smart competitors.

What the CEO Needs to Do

10

If a CEO asked me point-blank for advice on how to use price in the best way possible in his/her company, what would I say? That is not a rhetorical question. I do hear that question often, and I realize that a CEO is not looking for an answer that begins with "It depends on your situation ..." or "It's really complicated." They know that already. They want more.

One recent situation involved a CEO who had been promoted from within to run a global company with annual revenues of more than $50 billion. He explained that his company historically placed a huge emphasis on market share, to the point where that "obsession" had taken root in the company's culture. That may have been fine a few decades ago, but the company now served far more mature markets than growing ones, he noted.

"So what should I do?" he asked. "What is your silver bullet or secret potion?"

I admitted of course that I didn't have one. No one does. But I did have an answer.

"Lead your company with a strict profit orientation," I said. "And keep in mind that price is the most effective profit driver."

"Easier said than done," he responded, reminding me that his predecessor would publicly berate his direct reports who had lost market share. "That is incredibly difficult."

I advised him to repeat the "profit" mantra every day, as often as possible. He of course will hear the message every time he says it, but others hear it only once or twice and won't get tired of it. He also needs to follow his words with consistent, appropriate actions. One of the most important measures is to base the incentive systems of the country managers strictly on profit, not on revenue, volume, or market share targets.

There is also a tactical element which must reinforce the link between words and action. His company should not start any price wars. It should not respond to every aggressive move that competitors make. In countries or regions where the company has market leadership, it should pursue price leadership through a consistent communication campaign emphasizing the importance of price and value.

© Springer International Publishing Switzerland 2015
H. Simon, *Confessions of the Pricing Man*, DOI 10.1007/978-3-319-20400-0_10

Though the long-term profit orientation matters most, this CEO will need some successes in the short term. The goal, however, remains: direct the company's attention and energy resolutely to a long-term profit orientation. That requires a focus on value creation. The most important aspect of price is and will be value to customer.

"Good pricing has three prerequisites: create value, quantify value, and communicate value," I said in summary. "That is when you get the price you deserve, the price you need for a profitable business. And, last but not least, avoid price wars."

If a company can resist the temptation of price wars and eliminate the stigma of market share losses, it can improve the profit situation for an entire industry. In Poland, the company's subsidiary was number two. The new country manager ended a price war, which paved the way for price increases. The market leader followed. The net result for the number two-company was higher profits and a slight loss of market share. This success marked the first time the CEO did not criticize a country manager for losing market share, and this sent a powerful signal to the managers in other countries.

Price and Shareholder Value

We learned as early as in Chap. 1 that profit maximization is the only sensible goal for pricing. When people talk of profit maximization, they usually refer to one period, for example a year or a quarter. In reality, one's planning horizon should be longer and not limited to one period. The short-term orientation—in particular the typical quarterly fixation of publicly traded companies—is one of the most controversial aspects of capitalism.

Management should focus on long-term profit maximization. That is identical to saying that a company should increase shareholder value, or its market capitalization if the company is listed. Because price is the most effective profit driver, it follows automatically that price must take on a decisive role in management's efforts to increase shareholder value. This makes price a vital issue for top management. If a company's pricing drives its earnings, and earnings drive shareholder value, how can a CEO not make pricing one of his or her highest priorities?

Unfortunately, price does not appear to be a high priority for many CEOs. Former Microsoft CEO Steve Ballmer said that price is "really really important" but a lot of people "under-think it through."[1] Nor is price a high priority for the investment community at large. Though references to price have become more frequent in recent years, you still find them only rarely in commentaries, in equity analyst reports, or similar documents. One exception is this comment from investor Warren Buffett, who stated "The single most important decision in evaluating a business is

---

[1] Be all-in, or all-out: Steve Ballmer's advice for startups. The Next Web, March 4, 2014.

pricing power."[2] Even private equity investors, whose typical objective after taking over a company is to increase its value, rarely take advantage of price opportunities. Instead they typically focus on cutting costs or driving volume growth. Cost-cutting is internal and one sees the effects directly. Attempts to increase volume usually do not draw a negative reaction from customers. But price increases may put customer relationships at risk and the effects of price actions are often indirect. This risk aversion and the perceived lack of control over the outcome make price actions a less palatable option than cost-cutting and volume growth. The same thinking applies to executives and senior management, where the commitment to pricing is often lacking. We know that companies earn higher profits when their CEOs and the most senior managers get personally involved in price management; yet the attention that top managers actually pay to pricing is limited in most companies.

How Price Can Increase Market Capitalization

The relationship between market capitalization and after-tax profit is expressed as the price-earnings ratio, or PE ratio. As of May 16, 2014, the average PE ratio for all 30 companies which constitute the Dow Jones Industrial Average (DJIA) was 16.6.[3] In other words, the market valued the average company at 16.6 times its profit. The PE ratio can fluctuate sharply over time, but the figure of 16.6 is roughly in line with the long-term average for the DJIA stocks.

In Fig. 5.2 we presented the dramatic effect that a price of increase of 2 % could have on the profitability of selected public companies. Let's assume that this price increase sticks and the PE ratio remains constant. That allows us to calculate the effect a 2 % price increase has on a company's market capitalization. Figure 10.1 shows the results for the same companies we looked at in Fig. 5.2. The PE ratio for the selected companies is 17.93, slightly higher than the current PE ratio for the DJIA.

If Sony succeeded in implementing a price increase of 2 % across its entire product portfolio, its market capitalization would increase by $42.73 billion. On average the companies in Fig. 10.1 would see their market capitalization increase by $48.88 billion or by 26.7 % (based on the current average market capitalization of $182.8 billion). The effect that such a relatively small price increase has on a company's value should be the more interesting and more relevant performance indicator for top managers and business owners, because of its long-term nature. These numbers reveal in a very impressive manner the sheer massive potential that pricing has to increase the value of a company. I wonder how many leaders and business owners are aware of the leverage effect of prices, never mind actually inspire their organizations to tap that effect through professional pricing.

---

[2] Statement by Warren Buffett before the Financial Crisis Inquiry Commission (FCIC) on May 26, 2010.

[3] Market Data Center. The Wall Street Journal, May 16, 2014.

Company	Market capitalization in $bn	Price-earnings ratio	Increase in market capitalization through sustainable 2% price increase
Verizon Communications	124.1	18.7	246.37
BP	272.0	7.6	136.57
Exxon Mobil	671.0	10.7	100.89
Wal Mart	241.7	14.0	94.90
Nestle	458.8	18.0	59.99
AT&T	211.6	14.6	55.40
Toyota Motor	131.2	13.2	45.09
Bank of America	120.9	46.4	43.24
Sony	18.1	107.0	42.73
General Electric	237.4	13.8	38.46
IBM	407.0	12.6	38.44
CVS Caremark	77.9	14.1	36.88
Cardinal Health	22.0	12.8	33.26
Procter & Gamble	262.7	20.1	31.05
Apple	484.0	14.1	27.25
Siemens	95.6	14.0	26.95
Samsung Electronics	207.2	10.3	26.94
Boeing	73.8	14.7	23.19
Berkshire Hathaway	117.6	17.6	19.36
Allianz	62.6	9.2	18.60
Hitachi	22.6	13.5	17.56
Ford Motor	48.5	9.2	17.13
General Motors	38.2	8.9	14.06
BMW	61.4	9.4	14.00
Volkswagen	102.1	3.7	13.59

Fig. 10.1 Increase in market capitalization after a permanent price increase of 2 %

$120 Million More Through Pricing

The following case proves that the impact of price and profit on shareholder value is not the stuff of theory and dreams. It is absolutely real. A private equity investor was preparing to sell off one of the world's leading parking garage operators, a company it had owned for about five years. The investor previously exhausted all of its profit growth potential through conventional means such as cutting costs and adding more garages. However, it had not taken any systematic actions on the pricing side.

When a thorough analysis revealed potential for price increases, especially in large cities, the company acted swiftly. Instead of implementing an identical, across-the-board price increase, it took a differentiated approach, basing the increases for an individual garage on its attractiveness, capacity utilization, and competitive situation. The investor built the new prices into the contracts with the garage lessors, thereby locking in an additional income stream of $10 million per year. A few months after the implementation of the price increases, the private equity investors sold the company at a PE ratio of 12. In one fell swoop, the contractually secured profit increase of $10 million increased the company's value by $120 million, which means that they got

$120 million more than they had expected prior to the price increases. This case shows that price increases can quickly and massively increase the value of a company.

Price and Market Capitalization

The equity markets are considered the most objective evaluator of a company. The share price is supposed to reflect all information available in the market. That prompts the question of how price actions affect share prices. To my knowledge, no one has made a representative study of those effects. One reason for this may be the fact that information about the price situation of a company rarely if ever appears in a standard company report. Unusual price actions, in contrast, can often precipitate a significant change in a share price. In what follows we will look at a selection of case studies which show the sudden and dramatic influence that pricing can have on a share price.

The Day the Marlboro Man Fell Off His Horse

On Friday, April 2, 1993, Philip Morris, the maker of Marlboro, the world's biggest cigarette brand, announced a massive price cut for Marlboro cigarettes in the US market. The goal was to ward off no-name competitors, who had captured an ever-increasing market share. Philip Morris's share price fell by 26 % that same day, wiping out $13 billion in market capitalization and helping to drag down the share prices of other leading consumer goods companies such as Coca-Cola and RJR Nabisco. The DJIA declined by 2 % that day.

Fortune described "Marlboro Friday" as the day the Marlboro Man fell off his horse. Investors interpreted the price cut as a sign of weakness and a concession by Philip Morris that it was unable to maintain high prices in its fight against no-name competitors. The Marlboro Man, launched in 1954 and known worldwide as one of the biggest marketing icons ever, had lost a price war. Investors took his defeat as a general sign for the marketing inefficiency of leading brands. The declining market capitalizations of leading US consumer product companies in 1993 prompted a slight decline in advertising spending. That marked the first such decline since 1970. This event was considered to be the "death of a brand" and as a sign for the rise of a new consumer generation which gave more weight to the true value of a product rather than its marketing.

20 % Off on Everything: The Praktiker Case

Praktiker, a home improvement store chain in Europe with 25,000 employees, hundreds of stores, and about $5 billion in revenue, had a share price of over $40 in the middle of 2007. Building for years on its slogan "20 % off of everything—except pet food," Praktiker became Germany's second-largest chain in the category. Later

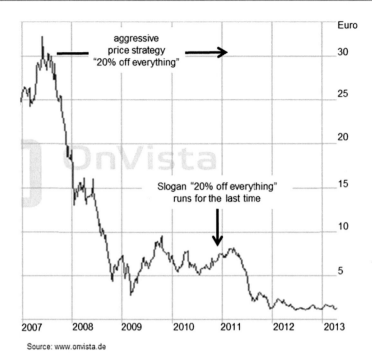

Fig. 10.2 Praktiker's share price decline

on, Praktiker began launching campaigns based on discounts for specific product categories, such as "25 % off of anything with a plug."[4] Another Praktiker slogan was "This is the price talking." Praktiker positioned itself as the hard discounter in the home improvement category and ultimately defined itself by these slogans.

Praktiker's aggressive price strategy led to disaster. By the end of 2008, its share price fell below $13. The hard discount strategy had led Praktiker astray, and they ultimately had to abandon it. The company took that bold step in 2010, running its "20 % off of everything" slogan for the last time at year's end. But the share price plunged again. In spring 2013 it was around $1.90. Figure 10.2 shows the share price decline from 2007 to 2013.

Praktiker's management was criticized for playing down the complexity of the transition away from a "discount culture," noting that "as soon as it became clear that the new positioning would take time and cost a lot of money, trust for the brand disappeared."[5] Another report said that "whoever boils down their magic formula to '20 percent off of everything—except pet food' doesn't get what it's about. Praktiker

---

[4] Frankfurter Allgemeine Zeitung, March 18, 2009, p. 15.
[5] Seidel H (2011) Praktiker: Es geht um 100 Prozent. Welt am Sonntag, July 31, 2011, p. 37.

is a soulless company."[6] Worth noting is that while Praktiker stumbled, the rest of the category flourished. From 2008 to 2010 the German home improvement chains saw their aggregate revenue rise by more than \$1.3 billion to \$24.7 billion. Praktiker filed for bankruptcy in 2013, and has ceased operations.

Dieter Schindel, the chairman of the retailer Woolworth, spoke of the "Praktiker syndrome," something which afflicted his own chain. Woolworth went into bankruptcy in April 2009 and then tried a completely fresh start in Europe. Under the new concept, the company consciously decided it would not succumb to the "Praktiker syndrome." It made direct, permanent price cuts on over 400 items, instead of making ongoing claims about aggressive discounts.[7]

The moral of this story: before committing a company to a positioning solely dependent on low prices, one should consider the potential consequences for profits—and thus for the share price. Following this statement, it should be observed that once committed, a company's attempts to move away from that policy can have disastrous consequences.

The Devastating Effect of Price Wars: The Potash Oligopoly Case

The global market for potash—potassium compounds which are an important additive to fertilizers—used to be dominated in relative peace by just three companies: Russia's OAO Uralkali, Canada's Potash Corp., and Germany's K+S. Prices were relatively stable at around \$400 per metric ton. That all changed at the end of July 2013, when Uralkali announced three moves which broke up the "informal cartel" and sent stock prices into a tailspin. In keeping with a new "volume over price" strategy,[8] Uralkali said that it would increase its production by 30 % in the next year, offer more favorable prices to China (one of the world's biggest consumers of potash), and break off its joint sales organization relationship with its Belarusian sister company.[9]

The effect on the Uralkali's share price was immediate and huge, as shown in Fig. 10.3. In a 2-day period, shares of Uralkali fell by 24 %. The other competitors suffered a similar fate: shares in Potash Corp. by 23 %, and shares in K+S by 30 %. The prospects for K+S seemed particularly dire, as one analyst saw prices falling to as low as \$288 per ton, which is roughly equal to the production costs of K+S. Another analyst group lowered its profit forecast for K+S by 84 % in the aftermath of the Uralkali announcements. A few months later, Uralkali effectively set a new floor for potash prices by signing a 6-month deal with a Chinese

---

[6] Freytag B (2011) Magische Orte. Frankfurter Allgemeine Zeitung, December 29, 2011, p. 11.

[7] Woolworth will zurück zu seinen Wurzeln. Frankfurter Allgemeine Zeitung, July 2, 2012, p. 12.

[8] Alpert LI (2014) Uralkali Signs Potash Deal With China. The Wall Street Journal, January 20, 2014.

[9] Uralkali bringt Aktienkurse in Turbulenzen. Frankfurter Allgemeine Zeitung, July 31, 2013.

Fig. 10.3 Uralkali's share price decline

consortium for $305 per metric ton, roughly 25 % below the prevailing prices in the first half of 2013.[10]

Pride Before the Fall: The Netflix Case

Netflix began as a DVD rental business. For a monthly fee, you could borrow as many DVDs as you liked. They would arrive by mail, and you would return them by mail when you were done. With this innovative business model, Netflix helped drive the huge DVD rental chain Blockbuster, which had thousands of stores nation-wide, into bankruptcy in 2009. Step by step, Netflix began to evolve into a movie streaming service, and kept its simple price model of a low monthly subscription fee intact. From 2010 onward the company was a true online star, boasting 25 million customers by the summer of 2011 and facing virtually no competition.

That such a successful company can fall victim to pride is no surprise. On July 12, 2011, Netflix announced a price increase of 60 % and attributed it to a sharp increase in its licensing costs. Those licensing costs, however, didn't interest Netflix

---

[10] Alpert LI (2014) Uralkali signs potash deal with China. The Wall Street Journal, January 20, 2014.

Fig. 10.4 The Netflix stock price after its large price increase

customers one bit. They responded negatively, though the company's net loss of customers was not so large in percentage terms. Investors were much less tolerant. They roughed up the company even more, causing the share price to plummet by around 75 % over the ensuing three months.

Netflix's market capitalization, which once topped $16 billion, eventually fell below $5 billion. Content suppliers cancelled their license agreements. A weaker Netflix also became vulnerable to stepped-up attacks from Amazon and Apple.[11] Figure 10.4 shows the movement of Netflix's share price in the three months after the price increase in July 2011. The moral: one should avoid arrogance in pricing, especially after a run of enviable success.

A Failed Attempt to Trade Customers Up: The J.C. Penney Case

In June 2011 the department store chain J.C. Penney announced that former Apple executive Ron Johnson would take over as CEO, effective November 1. Johnson wasn't just any ordinary manager getting elevated to a top executive job at a retailer.

---

[11] For a detailed description of this case, please see Stahl G (2011) Netflix Shares Sink 35 % after Missteps. The Wall Street Journal, October 26, 2011, p. 15 as well as the Harvard Business School case study on Netflix. In 2014 Netflix's market cap was $5.5 billion.

Fig. 10.5 The J.C. Penney share price

He was the man behind the spectacularly successful Apple Stores, which he nurtured and expanded since leading their launch in 2000. Prior to Johnson's taking charge, J.C. Penney sold almost three-quarters of its merchandise at discounts of 50 % or more. Without doing an advance testing of the potential effects, J.C. Penney implemented a radical change to its pricing on February 1, 2012. It eliminated almost all promotions and at the same time initiated a significant upgrade in merchandise to more expensive brands, which Penney would sell in more than 100 separate boutiques. In response to critical questions about the lack of advance testing, Johnson responded "we didn't test at Apple."[12]

J.C. Penney's revenue fell by 3 % in its 2012 fiscal year, while costs rose because of the implementation of the "trading up" strategy. These effects combined to turn an after-tax profit of $378 million in 2011 into a loss of $152 million in 2012. When the retailer announced the hiring of Johnson in the middle of 2011, its share price responded positively. As Fig. 10.5 shows, the share price started to

---

[12] Mattioli D (2013) For Penney's Heralded Boss, the Shine is off the Apple. The Wall Street Journal, February 25, 2013, p. A1.

decline sharply after implementation of the new price strategy began. Between January 30, 2012, and April 2, 2013, the company's share price plunged from $41.81 to $14.67, a decline of 65 %. During the same period, the DJIA rose by 16 %. This requires no further comment. And how did the story end? Ron Johnson was fired in April 2013. Until 2015 the share price fell below $10.

Discounts and Promotions: The Abercrombie & Fitch Case

In the third quarter of 2011, the fashion retailer Abercrombie & Fitch launched a campaign of discounts and promotions. The combination of the price cuts and a double-digit increase in unit costs put "significant pressure on our gross margins," said CEO Mike Jeffries. Because making a price increase—or rescinding the discounts—seemed feasible only after the holiday shopping season, the company expected that its profit would decline through the end of 2012.

During the financial crisis after 2009, Abercrombie & Fitch suffered revenue declines because the company steadfastly refused to undertake high-profile promotions. The promotions in the third quarter of 2011 did boost revenues, but the profit

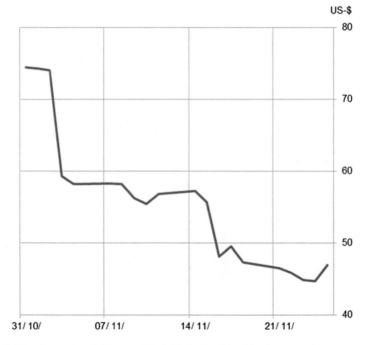

Fig. 10.6 The share price of Abercrombie & Fitch after launching its promotions

margins worsened. One investment firm downgraded the stock, and a retail analyst wrote: "We now see greater gross margin deterioration than we previously anticipated and believe the pace of margin recovery will take longer than expected, particularly given management's aggressive promotional stance in the domestic channel."[13] As Fig. 10.6 shows, Abercrombie & Fitch's share price fell by more than 30 % as a consequence of its price cutting. In 2015 it hovers around $20.

Price Discipline Increases a Company's Market Value: A Telecom Case

Now let's look at a positive case. The US market for data and wholesale voice services is famous for its price wars. Once a company puts its network cables in the ground, it has hardly any variable costs. This makes it very tempting to use aggressive prices to attract customers. One leading US company finally had enough of this strategy, after its share price fell by 67 % over a 2-year period. Simon-Kucher & Partners developed a comprehensive program to help the company stabilize its prices. The new program imposed strict price discipline on the sales force.

At an earnings press conference, the company announced that it had seen its first success with the new strategy. Its share price rose significantly that same day and

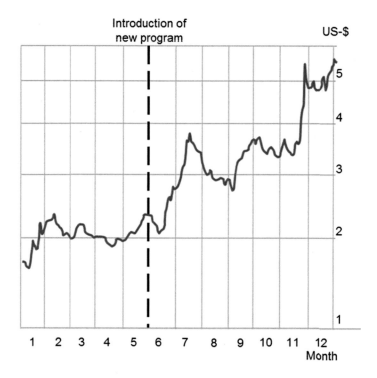

Fig. 10.7 Price discipline and share price for a telecom company

---

[13] Talley K (2011) Pricing Weighs on Abercrombie Margins. The Wall Street Journal, November 17, 2011.

eventually doubled within six months. Figure 10.7 shows the share price movement of the company before and after the introduction of the program. Some of its competitors witnessed the success and followed suit with their own form of price discipline, making this case a textbook example of strategic price leadership.

The company's management commented on the upward trend in the share price by saying: "We are pleased with the results of our continued disciplined approach to pricing. Third quarter performance reflects positive industry dynamics including continuing moderation of price compression." Analysts also praised the newfound price discipline: "The company's increase in wholesale prices is part of a general trend that price pressure is easing, a healthy pricing trend. More stable pricing should help all the players."

These cases show that price measures can have a dramatic impact on share prices and market capitalizations. It would seem prescient for senior management and investor relations departments to take the role of price more seriously, and communicate its importance more vigorously. Avoiding serious pricing mistakes would seem to be even more important than finding the right price strategy. Companies must absolutely avoid both kinds of mistakes: the ones with sudden short-term effects—such as Marlboro's, J.C. Penney's, or Abercrombie & Fitch's—as well as mistakes in long-term price positioning, such as Praktiker's. Taking the correct price decisions does not impact share prices immediately, but rather with some delay. That is because such decisions are normally not spectacular; they simply bring a company closer and closer to its desired price position. The effects are asymmetric. A poor price decision—as the previous examples showed—can have an immediate and devastating impact on a share price. A sound price decision often takes time to show its full effects, translating into a modest but steady improvement in share prices as the equity markets take notice.

Pricing and Financial Analysts

Analyst reports play a very important role for investors. After everything I have said above, one would expect that topics such as price level, pricing competence, and pricing power would appear prominently in analyst reports. But that is not the case. Only rarely do we see statements about prices in these reports, and when we do, it is usually some triviality such as the fact that a company is a premium supplier. When the reports do address pricing, they usually do so superficially.

But this seems to be gradually changing in the aftermath of the financial crisis. Analysts have begun to pay more attention to pricing. Perhaps the comment from Warren Buffett on pricing power has something to do with that. No one else's words carry greater weight or have a wider audience in the investment community than his.

One analyst report from a large banking group offers proof that the tide may be turning.[14] Entitled "Global Equity Strategy," the report goes into extensive depth and detail on the significance of price and pricing power for the evaluation of stocks.

---

[14] Credit Suisse, Global Equity Strategy, October 18, 2010.

It is worth reviewing a few key points of this study. The analysts concluded that pricing "is abnormally important: we calculate a price increase of 1 % point raises fair value on a discounted cash flow base by 16 %," a confirmation of what we repeatedly said in this book.

The report also analyzed individual industries with respect to their pricing power. It recognized high pricing power in premium cars, luxury goods, tobacco products, technology products, investment banks, software, and maintenance contracts. In contrast, it identified mass-market cars, tourism, airlines, consumer electronics (e.g., cameras), and media as industries with extremely weak pricing power. The analysts also assessed the pricing power of individual companies, attributing high pricing power to BMW, Imperial Tobacco, Daimler, Goldman Sachs, Oracle, and SAP. Companies they considered to have weak pricing power include Solarworld, Peugeot Citroen, Fiat, Nike, and the drugstore chain CVS.

There can be no doubt: factors such as pricing power, price position, and pricing competence are significant both for shareholder value and for evaluating stocks. But two reasons explain why these aspects historically receive only scant coverage in analyst reports. First, balance sheets and income statements do not contain any direct information on prices. Granted, this information does appear occasionally in the comments in annual reports, but such statements follow no standard format and are therefore hard to compare across companies. Second, the very high importance of price for shareholder value may not be fully understood, not only per se but also relative to other factors which determine shareholder value, such as capital costs.

The most important drivers of a company's value and its share price are profit and growth. Companies which deliver strong consistent results in both areas year after year will create shareholder value and become popular among investors. During Jack Welch's tenure as CEO from 1982 to 2001, General Electric's revenue increased from $27 million to $130 million. In the same period, profit increased sevenfold, with steady gains year after year. Adjusted for stock splits and dividends, GE's share price rose from 53 cents to $27.95 over that 20-year period. That is an increase of 5,273 % ... and not for some start-up, but rather for a company that has been a component of the DJIA since 1897. GE is the only company which can make that claim. For a time GE was the world's most valuable company, later eclipsed by Microsoft and Apple, two other companies with an amazingly long run of higher growth and higher profits.

One very compelling question is the following: How much does growth contribute to a company's value, and how much comes from profit? One would think that this question has been investigated thousands of times. But that is not the case. One of the few people to explore this question was the late investment banker Nathaniel J. Mass, who published his findings in an article in *Harvard Business Review* in 2005.[15] He developed an indicator which he called "relative value of growth" or RVG. The RVG showed how much 1 % of revenue growth contributed to shareholder value relative to 1 % of profit growth. For example, an RVG of 2 means that

[15] Mass NJ (2005) The relative value of growth. Harvard Business Review, April 2005, pp. 102–112.

revenue growth of 1 % would contribute twice as much to shareholder value as a 1 % improvement in margins, which a company could achieve through higher prices or lower costs. But Mass did not explicitly study the role that price plays in shareholder value. If we want to understand that role, we need to break down growth into its constituent parts.

The term "growth" normally means revenue growth. But revenue growth comes about in many different ways. If volume rises by 5 % at constant prices, revenue will increase by 5 %. If prices increase by 5 % and volume remains constant, this also results in revenue growth of 5 %. Company reports rarely distinguish between these two fundamentally different forms of growth. As we know from Fig. 5.3, these two scenarios have sharply different effects on profit and therefore on shareholder value. Using the example from Fig. 5.3, pure "price growth" results in profit growth of 50 %, whereas pure "volume growth" increases profit only by 20 %. In reality, these two growth drivers (volume and profit) could come in any conceivable combination (i.e., both go up, one goes up, the other down). If volume and prices both rise, as they did for a time in the oil market, revenue and profit will experience very strong growth. Revenue can grow when prices decline and unit sales grow disproportionately, and vice versa.

The study conducted by Mass did not distinguish between these different forms of growth. Implicit in his analysis, however, is the assumption that growth is purely volume based. It would be more revealing to distinguish between volume growth and price growth, but unfortunately that is difficult. Annual reports and income statements do not provide any data to go on. Analysts should try to include more price-related data in their studies, similar to the equity report I cited earlier. It is urgently necessary to devote more research on the link between price and shareholder value.

Price and Private Equity Investors

The typical business model of private equity investors involves acquiring a company at a favorable price, and then trying to raise its profits as quickly as possible. The first target of that effort is usually costs. Applying their experience, investors strive to achieve short-term improvements. In addition they typically tackle the topic of growth, usually focusing on entry into new segments or new markets, often foreign markets. In short the acquired company simply needs to move more units.

So we are talking here about volume growth. Private equity investors often shy away from trying to achieve profitable growth through higher prices. One reason is that the investors are often not very familiar with the markets the acquired company competes in, and therefore expend their energy on measures which are less risky than price moves. Furthermore, the people the private equity investors put in charge to oversee these changes normally have considerable experience with rationalization, but much less experience with marketing or trading up. The parking garage example earlier in this chapter proved, though, just how much potential lies in using price actions as a way to drive growth and profit. Private equity investors do not always recognize this potential, because it is harder to quantify than the effects of cost cuts.

One other explanation is that price measures—similar to innovation processes—require a longer term orientation. Often one doesn't get to a desired price level with one big move, but rather with a series of smaller ones spread out over years.

Private equity investors should also take this untapped price potential into account in their due diligence phase. It is not always easy to assess that potential, especially prior to an acquisition, but price and pricing power nonetheless remain vital factors in determining the potential shareholder value. One must not forget the comment of Warren Buffett on pricing power.

The attitude of private equity investors has also begun to change, though. Texas Pacific Group, which ranks as one of the largest private equity firms with more than $50 billion invested, treats pricing with great care and has frequently hired Simon-Kucher & Partners as a consultant. More and more private equity firms are recognizing the profit and value potential which pricing offers and have begun to examine it systematically. Particularly important to them is how stable and sustainable the price position is.

The Key Role of Top Management

Pricing belongs on the CEO's desk. That is clear, but reality looks much different. Simon-Kucher & Partners investigated deals for one of the world's largest automotive suppliers. In its negotiations with car companies, this supplier would usually set an internal minimum price or floor price at which a deal would still be accepted. We found out that nearly all of the contracts the supplier won came at the respective minimum price. As we showed these results to the supplier's CEO, he went berserk. He didn't know the details of the pricing process, especially the setting of a floor price. Otherwise he would not have been so surprised at hearing these findings.

The CEO of an engineering company, who found it tiresome to go through a price "chess match" for every new project, laid down the following rule for his sales force: every project with a gross margin of less than 20 % requires his personal approval. That sounds rational, doesn't it? He told me that one year later, his sales-people rarely submitted deals for his approval anymore. So far so good! Then I asked him what the margins on the deals looked like. "They are always at 20.1 percent," he said. "Before we had occasionally gross margins of 24 or 25 percent or even more. But not anymore." That was the natural consequence of such a one-sided process rule. Why should a salesperson make his life more difficult in a negotiation with a customer by pursuing a margin of 25 %, when a margin of 20.1 % is perfectly fine with his own CEO?

If one asks top managers for certain details about prices, such as price gaps to competitors or across countries, the managers will often pass. Of course one cannot expect a top manager to know every price and the details behind it. But he or she should be informed about fundamental facts, processes, and results.

Should companies reward top managers with price-based incentives? In principle that is possible. Managers could receive such rewards for achieving price increases, meeting or exceeding inflation rates, adjusting to competitors' prices, or reducing discounts. Sometimes companies formulate explicit price goals. Toyota uses a system of relative prices, under which they express their own prices relative to the average prices of the relevant competitive models. In some years, the company issued specific instructions on how managers should change these relative prices. Precise goals such as these can be good starting points to encourage and reward desired pricing behaviors.

Nonetheless, I generally advise against such incentives for top managers, although I do advocate them for salespeople. The business owner or the board which would grant these incentives generally does not know what price measures lend themselves best to increasing shareholder value. Companies should instead offer incentives based on increases in shareholder value and not on the individual instruments for achieving it, such as price.

The Toyota example leads to another insight, namely that creating a price metric for top managers to use can be very helpful. I consider relative prices to be a very meaningful indicator. One can calculate them not only at the individual product level, but also for product groups, for business units, for individual countries, or for the entire company. Using such "key pricing indicators," top managers can make a fundamental assessment of their company's price position and how it changes.[16]

My insistence that top managers devote more time and energy to pricing should not in any way imply that the CEO should involve himself or herself in all manner of price negotiations. In some isolated cases such involvement might be necessary, but it also has its disadvantages. The CEO of a large logistics service provider made a habit of visiting the CEOs of his customers in the automotive industry once a year. These CEOs regularly brought up the topic of price and managed to extract additional price concessions from the logistic company's CEO. These meetings undermined the months-long efforts of his sales teams. Simon-Kucher & Partners recommended that the CEO stop making these annual visits. He followed our advice, and his company's margins improved.

Fortunately there are CEOs who do indeed pay a lot of attention to pricing. One of these was Wendelin Wiedeking during his years as CEO of Porsche. He personally involved himself in important price decisions and was fully versed in the details. Extremely professional price management, including CEO involvement, is one of the reasons Porsche has become the world's most profitable automaker. In 2013, Porsche achieved an operating return on sales of 18.0 %, up from 17.5 % in the prior year. The numbers of all other companies in the automotive industry pale in comparison.

Pricing at General Electric also enjoys the close attention of top management. In 2001 GE installed Chief Pricing Officers in each of its divisions and had them report directly to the division leader. A few years later, CEO Jeff Immelt noted the positive effect these new positions had. Price discipline had tightened considerably, and the company did a better job of achieving its target prices. The Chief Pricing Officers

---

[16] Viele Preiskriege basieren auf Missverständnissen. Interview with Georg Tacke, Sales Business, January–February 2013, pp. 13–14.

had also taken on an instructional role, ensuring much better preparation for price negotiations. All in all, Immelt said that his expectations were exceeded by a wide margin.

Hidden Champions, relatively unknown world market leaders in their respective industries, are also characterized by heavy involvement of their CEOs in price questions.[17] Because of this focus, these executives know all the details of the business, which enables them to make qualified judgments and take on a leading role in resolving price issues. The prices Hidden Champions charge are usually 10–15 % above market levels; yet the companies are global market leaders. Their returns likewise outpace industry averages by a factor of 2.4.[18] The involvement of the CEO in pricing plays no small role in this level of success.

The Global Pricing Study, which Simon-Kucher & Partners conducted in 2011 and again in 2012, illuminated and confirmed the critical role of top management in pricing.[19] The 2012 study, which included 2,713 managers from over 50 countries and a large cross section of industries, took a deep look at the role of top management in pricing. Companies whose top managers took a strong, personal interest in pricing stood out compared to companies whose senior executives did not take on such an active role, as the following results show. For companies with strong CEO involvement:

- The pricing power was 35 % higher.
- The success rate for implementing price increases was 18 % higher.
- 26 % more achieved higher margins after the price increases, which means that they were not just passing on higher costs to their customers.
- 30 % had a special pricing department, which in turn had an additional positive effect on profits.

The study showed that companies with strong pricing power had 25 % higher returns than those who didn't. One should always be careful about causality assumptions when interpreting these kinds of results. But these findings do support the statement that higher profits are likely to result when the CEO gets involved in pricing. To say it one more time: pricing belongs on the CEO's desk!

---

[17] See Simon H (2009) Hidden champions of the 21st century. Springer, New York.

[18] Simon H (2012) Hidden champions – Aufbruch nach Globalia. Campus, Frankfurt.

[19] Simon-Kucher & Partners, Global Pricing Study, Bonn 2011 and 2012.

Name Index

A
Ahmed, Mumtaz, 79, 80
Albrecht, Karl, 52
Albrecht, Theo, 52

B
Ballmer, Steve, 9, 194
Becker, Gary, 27
Bloomberg, Michael, 24
Buffett, Warren, 24, 25, 194, 195, 205, 208

C
Cantillon, Richard, 117
Colvin, Geoff, 180
Cowger, Gary, 190

D
Dean, Joel, 38
Dolan, Robert J., 4
Drucker, Peter, 6, 7, 82, 84, 149

F
Friedman, Milton, 27

G
Gabor, Andre, 39
Ginzberg, Eli, 38
Govindarajan, Vijay, 61
Gracian, Baltasar, 14
Granger, Clive, 39

Grieder, Calvin, 61
Gutenberg, Erich, 82, 121

H
Hwang, Chang-Gyu, 64

I
Immelt, Jeff, 209, 210

J
Jeffries, Mike, 203
Jobs, Steve, 64, 173
Johnson, Ron, 201, 203
Joly, Hubert, 10

K
Kahneman, Daniel, 27, 28, 40, 41, 46, 47
Klein, Hemjö, 18
Kotler, Philip, 3, 4, 7
Kucher, Eckhard, 6, 37, 38, 110

L
Langton, Chris, 135
Lutz, Bob, 91, 92

M
Mahajan, Vijay, 57
Mass, Nathaniel J., 206
Mayer, Fritz, 61

© Springer International Publishing Switzerland 2015
H. Simon, *Confessions of the Pricing Man*, DOI 10.1007/978-3-319-20400-0

Mehdorn, Hartmut, 19
Miele, Markus, 66
Mirowski, Philip, 49
More, Roger, 189
Müller, Kai-Markus, 28, 47, 48
Murdoch, Rupert, 24

N
Nagle, Thomas T., 4
Negroponte, Nicholas, 59
Nimer, Dan, 4, 6

O
Oates, Dennis, 187
Obermann, Rene, 164
Ogilvy, David, 16, 17, 98, 107
Okuda, Hiroshi, 190
O'Leary, Michael, 170

P
Plenel, Edwy, 162
Prahalad, C. K., 57

R
Raynor, Michael, 79, 80

S
Samuelson, Paul, 27
Sandel, Michael J., 25, 26
Scherzer, Stephan, 162
Schindel, Dieter, 199
Schutz, Peter, 76

Sebastian, Karl-Heinz, 6
Selten, Reinhard, 2, 8
Shaich, Ron, 187
Simon, Herbert A., 1, 2, 4, 5, 9, 27, 51, 81, 97,
        121, 153, 177, 186, 193, 210
Stigler, George, 115

T
Tacke, Georg, 19, 179, 209
Tak-Uk, Im, 114
Tarde, Gabriel, 25
Telser, Lester G., 110
Thaler, Richard, 46
Trimble, Chris, 61
Tversky, Amos, 27, 40, 46, 47

V
Varian, Hal, 174
Veblen, Thorsten, 28, 70
Vickrey, William, 123, 174
von Goethe, Johann Wolfgang, 174
von Neumann, John, 112

W
Wagoner, Richard, 179
Welch, Jack, 206
Wengen, Liang, 73
Wiedeking, Wendelin, 67, 76, 179, 209
Williamson, Paul, 17, 18
Winterkorn, Martin, 15

Z
Zinkann, Reinhard, 66

Companies and Organizations Index

A

Abercrombie & Fitch, 203–205
Acer, 54
Air France, 170
A. Lange & Söhne, 71
Aldi, 51–53, 56–58, 102, 103, 113
Alibaba, 56
Allianz, 114
Amazon, 21, 55–56, 86, 134, 136, 159,
    190, 201
American Airlines, 180
American Express, 43, 73
Amtrak, 23
Angry Birds, 160
Anheuser Busch InBev, 113
Apple, 64, 82, 86, 134, 147-149, 173,
    201, 206
Asus, 146
AT&T, 23, 148, 173
Audi, 31, 146
Avis, 156

B

Bank of America, 172
BASF, 6, 155, 180
Bayern Munich, 144
Beats electronics, 173
Ben and Jerry's, 39
Bentley, 73
Best Buy, 10, 82
BIC, 65
BMW, 31, 132, 206
Boeing, 54
Bosch, 58
Bugatti, 74
Bühler, 61
Burj Al Arab Hotel, 73

C

Cartier, 72, 75
Chanel, 75
Chivas Regal, 28, 29
Columbia University, 38, 174
Crayola, 63
Cra-Z-Art, 63

D

Dacia, 58, 61
Daimler, 8, 206
Dell, 54, 56, 57
Delta Airlines, 95, 132-133
Delvaux, 28, 29
Deminex, 22
Deutsche Bahn (DB), 18, 172
Deutsche Telekom, 164
Dürr, 155

E

Easy Jet, 25
eBay, 56, 123, 146, 150, 174
Electronic Arts, 162
Emirates, 11, 12
Enercon, 63, 67–68
EnviroFalk, 155
E-Plus, 165

F

Farmville, 160
Ferrari, 28, 76
Fiat, 206
Ford, 91
Fortune, 24, 57, 59, 86, 173, 180, 197
Fürst von Metternich, 37, 38

© Springer International Publishing Switzerland 2015   213
H. Simon, *Confessions of the Pricing Man*, DOI 10.1007/978-3-319-20400-0

G
General Electric, 16, 61, 154, 206, 209
General Motors, 77, 86, 91–92, 94, 113, 143,
        179, 189, 190
German Management Institute, 6
German Railroad Corporation, 8, 16, 18
Gillette, 60, 65
Goldman Sachs, 206
Google, 140, 162, 173, 174, 190
Grohe, 62
Gulfstream, 73

H
HanaroTV, 156
Harvard Business Review Press, 162, 173-174
Harvard Business School, 4, 54, 201
Hela, 182
Hermès, 72
Hewlett Packard, 54, 146
Hilti, 157
Hilton, 141, 142
H&M, 53
Hoechst, 6
Honda, 58-59, 61
HUK-Coburg, 114
Hyundai, 114

I
IhrPreis.de, 166
IKEA, 52-53, 57
Imperial Tobacco, 206
INSEAD, 6

J
Jouyou, 62
Jumeirah Beach Hotel, 171

K
K+S, 199
Karl Mayer, 61
kayak.com, 12, 154
Keio University, 6
Kohlpharma, 138
Kupferberg, 37, 38

L
Lacoste, 77
Leegin Creative Leather Products, 137

Le Monde, 162
Lenovo, 54
Lexus, 145-146
LinkedIn, 160
London Business School, 6
Louis Vuitton Moët Hennessy (LVMH), 72
Lufthansa, 41, 42, 53, 124, 125, 171

M
Massachusetts Institute of Technology, 3
Maytag, 63
McKesson, 84
Mediapart, 162
MediaShop, 28
Memorial Sloan-Kettering Cancer Center, 148
Mercedes, 8, 31, 73, 74, 76
Michelin, 69, 155
Microsoft, 9, 64, 129, 148, 157, 190, 194,
        206
Miele, 15, 17, 63, 66, 70
MillerCoors, 113
Modelo, 113
Momentum, 124
Motorola, 82, 83

N
Nestlé, 60
Netflix, 200-201
Newnet, 146
New York Times, 26, 124, 137, 148, 161, 182
Nike, 206
Nokia, 148
Northwestern University, 3
Norwich Union, 155
Noweda, 84

O
Omega, 72
Opel, 77
Oracle, 206
Orica, 155

P
Pandora, 160, 173
Panera, 187
Pepsi, 17
Philip Morris, 197
Philips, 61
Phoenix, 84

Playmobil, 146
Porsche, 8, 66-67, 76, 179, 209
Potash Corp., 199
Praktiker, 55, 182, 197-199, 205
Priceline.com, 166
Procter & Gamble, 60, 65, 86
PSKS, 137

R
Raffles Hotel, 75
Renault, 58, 61
Richemont, 72-73
Ritz Carlton, 73
Rolex, 72
Rolls Royce, 73, 154
Ryanair, 53-54, 57, 132, 170

S
Saab, 77
Samoa Air, 134, 135
Samsung, 64, 86, 164
Sanofi, 148
Sany, 73
SAP, 206
Siemens, 61, 62
Simon-Kucher & Partners, 7, 17, 25, 35–37,
        65, 77, 84, 88, 89, 110, 120, 131, 138,
        139, 156, 162, 163, 165, 168, 169, 179,
        184, 185, 188, 189, 204, 208–210
Sirius XM Radio, 173
Sixt, 172
SK Broadband, 156
Skippy, 39, 63
Skype, 160, 161
Solarworld, 206
Sony, 86, 195
Southwest Airlines, 53
Spotify, 173
Starbucks, 48, 165
Strategic Pricing Group, 4
Swatch, 60, 72, 79

T
Tank & Rast, 158, 174
Tata, 58, 61
Tesla, 76
Texas Pacific Group, 208
Thomas Cook, 187
T-Mobile, 164
Toyota, 145-146, 190, 209
Trader Joe's, 51, 52
Tuck School of Business, 61
TUI, 8, 187

U
UniCredit Banca, 135
Universal Stainless & Alloy Products, 187
University of Chicago, 4, 46, 110
University of Michigan, 57
University of Notre Dame, 49
University of Texas, 54, 57
Uralkali, 199, 200

V
Volkswagen Group, 15

W
Walmart, 53, 81, 86
Welt, 2, 161, 198
Whole Foods, 52
Wilkinson Sword, 65
Woolworth, 55, 199

Z
Zalando, 55-56, 136
Zara, 53
Zipcar, 156
Zurich, 165

Subject Index

A

Advance booking, 138, 144
Advance purchase, 125
Advertising, 16, 17, 94, 95, 98, 119, 120, 143, 145, 161, 164, 174, 181, 197
After-tax profit, 53, 54, 67, 72, 83, 148, 195, 202
Aggressive prices, 10, 59, 186, 204
Airlines, 11, 23, 53, 55, 56, 98, 135, 141, 150, 170, 180, 187, 206
à la carte pricing, 172–173
Analyst, 52, 56, 194, 199, 203, 205, 206
Annual fee, 19, 43, 46, 73, 160
Annual pass, 163
Anti-gouging law, 143
Antitrust, 21, 24, 113, 186
Arbitrage, 127, 129, 138
Auction, 74, 123, 174–175
Automotive, 24, 31, 32, 58, 66, 76, 84, 99, 138, 155, 179, 185, 190, 208, 209

B

Bargain hunter, 143, 166
Bartering, 153
Base price, 98, 140, 159, 171
Behavioral economics, 10, 27, 49
Block booking, 129, 173
Bonus, 12, 45
Brain research, 48
Brand(ing), 13, 15, 16, 24, 28, 31, 34, 51, 52, 55, 62–64, 66, 67, 76, 77, 97, 109, 120, 136, 145, 179, 183, 197, 198
Break-even, 20, 69, 75, 78, 93
Bundling, 4, 10, 74, 130–133, 173
Business model, 9, 51, 53, 55, 56, 154, 156, 160, 200, 207
Business-to-business, 12, 16, 25, 30, 98, 102
Buying power, 24, 102, 135

C

Cannibalization, 55
Cantillon effect, 117
Capacity utilization, 53, 85, 125, 178, 183, 187, 196
Capital management, 52
Cartel, 24, 102, 199
Cashback, 76
Cash flow, 81, 155, 189, 206
Cash for clunkers, 181
CEO, 7, 9, 10, 15, 18, 19, 30, 60–62, 64, 67, 72, 76, 135, 164, 170, 172, 175, 179, 185, 187, 189, 193, 194, 201, 203, 206, 208–210
Chamberlin hypothesis, 115
Channel price differences, 136
Clearance sale, 138
Cloud computing, 157
Commodity product, 97, 189
Compatibility, 132
Competitive advantage, 70, 95
Competitive behavior, 143
Competitive reaction, 107, 111, 112, 114, 115, 188
Competitor, 79, 102, 103, 108, 110–112, 114–116, 185, 186, 188, 190, 191
Configure to order, 54
Conjoint measurement, 108, 109, 112, 153
Consumer goods, 90, 197
Consumer price index (CPI), 118
Consumer products, 16, 29, 60, 67, 90, 127
Consumer surplus, 121, 127, 133
Contagion effect, 145
Contribution margin, 88, 92, 93
Corporate culture, 78
Cost advantage, 57, 69, 79, 95
Cost function, 106, 121, 167
Cost management, 10
Cost-plus, 29, 93, 102–104

© Springer International Publishing Switzerland 2015
H. Simon, *Confessions of the Pricing Man*, DOI 10.1007/978-3-319-20400-0

Cost strategy, 53
Cost structure, 66, 88, 103
Crisis, 39, 76, 138, 177–187, 203, 205
Cross-price elasticity, 111, 154
Customer-driven pricing, 165–166
Customer lifetime value, 162
Customer relations, 10, 184, 195
Customer satisfaction, 54, 146
Customization, 55, 131

D
Data analysis, 141
Dealer, 91, 142
Demand curve, 4, 21, 27–30, 37, 99–101,
        103–106, 108–111, 115, 121, 125, 129,
        166, 167, 181
Design, 13, 16, 17, 29, 34, 62, 64, 67, 74, 77, 78
Desired price, 24, 25, 34, 205, 208
Differentiated good, 97
Discount, 8, 11, 16, 19–21, 31, 43–45, 54, 81, 84,
        86, 89–92, 129–131, 133, 139, 147, 148,
        163, 168, 173, 182, 183, 198
Discrimination, 129, 134
Distribution, 8, 74, 75, 77, 110, 121, 125, 132,
        137, 150, 165, 167
Distribution channel, 74, 110, 125, 150, 166
Distributor, 129
Durable goods, 60
Dynamic modeling, 4
Dynamic pricing, 139–141
Dynamics of price, 3

E
Early booking, 125
E-commerce, 56, 95, 109, 141, 165
Econometrics, 110
Economies of scale, 56, 85, 145
Efficiency, 52–54, 56, 57, 87, 155, 174
Emerging markets, 22, 23, 57, 59–62, 117,
        119, 165, 185
Employee discount, 94, 143
Endowment effect, 41
Enduring value, 75
End-user price, 136
Equilibrium, 21, 22
Ethical, 7, 26
Event-based price differentiation, 143
Exchange rate, 105
Experience curve effect, 145

F
Fast-moving consumer goods, 37, 125
Fencing, 126, 137, 138, 140, 150, 154, 161, 170
Field experiment, 38, 109
Fixed costs, 18, 75, 78, 88, 89, 92, 93, 103,
        115, 121, 124, 126, 133, 154, 177,
        178, 180
Flat rate, 161, 163–165, 173
Fleet management, 157
Forecast, 23, 141, 168, 199
Free shipping, 89, 90
Freemium, 146, 160–163
Full-volume discount, 133

G
Game theory, 2, 112
Gold standard, 118, 119
Government, 21, 23, 24, 117, 119, 158, 174,
        181, 182
Gray imports, 138
Gray market, 75

H
Hi-Lo strategy, 143
Historical data, 110, 111
Hog cycle, 22
Hybrid consumer, 78

I
Incentive system, 86, 167, 193
Incremental discount, 133
Indirect questioning, 108, 112
Individual prices, 11, 130, 163
Industrial products, 60, 63, 67, 88
Inflation, 39, 75, 117–120, 209
Innovation, 13, 51, 64, 65, 70, 148, 153, 158,
        174, 208
Intangible benefit, 15, 16
Introductory offer, 139
Introductory price, 146–148
Inventory, 52, 53, 94, 166, 177, 191

L
Last-minute, 138, 140, 144
Launch price, 145, 146
Law of declining marginal utility, 40, 101
Life sciences, 99

Limited edition, 71, 73, 77
List price, 12, 44, 45, 54, 133, 135, 161, 183
Location-based price differentiation, 154
Low-price strategy, 52, 56, 60, 79, 80
Loyalty card, 159
Lump sum, 45
Luxury, 13, 28, 29, 31, 63, 66, 70–78, 80, 145, 146, 171, 186, 206

M

Manufacturer-prescribed price, 136
Manufacturing base, 60
Marginal utility, 40, 101, 126, 127
Market capitalization, 56, 64, 91, 194–197, 201, 205
Market-clearing price, 21
Market dynamics, 8
Market penetration, 145
Market share, 21, 31, 59, 61, 63, 65, 67, 72, 77, 82, 84, 85, 90, 91, 94, 110, 112, 113, 119, 120, 149, 167, 178, 181, 186, 189–191, 193, 194, 197
Mark-up, 102
Maximum price, 101, 104, 105, 108, 122, 123, 125, 126, 129, 130, 133, 151, 167
Minimum balance requirement, 160
Mixed bundling, 130–132
Money supply, 117
Monthly payment, 46
Moon price, 44
Multi-person pricing, 10, 133

N

Name your own price, 165, 166
Negative utility, 40–46, 48, 165, 172
Negotiated transaction, 101
Neural economics, 48
Neuro-pricing, 47, 48
Nobel Prize, 2, 27, 39, 115, 174
Non-linear pricing, 4, 10, 101

O

Odd prices, 37
Oligopolistic market, 112
Oligopoly, 112, 115, 116, 186
One-off payment, 45, 46
One-time fee, 159
One-time payment, 46

Optimal price, 29, 51, 95, 100, 103–106, 115, 116, 121, 122, 124, 127, 130
Optional accessories, 131
Overcapacity, 185–187, 189
Oversupply, 1, 22, 23

P

Pain center, 47, 48
Parallel imports, 138
Passed-up profit, 122
Patent, 140
Pay what you want, 166, 167, 171
Peak-load pricing, 139
Peak pricing, 135
Penetration strategy, 145, 146, 160
Penny gap, 161, 162
Perceived value, 13, 15, 17, 18, 64, 66, 70, 93, 101, 183
Person-specific price, 134–136
Placebo effect, 30, 31
Positive utility, 40–45, 147, 165
Potential buyer, 41, 76, 122, 125, 126
Premium customer, 162
Premium manufacturer, 59
Premium price(ing), 24, 63–67, 69, 70, 78, 79, 97
Premium product, 63, 64, 66, 70, 78, 112, 161
Premium segment, 59, 60, 66
Premium strategy, 60
Premium supplier, 60, 70, 102, 205
Prepaid, 165
Prestige effect, 29, 32, 70, 77, 108
Price anchor, 32–34, 36, 45, 123, 155
Price bundling, 4, 129, 132, 133, 163, 173
Price category, 150
Price change, 8, 9, 11, 86, 90, 93, 99, 102, 104, 105, 107–109, 111, 115, 119, 141, 162, 180, 190
Price comparison, 124, 154
Price competition, 24, 102, 124, 190
Price concession, 180, 181, 209
Price consulting, 5, 7
Price corridor, 138
Price decline, 177, 189, 198
Price decrease, 94, 107, 181, 182, 187
Price difference, 30, 63, 64, 69, 105, 108, 110, 124, 138, 153–155, 157
Price differentiation, 30, 44, 120, 122, 124–127, 133–135, 137, 138, 149–151, 158–160, 163, 173, 184

Price discount, 181, 183
Price elasticity, 3, 4, 38, 93, 94, 105–107, 110,
    111, 139, 143, 170, 172, 181
Price erosion, 74
Price gouging, 24, 142
Price increase, 20-21, 28–30, 35, 37–39, 73,
    75, 86–88, 94, 105, 108, 112, 113, 116,
    120, 143, 145, 162, 170, 181, 183, 184,
    186, 187, 194–196, 200, 201, 203, 206,
    210
Price information, 12, 47, 153, 154
Price interval, 106
Price leadership, 112, 113, 115, 193, 205
Price level, 33, 76, 103, 118, 148, 155, 168,
    180, 182, 188, 189, 191, 205
Price list, 11, 12, 48, 184
Price management, 5, 7, 28, 85, 99, 186,
    195, 209
Price metric, 45, 69, 156, 157, 209
Price negotiation, 44, 209, 210
Price parameter, 98, 157
Price perception, 32, 37, 45, 47, 117, 119
Price positioning, 29, 31, 51, 57, 59, 60, 63,
    66, 78, 205
Price pressure, 183, 205
Price promotion, 10, 143
Price reduction, 37, 147, 181, 182
Price-response function, 99, 115
Price sensitivity, 3, 107, 108, 135, 136, 184
Price setting, 13, 23, 36, 78, 85, 98, 99, 101,
    109, 113, 174
Price spiral, 114
Price stimuli, 47
Price strategy, 78, 79, 143, 144, 148, 160, 198,
    203, 205
Price structure, 10, 12, 17, 18, 36, 43, 45, 116,
    127–129, 131, 139, 149, 160, 162
Price test, 162
Price threshold, 37–39, 166
Price transparency, 7, 8, 11, 12, 153, 154, 183
Price trend, 22, 69, 147, 168
Price-value relationship, 31, 70, 146, 148
Price variable, 11
Price war, 9, 84, 87, 95, 99, 113, 114, 116,
    181, 188–191, 193, 194, 197, 204
Pricing lever, 10
Pricing policy, 149
Pricing power, 24, 25, 195, 205, 206, 208, 210
Pricing process, 98, 102, 208
Pricing theory, 6
Pricing wisdom, 12
Primary brand, 55, 74
Private equity, 195, 196, 207–208
Procurement, 52–54, 56, 58, 174
Product life cycle, 3, 132

Product line, 53, 148
Product portfolio, 98, 195
Product quality, 51, 68, 70, 74, 77, 109
Profitability, 7, 25, 56, 72, 79, 82, 84, 85, 93,
    144, 185, 195
Profit contribution, 127, 142
Profit driver, 17, 87–88, 92, 177, 193, 194
Profit improvement, 88, 132, 184
Profit increase, 86, 87, 123, 130, 133, 151,
    196, 206
Profit margin, 33, 53–55, 63, 81, 83, 85, 86,
    92, 148, 168, 169, 178, 203
Profit maximization, 194
Profit-maximizing price, 103, 105, 109, 121,
    127, 130, 167
Profit-optimal price, 130
Profit-oriented incentive, 168
Profit potential, 121, 122, 127, 128, 130, 138,
    150
Profit rectangle, 122, 123, 128, 136, 138, 149,
    151, 156
Profit triangle, 122, 123, 128, 129, 136, 138,
    149, 151, 156
Promotional price, 143
Prospect theory, 27, 40–42, 44–46, 164, 172
Purchasing power, 25, 57, 73, 78, 117, 118,
    135, 136, 138
Pure bundling, 130, 132, 172

R
Rebate, 44, 133, 158
Recession, 24, 72, 75, 178, 180, 185
Reimbursement, 158
Relative price, 108, 110, 111, 119, 209
Reminder effect, 43
Resale price maintenance, 136
Reseller, 75, 100, 182
Reservation price, 101
Retail, 10, 38, 90, 92, 95, 98, 102, 113, 136,
    137, 143, 166, 182–184, 203
Retailer, 44, 52, 54, 55, 90, 102, 103, 136,
    137, 143, 159, 166, 199, 201–203
Retail price, 92, 137, 183
Return on sales, 39, 52–54, 56, 64, 67, 72,
    148, 209
Revenue management, 141, 142
Risk sharing, 67, 68

S
Sales, 1, 6, 9, 10, 15, 18, 20, 21, 28, 30, 31,
    33–35, 37–39, 43, 52–56, 62, 72, 73,
    76, 81–83, 85–88, 90–95, 98, 103–107,
    109–112, 114, 116, 140, 143–146, 155,

160, 168, 177, 178, 180–182, 185, 186, 189, 190, 199, 204, 208, 209
Sales volume, 9, 90, 94, 105, 109, 111, 144
Sanifair, 157-158, 169
Scarcity, 22, 34, 71, 117, 118, 142
Seasonal price, 138
Second-order effect, 15, 16
Self-control, 76
Shareholder value, 194, 196, 206–209
Share price, 55, 148, 185, 197–206
Sherman Antitrust Act, 137
Signaling, 112, 114, 186, 190, 191
Skimming, 145, 147–149
Spare part, 11, 76, 184
Specialty store, 75
Standardization, 131, 132
Store traffic, 144
Suggested price, 167
Sunk costs, 42, 46
Suppliers, 12, 22, 24, 52, 58, 59, 62, 63, 135, 153, 155–157, 166, 184, 185, 201, 208
Supply and demand, 1, 9, 21, 73, 97, 99, 139, 168, 177
Supply curve, 21
Surcharge, 156, 169–172

T
Tax-free shopping, 90
Telecommunications, 36, 159, 161, 163, 164, 174
Time-based price differentiation, 139–141, 143, 144, 170
Tip, 171
Transaction cost, 42, 46
Two-dimensional price, 19, 21

U
Ultra-low price, 57–59, 78
Unbundling, 132, 173
Uniform price, 121–123, 125–128, 133, 138, 149, 151
Unit contribution, 102, 122, 126, 180

Unit margin, 28
Unit sales, 28–31, 49, 87, 105, 110, 207
Upfront investment, 95
Utility optimization, 27

V
Value-added service, 132
Value chain, 57, 58, 60, 77, 78, 132
Value communication, 16
Value creation, 194
Value difference, 105, 150
Van Westendorp Price Sensitivity Meter, 108
Variable costs, 18, 75, 78, 88, 92, 103-104, 155, 167, 178, 204
Variable price, 98, 159
Variable quantity, 100, 101, 108, 126
Veblen effect, 70
Vickrey auction, 123
Volume, 11, 12, 21, 22, 38, 39, 52, 59, 60, 63, 64, 71, 72, 76–79, 85–91, 93, 94, 99, 100, 105, 107, 110–112, 115, 116, 125, 128, 133, 134, 145, 148, 159, 160, 162, 164, 167, 168, 177–184, 190, 193, 195, 199, 207
Volume decline, 38, 91, 177, 178, 180
Volume discount, 89, 125, 133, 134
Volume increase, 91, 181

W
Wholesale price, 89, 92, 205
Willingness to pay, 13, 15, 17, 18, 21, 34, 36, 48, 75, 78, 101, 102, 105, 121–127, 129, 130, 132, 133, 135, 136, 139, 142, 148–150, 166, 170, 172, 174, 184
Word of mouth, 145
World market leader, 55, 58, 61, 148, 155, 159, 180, 210

Y
Yes-no decision, 100
Yield management, 141